KT-577-970

HOUSE OF LORDS

Changing Perceptions
of Economic Policy

Changing Perceptions
of Economic Policy

Essays in honour
of the seventieth birthday of
Sir Alec Cairncross

Edited by Frances Cairncross

Methuen
London and New York

First published in 1981 by
Methuen & Co. Ltd
11 New Fetter Lane, London EC4P 4EE

Published in the USA by
Methuen & Co.
in association with Methuen, Inc.
733 Third Avenue, New York, NY 10017

Typeset by Scarborough Typesetting Services
and printed in Great Britain at the
University Press, Cambridge

British Library Cataloguing in Publication Data

Changing perceptions of economic policy.
1. Cairncross, *Sir* Alec   2. Economics −
Addresses, essays, lectures
I. Cairncross, Frances   II. Cairncross,
Sir Alec
330   HB171

Library of Congress Cataloging in Publication Data

Changing perceptions of economic policy.
Based on a conference held at St. Peter's College,
Oxford, at the end of Mar. 1981.
Includes index.
1. Great Britain − Economic policy − Congresses.
2. Economic policy − Congresses.   I. Cairncross,
Alec, Sir, 1911−
HC256.6.C42   338.941   81-11286
AACR2

ISBN 0-416-31550-X

Contents

Preface

This book is based on a conference held at St Peter's College, Oxford, at the end of March 1981 to celebrate the seventieth birthday of my father, Sir Alec Cairncross.

The plan of the conference was to contrast the views of two generations of economists — most of them with experience of the shaping of policy — on the ways in which perceptions of economic policy had altered over the seventy-year span of my father's lifetime. The main papers were written, with a few exceptions, by economists of his own generation. Each discussion session was opened by a younger economist, while the author of the paper summed up. One author, Dr Lamfalussy, Economic Adviser to the Bank for International Settlements, was unable to come: his place at the conference was taken by Mr Michael Dealtry, also of the BIS.

This book would never have existed without the help of a number of people. The conference was funded largely by the Treasury, the Social Science Research Council, the Department of Employment and the Bank of England. It was planned with a great deal of help from Professor Robin Matthews, who also chaired it. The discussions were recorded by my husband, Mr Hamish McRae, and most of them were transcribed by my father himself. To all of them I am very grateful; and also to the contributors and the participants. This book is really their work.

Frances Cairncross

Introduction

FRANCES CAIRNCROSS

Perhaps the most remarkable aspect of the conference from which this book emerged was the way it brought together many of the economists who — both in the universities and behind the scenes in Whitehall — had helped to shape and direct British economic policy in the thirty years after the Second World War. In the papers, and more pointedly in the discussion, they looked back over the policies which they helped to form and asked themselves how far they had succeeded.

Among the participants were several generations of what might be called the Keynesian Establishment of British economists. They included five former chief economic advisers to post-war governments. But neither British monetarism nor the New Cambridge school of economists were well represented, and a tone of scepticism about Conservative economic policy ran through much of the debate. Dr Alan Budd, the lone British monetarist at the gathering, described the conference as 'being held in exile': and indeed the day after it ended, the names of several of the participants appeared among the 364 signatories to a letter of protest at the Government's economic strategy. However, the conference was saved from cosy Keynesian consensus by the presence of a number of distinguished foreigners, both among the contributors and the participants. 'I never fell under the spell of Keynes', one of the European contributors remarked in the course of discussion.

The question which the conference was intended to examine was: how have perceptions of economic policy changed over the past seventy years? Have new departures in policy usually been matters of fashion, or have they followed advances in economic thought, or have they simply been responses to uncontrollable forces in the world outside? As so often happens, the conference did not answer the question: it suggested rather that perceptions of policy, at least in the way economists look at the world, have changed very little, except perhaps in the field of demand management.

Even there, few of the participants chanced their arm at the reason why active demand management policy had, in the words of Sir Bryan Hopkin's paper, 'lost a good deal of the glamour which had once invested it'. The fullest attempt came, not surprisingly, from a representative of the 'new perception' – from Dr Budd – whose discussion of Sir Bryan Hopkin's paper put forward the theory of the 'searing experience'. The prejudices of economists are formed by the powerful experiences of their youth. For the generation which had been responsible for policy making since the War, the searing experience was the pre-war Depression, of which there is a vivid personal recollection in Sir Arthur Knight's paper. For the younger generation, the searing experience was the inflation of the 1970s, an experience which they were determined should never be repeated.

If the discussion suggested that most of the participants had not changed their perceptions of policy, it also emerged that the perception of government and of its competence had altered. The post-war period had been marked by an ambitious view of what government could do and thus of what economic policy might achieve. But repeatedly, in a wide range of policy areas, it became clear that economists were now more cautious in their attitude to what government might reasonably be expected to achieve.

For most of the participants, their perception of history had also altered, giving them a new interest in the experience of the inter-war years. Again and again, the conference found itself dividing Britain's recent history into three periods: the difficult 1920s and 1930s, the era of stability and of relatively fast growth in the 1950s and 1960s, and the most recent decade of accelerating inflation and disintegrating order. There was a feeling that the experiences of the inter-war period might have lessons for our present difficulties: and there was also a concern to discover whether we had made mistakes in the immediate post-war period which might account for some of the problems which had surfaced in the 1970s.

Of course, the role of economists in shaping economic policy changed out of all recognition between the inter-war years and the post-war period. This was one of the themes of Sir Alec Cairncross's opening paper on academics and policy makers. He was concerned to chart the development of the channels of communication between professional economists and those who form policy. Inevitably that led to a discussion of the role of the economic adviser: the man who stands between the academic economist and the government minister.

It was Sir Bryan Hopkin's paper on demand management which gave the conference its core. Through it and through the discussion which followed ran two main questions. Was the post-war boom, with its stable levels of employment and its historically high growth rate, the result of the pursuit of sound Keynesian policies? Or was it simply fluke – the lucky result of the international economic conjuncture? Secondly, why had post-war demand management been abandoned? Had it failed – or had governments misused it? From the discussion, it was clear that part of the answer to the second question lay in the change which appeared to have taken place in the behaviour of the labour market in the late 1960s – what Sir Henry Phelps Brown later referred to as 'the hinge' (p.89).

Sir Henry's paper on the labour market and industrial relations clearly fitted closely with the discussion of demand management. Sir Henry charted the way in which governments had been forced, in the post-war era, to change their view of the correct policy towards the setting of pay rates and towards trade unions, in the first case by experimenting with incomes policy, and in the second by attempting to reform industrial relations through legislation. But it was on incomes policy that the subsequent discussion concentrated: inevitably, as incomes policy offered the only hope of curbing inflationary pay rises apart from what Sir Henry described as 'a return to the economics of the trade cycle, and restraint by a steep rise in unemployment, as in 1921 and 1932'.

Sir Arthur Knight's paper on industrial policy raised, in microeconomic terms, a similar point to Sir Bryan Hopkin's macroeconomic contribution. Had the great extension of the government's policy ambitions in the post-war era been born out by success? Sir Arthur was broadly sympathetic to the view that imperfections of the market meant that government ought to step in to help potentially successful industries and firms. But as those who had tried to pick winners during their time in Whitehall confessed in the discussion, it was not always as easy as it might appear.

Industrial policy appeared in a different light in Dr Tumlir's paper on the evolution of the concept of an international economic order. He argued that the stability of the first two decades after the

Second World War had been due not so much to deliberate government policy as to the limits which governments had accepted on their freedom of action, limits institutionalized in the GATT and the IMF which had made government policies more stable and predictable. It was the disintegration of these self-imposed restraints – as seen, for instance, in the revival of protection – which was so disturbingly reminiscent of the 1920s and 1930s. He argued that the extended involvement of government in the structure of the economy – the sort of intervention which Sir Arthur Knight's paper had described – was a way of deliberately avoiding economic adjustment. If domestic economies were not able to adjust to the shocks imposed on them from without – shocks which had been so powerful in the inter-war period and again since the rise of oil prices – then it became impossible to maintain international stability.

Dr Lamfalussy, examining capital movements, covered a rather smaller corner of the international canvas in more detail. He looked at one of the main ways in which governments respond to external economic pressures: through allowing or trying to prevent movements of short-term capital. He argued that there were some circumstances in which such controls might be appropriate. But in the subsequent discussion, several participants argued that the British experience had been that short-term capital movements were extremely hard to control.

In the final paper, by Dr Guido Carli, the conference focused on what appeared to many to be the central issue. Why has the British experience been so different from that of other industrial countries? Dr Carli saw the answer in terms of the early industrialization of Britain, the burden of the class structure, the dominance of the City and the growth of the public sector. But in the important discussion which followed, participants found it hard to arrive at such specific conclusions. After all the popular explanations of poor performance had been examined and rejected, two possibilities remained. One was that the slow growth of resources – particularly of the industrial workforce – might have been more important in holding back the growth of productivity than had been previously realized. The other was that the causes of slow growth were social: and not explainable in the language of economists after all.

Introductory remarks

SIR ALEC CAIRNCROSS

In setting out to discuss changing perceptions of economic policy, perhaps the first question we need to ask ourselves is: whose perceptions are we talking about? Are we talking about the public? After all, we live in a democracy, and the public's perception is supposed to dictate the policy in the long run? Are we talking about ministers, or their advisers? Or are we talking about economists? There are times when I ask myself whether economists' perceptions are all that important. If they do not connect with policy, then it does not matter very much what economists perceive. So we have to ask ourselves: how do the perceptions of economists translate into actual changes in policy?

It is here that one of the biggest changes has taken place in the last seventy years. There has been an enormous multiplication of economists. Indeed, sometimes I am tempted to ask what they all do. Why do we need so many economists? There was a time in my life when I thought we would live to see a day, perhaps about 1981, when we were all so well off that there would be less interest in economic affairs. If there was less interest in economic affairs, I used to think, there would be less need for economists. But on the contrary, the better off we become, the more economists we have, and the more complicated economics becomes, and the more unintelligible to the average man.

During this conference we should ask ourselves whether this is inevitable. What influence have economists actually had? Are we quite sure that the way things have gone over the last seventy years has been to any extent dependent on their insights and perceptions? Or has economic policy been largely a reaction to events, which might have occurred even without the advice of economists?

So we need to look at the question of intermediation: at the connection between economists writing technical papers in technical

1

journals, and the actual formulation of policy by people who may be quite incapable of understanding a word of these papers — ministers who are elected by a public which certainly does not understand a word of most of the contributions which economists make. How does this relationship fit into a democracy? After all, the public is supposed to call the tune. Are we to take the technocratic view that because economists are experts of a sort, their perceptions should dictate what is finally done? Or may there not be a need for the economists to put themselves in the position of ministers who have to handle policy, and try to see what is practicable and what policies are acceptable to the various interest groups which make up the electorate. The answers may not be quite the same as those which theory offers.

Now seventy years is a long time — time for a lot to happen. And a lot has happened. As economists, we look back with an eye on the future — to see what we can learn from the way in which policy making has gone. Many of us at this conference have been engaged in policy making. If you go back that far, you certainly have the impression that economists were thinner on the ground and that policy was very different. Almost all the papers deal with issues which had no counterpart in 1911. There was not much that you could call demand management, or labour market policy, or even industrial policy — except perhaps in the form of tariffs. As for capital flows, who tried to check them in 1911? Trade policy is the exception: it did exist, but all that people argued about was imperial preference. Perhaps Dr Carli's subject is the one which would have been of most interest in 1911. In those days the British tended to think that they were unique. Now they are anxious to pretend they are not. They like to feel that other people have the same problems.

If you think of what has happened to economics over the past seventy years, a great deal of the developments have been in these areas of policy where very little had been done at the start of this century. We have also seen a lot of work on devising tools to implement policies such as these. Take economic forecasting. Malthus may have tried economic forecasting of a kind — but it was very long term. There was no short-term forecasting in the nineteenth century. Or take the question how to run a nationalized industry. When coal, steel and other industries in this country were taken into public ownership, the ministers concerned did not have the faintest idea about how they ought to be run — and said so.

Economists had the job of working out what happens when an industry passes into the public domain.

Are there areas of that kind now, where policies will have to be developed to deal with issues which have not yet arisen? It seems more than likely to me that the objectives of policy may change. All those things that we have put in textbooks – growth, stability, greater economic equality – may be supplemented by new goals, which call for new policies to achieve them.

There are a number of questions about the contribution economics can make to policy making on which our discussion may throw some light. Are theory and practice too far apart? Or have other disciplines now got a more important contribution to make to the policy debate? How great an influence have economists had? Were the years of post-war prosperity the results of successful demand management, or was there just a great international boom which made everything easier? Of course, there are areas where policy has clearly been shaped by the ideas of economists. Incomes policy is one example – but it has not been terribly successful. There are areas, too, where economists have contributed too little – such as industrial policy. That may have been more important than some of the other fields of policy where economists were more involved. We have to ask ourselves the question quite brutally: are economists a plus? Can economists conclude that their influence has, on balance, been for the better?

We have a series of papers before us. Demand management is the subject of the paper by Professor Sir Bryan Hopkin, and it is an area where there is now real debate, while there was very little debate in the first twenty years after the war. We ought to consider whether there is likely to be some kind of synthesis between the new ideas of demand management and the old. The area of labour market policy covered by Sir Henry Phelps Brown is one where we are still experimenting. Do we have changing perceptions of what is feasible, or of what is theoretically desirable? Will institutions have to be revamped? Economists do not really set up in business to revamp institutions. But if they do not, who should? This is a question relevant to a great many other issues of policy. Take nationalization. Who makes sure that there is some element of competition, even after you have nationalized? Or take incomes policy. If you did achieve a successful incomes policy, how would economists come to grips with the kind of changes that would imply?

3

We have papers on capital flows and on trade policy by two distinguished economists from overseas. I hope that we will cover exchange rates in our discussion of Dr Lamfalussy's paper, because there has certainly been a big change there. We have moved from fixed exchange rates to floating rates: from exchange controls to no exchange controls in many countries: from a world in which we could believe that devaluation could change the structure of an economy to one where people argue that real exchange rates cannot be altered. Industrial policy is another area where we have discovered that things are more complicated than we used to believe. Economists used to feel happy if they had worked out some simple rule such as 'price equals marginal cost'. Now we have found that there is much more to price-setting and running a business than we imagined.

But the first paper, which I have written, deals not only with policy but with the policy-making machine, and with the way in which economists' ideas ultimately become accepted in practice.

1

Academics and policy makers

SIR ALEC CAIRNCROSS

Economic policy making is an activity like any other activity which involves producers competing to supply a market and consumers hoping to find their wants supplied. Economists may produce ideas and their ideas may be drawn upon at the official or the ministerial level. But what guides policy may have very little to do with the ideas that economists put forward. It may be dominated by non-economic considerations or by the views of non-economists or by doctrines refuted long ago or in widespread disrepute. What economists have to say may be neglected because its bearing on policy is obscure, contested, ambiguous, or insufficiently precise; because economists' conclusions rest on mistaken or inappropriate assumptions; because they are not adapted to the needs of the policy maker; or because, for that or any other reason, they simply fail to gain a hearing. Policy makers, as a rule, are slightly deaf: there is too much noise.

In a seller's market, in which economists are credited with the capacity to change the world and enjoy the prestige that comes with success, these non-economic resistances to the spread of their ideas may be submerged or attenuated. But when events are clearly in the saddle and economists seem impotent, they lose the favour and attention they were previously accorded. Such swings in fashion, so apparent since the Second World War, are a commonplace of competitive markets.

Market resistances of another kind may also come to the fore through product differentiation. Competition in the supply of a homogeneous product is one thing: economic advice grounded in a common orthodoxy may find unchallenged acceptance. But when economists compete with one another in brands of theory, their hold tends to be confined to their own special market which may or may not embrace the centres of policy making.

5

It is easy for economists to bury themselves in research and development and lose themselves in admiration of their products regardless of any link with policy. But product development, whether it relates to stabilization and demand management or to the labour market, or any of the matters discussed in the papers to be presented at our conference, is only part of the business. If we are to master our trade thoroughly we need to study the market and its characteristics, the way in which policies take shape and gain acceptance, the changes that are in progress among producers and consumers and the role of intermediaries between the two.

THE MARKET IN 1911

Let us start by looking at the consumers. Seventy years ago their requirements were modest. Ministers felt in no need of the services of professional experts. The objectives of government were limited, readily translated into policy measures and essentially long term so that there was ample time for debate of the underlying issues and the decisions to be taken were infrequent and lacking in complexity. There was no suggestion that the government should manage the economy, which was seen as fundamentally self-regulating. Since market forces were taken to be almost wholly beneficent there was correspondingly limited scope for government intervention to promote economic growth; the idea of using public works in order to stabilize employment had just surfaced; inflation was a matter for the (privately owned) Bank of England rather than the Treasury; protection and subsidies to particular industries were alike anathema; the welfare state lay almost entirely over the horizon.

The limited scale of government operations seventy years ago is evident from the size of the budget. In 1911 the rate of income tax had only recently been raised dramatically by Lloyd George from 1/- to 1/2d. Current expenditure by public authorities, central and local, was running at £200m., a year − about 10 per cent of GNP − and about half of that went in paying for past wars in debt interest or possible future wars in defence expenditure. It would have been unthinkable that manual workers should be asked to pay income tax (though not at all unthinkable that they should pay indirect taxes or that indirect taxes should be the main source of government revenue).

The same point can be made in terms of employment. The central government employed 1.5 per cent of the working population (excluding the armed forces which were rather more numerous) and the local authorities employed just over 3.5 per cent (including teachers, police, etc.). There were less than a million workers, full-time and part-time, in the two groups together. But things were changing fast, for in the previous twenty years the number had more than trebled.[1]

Under these circumstances it is hardly surprising that in 1911 practically no government or government department had ever knowingly hired a professional economist. The central government machine in Britain (as in India) was miniscule. Governments employed few administrators and were even more sparing in their use of experts of any kind. There were years, even in the 1930s, when there were no new entrants to the Administrative Class of the British Civil Service. The Treasury got along before the First World War with an administrative staff of twenty (many of whom survived into their nineties). It is true that they included Hawtrey and for a time Keynes. But neither Hawtrey nor Keynes ever sat a university examination in economics and neither would have described himself in 1911 as an economist.

The same absence of demand was apparent in business. The typical business was small and felt little in need of advice from economists. The first multinationals had just been born; macroeconomics had not. The market environment, uncomplicated by sporadic and widespread government intervention, was more stable, more predictable, and above all, more comprehensible.

The lack of demand was mirrored on the side of supply. Virtually no British economist (except Bowley?) held a PhD or other higher degree in economics before the First World War. In the 1930s when Cambridge was the leading centre of economic study in the world, no member of the staff had a higher degree in economics and at the beginning of the decade there was no living PhD in economics of the University. Indeed when Ronald Walker was awarded the degree in 1933, the research students who had come up the previous year gave him a dinner to celebrate. The number of chairs in economics in the entire country was not more than about twenty, some universities having none at all. Had the government set out to recruit a dozen trained economists of academic standing it would have had a hard time.

Not that the government thought of doing any such thing.

Economists busied themselves teaching and the government went on administering, without any interchange between the two except in wartime. Now and again an economist would be appointed to a committee of inquiry or a Royal Commission and the report might be acted upon after the usual lag of a generation. Communication was either at the personal level, or through the press. There might be contact at meetings of the Royal Statistical Society or of the Political Economy Club. But in general the few economists who took an interest in policy had to content themselves with a letter to *The Times* if they wanted to bring their views to the attention of the public.

The economic and financial press was less rudimentary. Business news was carried in the more serious newspapers and the subject of comment in the daily press, in *The Economist* and *The Statist* among the weeklies and in some of the magazines and journals like *The Banker*. But there was very little that would pass as economic analysis and nearly all the commentators with any detailed knowledge were interested in specific industries or specific problems. None of the financial journalists would have claimed any standing as an economist except possibly Sir Robert Giffen (who gave up financial journalism long before 1900), Hartley Withers, the editor of *The Economist,* or his successor Walter Layton.

The fact is that contemporary issues of policy rarely called for refined economic analysis. In any event, economics as a subject was not designed for immediate application to practical issues. The matters of controversy in economic policy had been largely confined to issues about the currency (paper money and the return to gold in 1821, regulation of the banks, bimetallism, centralization of the gold reserves) or protection (the Corn Laws, Imperial Preference) or income distribution (the relief of poverty, progressive taxation, etc.). Many of these controversies had been forgotten or were regarded as settled and those that were still active were highly political. Few of them featured in what textbooks there were, and there were very few. Economics did not supply ready-made answers to the problems posed in these controversies. It was essentially 'a moral science and not a natural science' in that it employed 'introspection and judgements of value'.[2] It was a preparation for thinking about economic problems through the construction of models from which the real values of the variables were necessarily missing. As customarily taught and studied, it was an exercise in logic that

8

was almost always long-term logic and had little or no bearing on the day-to-day problems confronting government.

An important reason for the abstract character of economics was the limited availability of statistics. Indices of prices and wages were in their infancy; production statistics, as Giffen complained, hardly existed (the results of the first Census of Production were just appearing); calculations of the national income and the balance of payments were primitive and unfamiliar; nobody had ever heard of the terms of trade, or domestic capital formation, or the public sector borrowing requirement. A large proportion of the available statistics were annual or even decennial. Any picture of what was happening to the economy from month to month would inevitably have been impressionistic and non-quantitative. Even what data existed were rarely pieced together so as to introduce some degree of coherence and consistency.

THE MARKET TODAY

Things have obviously changed a great deal since 1911. The pace has been set by demand but, as usual, demand and supply have inter-acted on one another. Economists have been diligent in proposing new activities for government, in detecting weaknesses within both the private and public sector, and in propounding the need for management of the entire economy, whatever the line of division between the two sectors. We need not enquire here into the reasons for the enlargement and growing complexity of government opera-tions nor detail the part played by economists in the changes that have occurred. We need only note the contrast with seventy years earlier. Government expenditure now absorbs half the national income. Nearly half the capital investment of the country is public investment. The aims of government have become far more ambi-tious, its responsibilities far heavier, its influence enormously more extensive. Governments control or seek to control the level and direction of economic activity. They are involved, in an increasingly detailed and complex manner, in almost every kind of economic activity in the discharge of one or more of their various functions: either in carrying on the activity itself or in regulating the terms on which it can be carried on or in buying the product or in taxing any profit that is made or in many other ways.

They are involved because they have an active economic policy in pursuit of the objectives of growth, stability, greater economic equality, etc. for which previously they took little or no responsibility. It is not only that the scale of their activities has grown. It is that these activities are largely dominated by economic factors, that it is increasingly difficult to secure consistency and coherence in the whole range of activities, and that many of the issues calling for decision are highly complex. The more control over the economy is centralized the greater the need for expert analysis of these issues; and naturally economists regard themselves as equipped to fill the role. We shall discuss later how far that self-confidence is justified.

But of course it is not only in government that the need for expert advice on complex economic issues arises. Business is faced with the same problems, largely because it has to reckon with the activities of government. While the economists in government seek to unravel the mysteries of the private sector and what it will do, business economists bend to the even heavier task of unravelling the mystery of what governments will do. Economists come to be recognized as the great map readers of the modern economy, without whom navigation is far more difficult and, as a result, the demand for their services expands steadily.

There has also been an expansion in export demand and in distribution. If economic management was in its infancy before the war, international economic management had not even been born. In the last generation new international agencies by the dozen have sprung up, the multinationals of the economics business. Since their functions are almost exclusively economic, it is hardly surprising if they have raided the economics profession throughout the world for staff. In addition, an important export industry has grown up: the advanced countries supply economic advisers to the less developed and offer in their universities and institutes training in economics for foreign students.

Another type of expansion takes the form of intermediation. If policy is dominated by economics and framed by economists, the public has a natural curiosity in what is going on. There is a need for economists who can translate what their fellow economists are saying into language intelligible to the layman and communicate their contentions through the press, on the radio, on television, and in other ways.

It is not a long step from intermediation to missionary activities.

The economist in government is looked to for a gospel that will permit consensus. The economist in business is expected to provide a rationale for the life of the business man. The economist abroad is welcomed as an up-to-date replacement for the medicine man. The economist employed by the media is supplied with a pulpit and asked to produce a weekly flow of sermons.

We turn next to the impact on economics and on economists of the new market environment. The main effect can be summed up as professionalization. It is now increasingly taken for granted that a professional economist will have a higher degree in the subject. Where not so long ago a chair in economics might be filled by someone without even a first degree, now applicants are expected as a rule to have a second. Very little that an economist had to say seventy years ago was unintelligible to the layman. Now very little is intelligible. The expansion of the market has also had the usual effect on the division of labour. Separate markets break off and are supplied by transport economists, health economists, monetary economists and a long list of other specialists. More and more journals cater for each group of specialists; and more and more use a language, including the language of mathematics, that confines the readership to a priestly few even when the issue under discussion affects the lay multitude. However, a parallel process allows each issue to be treated in ascending order of professional sophistication in the daily press, the trade press, the bank review, the conference paper and the learned journal. Communication is still possible between different groups of economists and between them and the weaker brethren in politics, business or ordinary life.

At the same time the sharp division between those on the inside and those outside the policy making machine has been greatly softened. There was a time in many countries – and it remains true in some – that economists in the universities were concerned primarily with ideology and eternal verities. A visitor to Japan would be asked on arrival whether he was a Marxist or a Keynesian as if economics were a form of religious belief. On the other hand, the Bank of Japan and the Ministry of Finance employed economists whose work was indispensable to economic policy making. In Britain in the inter-war period there might be a few grandees within the machine who held the title of Economic Adviser, one or two like Sir Sydney Chapman who were academic economists and others like Sir Frederick Leith-Ross who were not. The beginnings of an association

11

between economists in academic posts and the business of economic advising go back to the Economic Advisory Council and the Committee on Economic Information which emerged from its entrails. In war and post-war years the Economic Section of the Cabinet Office (from 1953 of the Treasury) brought academic economists within the administrative machinery of government much as, in the United States, the Council of Economic Advisers marked a decisive change. But the existence of the Economic Section did not by itself guarantee movement between academic life and government. That movement on a regular footing came later when in the 1950s and 1960s provision was made for recruitment of economists on a 2–5 year basis and when, under the Labour government of 1964–70, large numbers of economists entered government departments, usually on temporary appointments.

There is therefore, in Britain and other countries, an increased reliance on expert economic advice, tendered by people who regard themselves as professional economists and may expect to resume an academic career in due course. In some countries, however, there is no deliberate segregation of economists from other administrators and efforts are made to ensure that those who discharge economic functions have at least an elementary knowledge of economics.

Whatever the position in government, banking (and especially central banking) and big business generally make extensive use of staff trained in economics and no longer confine such staff to the assembly of economic information, speech writing, etc. A large and growing component of management in every sphere is literate or numerate in economics. And there is far more coming and going between the universities, business, banking and government than there used to be.

If economists have come to regard themselves more as practitioners, they have also had to recast their subject in more operational terms. This means, first and foremost, an increased preoccupation with problems of the short term; secondly, an enormous expansion in data analysis via econometrics; and thirdly, an effort to narrow the gulf between the empyrean of pure logic and the nitty gritty of the real world. Success in all these efforts is of course contingent on a recognition that economics is by no means the whole story and that there are other studies of human behaviour with which economics has to make common cause. There is space for only a few illustrations of how these changes are working out and how the teaching of the subject still fails to prepare economists for the realities of economic policy making.

An example of the first is economic forecasting. The horizon of such forecasting is usually limited to eighteen to twenty-four months so that the models on which the forecasts rest incorporate short-term relationships. These relationships had not been the subject of any extensive investigation before the 1930s partly because much of the necessary data did not exist but more fundamentally because the focus of government policy was traditionally long term. It is hardly necessary to point out that the kind of economic analysis used in, say, the *Economic Review* of the National Institute of Economic and Social Research or the *Economic Outlook* of the London Business School is almost entirely post-war.

The need for economic forecasting arose out of the change in government objectives after the White Paper on Employment Policy (Cmnd. 6527) in 1944. Forecasting is a tool of management indispensable to the framing of policy; and it was the development of economic management under the influence of Keynesian ideas that produced so much emphasis on economic forecasting. Whether Keynes himself would have approved of this emphasis is another matter.

So far as the training of young economists is concerned, the preoccupation with the short term has obvious drawbacks. It involves a concentration on shifting and uncertain relationships, an immersion in masses of statistics and refined statistical analysis and a preoccupation with macroeconomic model building that make heavy intellectual demands on comparative beginners and may work to the detriment of the more historical and philosophical elements in an understanding of the economy.

Economic forecasting leads inevitably into econometrics to which somewhat similar comments apply. Given the vast amount of economic data it is difficult to see how it can be handled satisfactorily without econometric analysis. The danger is that a greater degree of permanence and weight may be attached to the values of the parameters than is justified. As we all know, a variety of explanations, however dressed up in mathematics, may fit the facts almost equally well. Keynes would certainly have wished to warn us against over-investment in techniques more appropriate to the natural sciences especially if this were done in order to make economics more scientific than it really is.

It is when we turn to the gap between the generalizations of theory and the complexities of real life that the major problems arise. Since illustrations of the gap will abound in other papers it is unnecessary to dwell at length on it here. Three important characteristics of theory limit its value to the policy maker.

First of all, theory starts from definite and stated assumptions and follows its own logic to the bitter end. It assumes that we know exactly where we are, free from uncertainty of the kind so familiar to policy makers when, for example, the figures are not available, are inconsistent with one another, or are subject to seasonal and other adjustments that are themselves uncertain. From precise assumptions theory allows us to draw precise conclusions. But the policy maker cannot rest content with hypotheses. He has to take the situation as he finds it, in all its vagueness and uncertainty, and decide what to do about it. Action to deal with a specific problem takes precedence over intellectual speculation that is free to begin and end where it chooses.

There is the further difficulty that theory is content to handle things one at a time that do not arise in this isolated conditions in the real world. Where, for example, activities form part of a network or system, the cost or price of each activity cannot be arrived at in abstraction from the way the different activities are interconnected within the network. The young economist who has been taught all about marginal cost is rarely prepared for the complexities that arise in trying to apply the theory to the pricing policy of public utilities and nationalized industries: all the more because he is not warned that there is a multiplicity of margins to be considered, not just a simple margin at the production frontier. The fact that real world decisions are interrelated with one another makes them much harder to take than the one-at-a-time decisions of the textbooks.

Economic theory is also no more than a partial analysis of human behaviour. But those who have to manage an economy or a business have to deal with real men and women whose responses to policy may not be those postulated by theorists. How a policy works depends to some extent upon how it is received; and Ministers who have occasion to consult their economic advisers may show at least as much interest in the likely response as in the case for the policy itself. Economists now show more interest in how expectations are formed. But economic theory has little or nothing to say about other aspects of behaviour upon which economic performance may be critically dependent: for example, the mood of the working man; his attitude to his job, his employers and society at large; his readiness to accept technical and other forms of change; his fits of bloody-mindedness and militancy.

Even if a problem is the subject of some branch of economic theory, we are not necessarily much the wiser in deciding what to do about it. It is only too easy to confuse the economic context of awkward social problems and the ability of economists to solve them. The fact that economic development changes economic magnitudes, for example, does not make economic development respond to the instruments of economic policy. It may respond more readily to quite different things: preservation of law and order; political leadership; contact with abroad. Similarly, while inflation is an economic phenomenon, the causes of inflation do not necessarily lie in some form of economic malfunctioning. There may be very little that economists can contribute to its control.

CONTEMPORARY PROBLEMS

Let us turn next to the problems posed by the expansion of the market and by the sheer scale and complexity of modern policy making.

One of the central problems, if not *the* central problem, is the information explosion. The volume of statistics has grown inordinately and there are whole digests which are hardly ever looked at. An over-abundance of raw material is not, however, a source of great difficulty. What matters is the torrent of comment and analysis at all levels from the purest of pure theory to articles in the daily press. Seventy years ago there was a single economic journal in the United Kingdom and perhaps half a dozen others in the rest of the world. Now there are more journals than any economist could name, much less read, and the number continues to grow. It is said that, on the average, articles published in a learned journal have about five readers each. What is certain is that nobody can hope to read more than a very small fraction of what appears and that the fraction diminishes the further we move from theory to policy. No less massive are the official papers of all kinds: reports of government committees and testimony before them, bulletins, press releases, speeches, answers to parliamentary questions, etc., etc. Then there are the bank reviews, the writings of financial journalists, letters to the editor, press reports and contributed articles. And all this has to be multiplied by the number of countries issuing relevant material, either at the theoretical level or on economic affairs. With such a din going on it is almost a matter of chance what one hears.

A number of consequences follow. One is that books give way to articles and articles to abstracts. Economists read a decreasing number of books annually from the time they embark on their studies and (for a time at least) an increasing number of articles. Policy makers rarely read books on economics although there is one ex-Minister who read three well-known textbooks on a long sea voyage and one ex-permanent secretary who took Marshall's *Principles* with him to Naples to read on holiday.

A second consequence is specialization. It becomes almost inevitable that economists who have to select what they read, as we all do, should come increasingly to limit their field of view. Yet we are all conscious that in an economic system everything interacts and we can only understand the parts by keeping an eye on the whole.

Another consequence is increased dependence on word of mouth. Ideas circulate much faster in personal contact than when one is ploughing almost at random through the 'literature'. In any event Ministers and officials have rarely time to read the 'literature' and would have difficulty in understanding it or in extracting from it new ideas relevant to policy. Even economists in government service can devote very little time to study of the learned journals and tend to draw heavily on intellectual capital accumulated earlier or derived from their own recent experience. Hence they are always at the mercy of obsolescence and of such contacts as they are able to preserve with economists who are still in academic life or at least have enough leisure and incentive to follow current theoretical controversy. Not that government economists fail to develop their own theory: sometimes they do so in advance of other thinkers because the pressure is greater and the material more readily available.

A third consequence is the rise of the conference. If ideas circulate best by word of mouth, conferences are an effective way of spreading them. Some of us who have virtually abandoned reading find conferences an ideal way of catching up or, more commonly, catching a glimpse of changes in progress. But even conferences have their limitations. If the natural sciences are anything to go by, we may yet see conferences of 10,000 or more at which the authors of the main papers are given ten minutes to make their contribution while other authors line the walls of the corridors leading to the lecture room with typed summaries and abstracts for their colleagues to glance at on their way to the next session.

The information explosion is coupled with an enormous expansion in numbers. The universities turn out economists of one kind or another by the thousand every year and some hundreds of them go on to advanced study and a professional career in government, finance or industry. Similarly the business of management in each of these spheres expands the number of consumers, many of them themselves trained economists.

It is a nice question how demand and supply should be married within the policy making machine. Should there be strict segregation within two separate career structures, the economists within an economic service and the administrators and managers within a separate administrative or managerial structure? The answer depends in part on the nature of economic expertise and how easily it can be disengaged from the other forms of expertise and knowledge necessary to administration and management.

The tradition until the 1930s and the later coming of econometrics was that the arguments as well as the conclusions of economists should be capable of being expounded and defended in terms within the comprehension of the intelligent layman. There was very little that mattered in economic theory that could not be mastered by the layman in the course of his career as he came face to face with one economic problem after another. The idea that a short period of study of the subject in late adolescence gave a man an invincible advantage over those who had wrestled for a couple of decades with the matters discussed in the textbooks would have seemed somewhat questionable. There were no doubt some controversial issues of great complexity where it was useful to consult leading economists in some form of Economic Advisory Council or Committee. But until the post-war period, administrators were assumed to be capable of advising on economic, as on other, issues without the assistance of professional colleagues; and the only professional economists in Whitehall were those attached to the Committee on Economic Information.

In the post-war period a different balance was struck and the Economic Section was continued in being first under James Meade and then under Robert Hall. The basic assumption was that a small group of economists would be able to inject economic advice at the point where the key decisions were being formulated and would at the same time help to educate their colleagues in modern economic analysis. Since economists become progressively out of date and the difference between the technical expert and the layman tends to narrow, provision was also made for a circulation of economists between academic life and Whitehall, usually on the basis of a two-year spell in the Treasury. This had the double advantage of familiarizing an increasing number of economists with the practical issues of economic policy and bringing fresh minds and fresh ideas to those issues.

Over the past decade all this has changed and it is very doubtful whether it has changed for the better. The circulation of economists between universities and departments has virtually ceased. A growing economic service advises on a diminishing number of decisions alongside administrators who are increasingly sophisticated in economic issues. Is there really scope for a hundred economists in the Bank of England and nearly as many in the Treasury or are they not inevitably steered into research functions better carried on elsewhere or alternatively underemployed and disgruntled as policy advisers? Would it not be preferable to lay more stress on picking qualified economists to fulfil administrative roles and devoting more effort to the training of administrators in economics? Is there not something to be said for limiting the role of economists in government to advising on the major issues and drawing for this purpose on the leading academics, with no more than a quite limited number of economists spending their entire career in Whitehall?

Whether because of the scale and complexity of modern policy making or for other reasons there is a strong tendency toward over-simplification of the issues and their resolution in ideological terms. The public, the government and, from time to time, economists too grasp at fashionable nostrums and give direction to policy by espousing one myth after another. In the post-war period the British have taken as exemplars a succession of countries of whose institutions, attitudes and policies they were grossly ignorant. First came the United States to which productivity teams were despatched soon after the war: efforts were then made to match American achievements in technical development that were out of keeping with the commercial limitations of the British economy. Then came

France and the French system of indicative planning. Why the British who had learned all that needed to be known about planning in wartime should have been so fascinated by French planning just when it was about to enter an inevitable decline is a great mystery. Since then, Germany and Japan have been held up to admiration. The one country whose achievements are belittled and largely ignored is the United Kingdom.

The role of myth and fashion is even more apparent in the succession of policies in favour. There are recurrent themes which it is not possible to do more than mention. Planning first of all: often to the neglect of such planning as was really possible or of circumstances that made the plan itself an absurdity; rarely with any recognition of the simple truth that the essence of good planning is re-planning since planning has to be a continuous process and is, at bottom, a way of handling uncertainties. Investment next: as if investment would not occur naturally if other conditions of growth were present. Emphasis on investment was the lazy economist's way of sticking to parameters he could introduce into his models and turning his back on the non-economic factors limiting the return to be expected from new equipment. Then stop-go, blamed for the level of investment which was said to be low but which, seen as a fluctuation around a disappointing trend, was no worse than in other countries: in retrospect, it was not without some advantages as an anti-inflationary device. Devaluation and floating rates, one or other of them regarded as a cure-all and now dismissed just as foolishly as curing nothing at all. Export-led growth, the last survivor from the testament of post-war growth: no doubt a credible doctrine if one believes in the sovereign value of an expanding manufacturing sector but not particularly easy to bring about under British conditions and now regarded as disastrous when the export that makes the running is North Sea oil. Finally, and far more disastrous than any of these, a return to the myths of the past, when governments had not yet learnt to lend an ear to economists, the quantity theory of money and its corollaries.

THE EXTENT OF ECONOMISTS' INFLUENCE

The influence of economists on policy fluctuates and it is never easy to say what that influence is. There are many economists and among them are always some whose views are in keeping with those of the government in office. But coincidence of view is no proof of influence. On the other hand who can say from what source Ministers draw their inspiration? And whatever the source, who can be confident of tracing the impact of Ministers on the march of events? It is all too easy to gain credit by making speeches or taking measures in support of outcomes that are already in the bag. The writings of economists may equally appear to exercise a dominant influence when they are little more than a Greek chorus to events that have a quite different origin. No one could deny the great influence of Keynes: but there are good grounds for doubting whether the acceptance of Keynesian ideas would have done much to accelerate economic recovery in Britain from 1932 onwards and for attributing most of the success of governments in maintaining full employment after the Second World War to other circumstances.

Yet governments do listen to economists, particularly those who claim to know what should be done. Once they give priority to controlling inflation, governments are inevitably less attracted to theories in which inflation does not figure and are readier to accept, for the time being, doctrines assigning little or no role to governments in relation to other objectives, such as full employment, faster growth, balance of payments equilibrium, etc.

So far as the public is concerned, the standing of economists, at its zenith in the thirty years after the war, is now back again at its pre-war low. But it is not only economists who have lost influence. We live in a society in which all forms of management and leadership, however advised, are under constant challenge. Constructive efforts can be frustrated and brought to a halt with remarkable ease and in a multitude of different ways. The power of the negative is in the ascendant. Consensus and cohesion in the execution of policy are increasingly hard to achieve. In wartime a common effort was possible because there was a predisposition to common sacrifices. Even in peacetime such a predisposition is an essential ingredient in the life of the community if it is to survive as a community. Without a readiness to make sacrifices a country can neither face the burden of change – which imposes sacrifices – nor reach the compromises that allow it to keep in temper.

Where shibboleths and myths do duty for reasoned argument any sacrifices called for are seen out of perspective and the management of the economy is correspondingly more difficult. Debate can descend to the non-professional level with marches, demos, violence and eventually terrorism. Or it can be left at the political level in parliamentary debate and lobbying by pressure groups. There can be no abstracting from the exercise of power in any of these ways. But there is room also for professional debate and economists have a duty to organize such debate so that at least the intellectual merits of different lines of policy are made clear to all concerned. If we are to do battle with the Minotaur in the maze of economic policy we need to be assured of the reliability of the thread that guides us.

There are a number of ways in which, over the past ten years or so, improvements in the organization of debate have been made. For example:

i The National Institute now runs a series of conferences in conjunction with the SSRC on controversial issues and publishes the proceedings. These conferences have much in common with the panel meetings preceding the publication of Brookings Economic Papers but are more elaborate and less regular.

ii The SSRC also supports a number of specialized study groups bringing together economists from different places with an interest in particular areas.

iii Although the London and Cambridge Economic Service is no more, the Clare Group of economists operates in a similar way, issuing a critique of current policy in the *Midland Bank Review* after discussion among themselves.

iv The new system of Select Committees of the House of Commons brings together more frequently than before the views of economists and others on current economic policy.

v The press devotes much more space to contributions from economists on issues of policy.

vi There are the publications of various bodies studying economic policy: the National Institute, the London Business School, the Cambridge Economic Policy Group, the Institute of Fiscal Studies, the Trade Policy Research Centre, the Policy Studies Institute.

In these and other ways there are now ample facilities for debate — far better than at any previous period. It is for economists to make use of these facilities and with the help of the media raise the level of public understanding of policy alternatives. They cannot complain that the remaining market imperfections deny them a hearing.

21

CONCLUSIONS

Economics is now the *lingua franca* of national and international economic management. Management has expanded enormously. So has the economics profession.

We must recognize the limitations of economics in the making of economic policy: don't let's pretend to be more scientific than we really are.

We need to concentrate on the organization of debate on the central issues.

NOTES

1 M. Abramovitz and V. Eliasberg, *The Growth of Public Employment in Great Britain*, Princeton: NBER, 1957.
2 Lord Keynes to R. F. Harrod, 1938, in J. M. Keynes, *Collected Writings,* vol. XIV, London: Macmillan, 1973, pp. 296–7; quoted by Professor B. Corry in A. P. Thirlwall (ed.), *Keynes and Laissez-faire,* London: Macmillan, 1978.

Comments by
John Wright

The paper provides us with a rich and useful metaphor – the market in economic advice – to which these opening comments will be attached. I am, in particular, concerned with the imperfections in this market.

PRODUCT DEVELOPMENT

The paper suggests that development of the product by those responsible for academic research does not always seem very responsive to what is needed.

One response is that of the pure academic: that the consumer does not know what is needed: and that in the long run the unharried development of a pure academic discipline will be in the interests of all. This is not my own view since I believe that even as an intellectual discipline economics has a distinctive value only in the special challenge it provides to juxtapose reasoning with the facts of the economic world.

Nor do I think that academic studies unrelated to actual economic problems are, for that reason likely to be unbiased in their development. In a subject in which logical deduction must play an important part, the development of a particular line of thought acquires a momentum of its own in the thinking of its originator. Powerful lines of argument impress seminars. Again certain parts of economics are more amenable to cut-and-dried presentations in textbooks. Often they seem to provide better examination material in that they discriminate more clearly between those who understand and those who do not.

These factors are much more important than they used to be when economics was less widely studied at undergraduate level and was not studied at all in schools. Perhaps the imperfections to which they give rise have to be accepted as inevitable − but they do raise the question of the most suitable subsequent apprenticeship for those who on graduation have an over-developed faculty for logical deduction.

Nor is it the case in the long run that product development has responded well to needs. Over the past seventy years there has been, to say the least, some incompatibility between the actual form of development of economic institutions and the development of economic thought. The increase in size of businesses and the consequent growth in the scale of individual business decisions and bargains should *prima facie* make some of the older assumptions of economics less relevant − for instance, the assumption that the irrational content of individual action is random and will cancel out in the aggregate, or that it will be eliminated by a competitive evolutionary process. Labour economics has been left on the edge of the subject; the economics of the firm have been primarily derived as corollaries from the theory of price; and many of the most interesting, and in the long run, most important aspects of economic behaviour have either been ignored, or have been recognized only to be relegated to the rag bag of 'X-inefficiency'.

THE MARKET

Who are the customers and what do they want to buy? Let us first note the range of products supplied: fairly pure statements of economic doctrine supplied by publication to the public; economic doctrine and technique embodied in young graduates (rather like

23

Midland farmers buying in sheep from the Borders and Yorkshire); commentaries on current economic problems by economists – whether widely broadcast or prepared for individual customers; specific advice given by economists called in to participate more closely and continuously in decision making.

Of these products it is the last three that have emerged in the past seventy years. Their relative importance and the more detailed form of their development can be partly explained by changes in the economic environment. But we also need to note the character of those responsible for consumption decisions. In the case of politicians the distinctive characteristics of the consumers have often been recognized, but we also need to consider the role in government decisions of line administrators, or if we turn to a microeconomic level, of line managers. None of these consumers are detached seekers after truth or even disinterested about the form of solutions to their own problems. If they cannot be seen to provide their own answers they will prefer it to seem that the answers have come from persons or bodies within their own control.

We also need to take account of the vagueness of the boundaries inside which the advice of economists is likely to be useful in practice. Simultaneously there exist the better defined areas of expertise of other professions – of bankers and financiers or, at the microeconomic level, of lawyers, management consultants, systems analysts, consulting engineers and, not least, accountants. Most of these professionals have also been increasing in importance in our managerial society. Many of the matters on which economists can most usefully comment overlap the natural territories of these professions. Moreover, some of the things, and often the most useful things, that economists have to say will not be based on an additional complementary expertise but on pointing out the limitations of the dogmas of the other professions. It is not surprising therefore that economists will often be unpopular. While their advice may be accepted in the short run, there will be attempts in the longer run to bring them under control both by giving them more regular employment and by incorporating elements of economics in professional training. Of course there may be some rationality in these moves by the customers to bring the production of what they consume more under their control; but the moves are likely to be pushed irrationally far.

There will always remain, however, some role, and from time to time an important role for the independent economist, working from simple principles:

i nothing has a single absolute value – because every good has a marginal utility that diminishes with its quantity;
ii relative values shift with circumstances;
iii maxims appropriate to individual action are not necessarily true in the aggregate;
iv nothing can be extrapolated with confidence since recognition of a relationship will modify the actions that determine it.

I suspect that it was their recognition of these sorts of simple truths that accounts for the success, as men of affairs, of Sir Alec and others of his generation. (What was it that made economists such good administrators in wartime?).

Yet it needs to be remembered that such truths, although simple, are not always willingly recognized because they are subversive of the more orderly views that non-economists prefer to have of the world.

Thus simple truths require active and effective propagation and I can think of no more successful purveyor of them than Sir Alec himself.

Discussion

With four former chief economic advisers to the government present, the debate on the opening paper inevitably ended up focusing on economic advice to governments. Before it reached that point, however, *Professor Alec Nove* of Glasgow University drew attention to the ways in which the shortcomings of economics textbooks might be held responsible for some of the mistakes of economic policy. He pointed out that particularly when they dealt with microeconomics, textbooks often gave a quite unrealistic picture of the way the economy worked. If one looked up the words 'quality', or 'goodwill' or 'sub-contractors' in the index of any standard textbook, the chances were that the word would not be there. The word 'quality' might appear in the irrelevant context of product differentiation. Paul Samuelson mentioned 'goodwill' only to say – without explanation – that it was something which could be sold. Yet all of these concepts played an important part in the real microeconomic world.

To illustrate the connection with government policy, he pointed out that a nationalized industry was very often in a monopoly position, and if instructed to behave 'commercially' could 'improve' its performance through a deterioration of quality. A nationalized industry operating within a commercial framework had no great incentive to preserve goodwill.

Words like 'duty' and 'object' or 'purpose' also tended to be ignored in standard works on microeconomics. He wondered whether this might explain the sort of statement made by an adviser to the Ministry of Transport before a House of Commons Select Committee that anyone who insisted that London Transport had some kind of social contract with Londoners would thereby make it impossible to provide efficient public transport. How on earth, Professor Nove asked, could one even begin to provide efficient public transport unless the object of the exercise were included in one's consideration of efficiency? It all reminded him of the behaviour of the bus service in the Russian town of Oryol. The service had been instructed to improve its commercial results, and therefore the driver was instructed that if on a journey to the outer suburbs he had fewer than seven passengers, he should throw them off and turn the bus round. Why, on conventional criteria, was this wrong?

Professor Sir Austin Robinson argued that economists ought to think much more about adaptation to change. In and around the year 1911, the year of Alec Cairncross's birth, he pointed out, Bleriot flew the Channel for the first time, Ford built the Tin Lizzie and Marconi communicated between Cornwall and Nova Scotia. This then was the new technology. Most of the industries in which people work today barely existed seventy years ago: petrochemicals, electronics, electrical engineering, aeronautics, automobiles. The integration of town and country was one of the most important single changes, and one which had been brought about by the invention of the internal combustion engine. One of the most difficult problems for economists, he argued, was to think about adaptation to change, whether it came from technical developments or from things which were happening to other countries. He wondered whether much of what passes for industrial trouble was not really worry about change.

Professor Sydney Checkland noted that the year 1911 had not been one when all was placid and quiet. It was the year of the National Insurance Act, and a year of great industrial disturbance – a time when Britain's industrial lead was palpably failing. He was also anxious that the conference should not underestimate the amount of thinking and discussion which was going on at the time: Alfred Marshall had been on the scene then, and had had much to say about contemporary problems.

It was *Lord Roberthall* who turned the discussion to economic advice for governments. The calculations of politicians, he pointed out, had to be done largely in terms of votes. The politician did not usually want to be presented with a lot of complicated assessments of the economic effects of policy. In Lord Roberthall's experience, an economic adviser could not be any good unless he was prepared to think about the problems as a whole, and to try to think himself into the politician's mind.

Lord Roberthall was also worried by the direction economics had recently taken. He was concerned about the advances in mathematical economics and in econometrics, because he felt that they forced terms to be defined too exactly to correspond to reality. He was also disturbed by the divisions among economists over the role of money in the economy – a subject which had been discussed exhaustively for over two hundred years. The present state of the debate, he said, was a disgrace to economists.

A younger participant took up this point. He was troubled that the heart of economic policy should be something so intensely technical as monetary policy in its present form. He had the impression that the senior generation of professional economists had some difficulty understanding what their junior colleagues were doing with their economic forecasting models. He was worried by the separation of economics from other social sciences. He felt that inflation was discussed too much in purely economic terms. The present inflation was a new historical phenomenon, with its social roots in the very prosperity of the 1950s and 1960s.

Professor Herbert Giersch drew attention to some aspects of the economist's job which had not yet been mentioned. He pointed out that the economist could help in international negotiations by using his insight to bridge gaps. He could also use his judgement to allay fears when people felt that there was an economic crisis. In cases of international conflict, the economist could act as an arbitrator,

27

finding formulas which would reconcile conflicting views. The imprecision of the English language gave British economists a particular advantage in this kind of work.

He also drew attention to the influence economists could have on policy making via public opinion − for example, by serving on Royal Commissions. The German Council of Economic Advisers (on which Professor Giersch had served) was obliged to report to the public. Its influence depended on communicating with the public. If the public cannot understand what the economist says, the economist can have no influence on policy making. He thought that as economics became more sophisticated, so it would become more difficult to translate the technical discussions of economists into language intelligible to journalists and then to the general public. This is especially important in a democracy, where politicians follow the swings of public opinion.

Dr Alan Budd, who served in the Treasury in the early 1970s, attacked what he called the 'piling up' of economists in Whitehall. He admitted that he found it irritating to see people doing academic work on civil service pay, but he also objected simply on grounds of liberal principle. Academic work should be done in the open, and it was not easy for this to happen in the Treasury. He wished that the debate on economic policy were conducted in the open, too. Any debate with the Treasury was inevitably one-sided. You put in your views: the Treasury then shuts its doors and goes into a huddle: a week or so later, you realize that your ideas have been either ignored or accepted − usually the former. But the academic economist could not discuss the Treasury's reaction with officials, because that normally involved a breach of secrecy.

Dr Budd also argued that the Treasury's enormous forecasting machinery might not be a benefit to the country. If the Treasury forecast did not take place inside Whitehall, it might be easier for a more equally balanced debate to take place. One possible forum for such a debate would be the House of Commons Treasury Committee (from which Dr Budd had recently resigned as a special adviser).

Lord Croham pointed out that the enormous expansion of economists in Whitehall had come mainly after 1964, and had been largely due to the change of government. That did not quite square with Lord Roberthall's belief that the expansion had been due to a change in the function of Whitehall economists. There had, of course, been an enormous expansion in forecasting. Taking up

Dr Budd's theme, Lord Croham argued that the reason why people paid attention to the Treasury forecast was because they believed the Treasury paid attention to it: if the forecast were taken out of the Treasury, then the Treasury might not pay much attention to it – and that might be a very good thing.

One of the most important jobs for economists in Whitehall, he argued, was to bring home to Ministers the message that 'you can't have your cake and eat it'. Economists had the essential job of pointing out that resources which were used for one purpose could not simultaneously be used for another. On the other hand, Lord Croham disagreed with Sir Austin Robinson's view that economists should think more about change. He thought economists were no better at forecasting changes – particularly social changes – than anybody else. Economists' models were based on projecting what would happen if things went on as before. Economists certainly could not have forecast the social changes brought about by technological changes such as the internal combustion engine, the radio and atomic energy.

Was the job of giving economic advice to a politician, he asked, a science or an art? He thought it was an art. He agreed with Lord Roberthall on the importance of trying to get inside the skull of a politician, and to see the situation he had to deal with. Lord Croham, who was Permanent Secretary to the Treasury from 1968 to 1974, said that it was often the individual's contribution which mattered, rather than something which might be called 'economics'. The academics who came into Whitehall and made a successful contribution were those who were able to synthesize the thinking going on around them, and the contributions of their colleagues, and to translate that into practical terms which would allow a government to formulate policy, and to explain what it was doing. Very few people who came into Whitehall from outside mastered that art.

Professor Erik Lundberg took up another quality of the successful economic adviser: what he called the 'optimum political naivety'. He agreed that the adviser must not be too divorced from political reality. But an economist who was too politically realistic was also not very useful. An economist had to decide how to reply when a politician claimed that a policy was not feasible, or politically impossible. Often, the right answer was not to give up, but to argue for working on a policy over a longer period.

When he had been working as an economic adviser, he had felt satisfied if he simply got people to consider aspects of a problem which they had forgotten to take into account. Sometimes the most useful thing an economic adviser could do was to make people question their preconceptions and their fixed ideas.

Mr David Worswick drew attention to the importance of the Centre for Administrative Studies – now absorbed into the Civil Service College – set up less than twenty years ago. It had meant that entrants into the civil service were all exposed to some elementary economics as part of their training, whatever their subject at university. He thought that this was an advance, and he hoped that it allowed the ordinary civil servant to distinguish between one economist and another. We were, he pointed out, almost at the point where very few senior civil servants had no acquaintance with economic literature.

But he shared the worries which had been expressed about the number of qualified economists 'locked up' in the Treasury and in the Bank of England. He had the impression that there was sometimes a lack of communication within Whitehall between the professional civil servants and the economic advisers. He admitted that this might be a passing phase, and a problem which would not affect younger civil servants and economists. But he also felt that the value of research work was greater if it were done for the public rather than for the government machine.

Professor Robin Matthews briefly put the other side of the issue by noting that one of the advantages that academic research in economics had over other social sciences was that there were enough people in Whitehall who could understand and respond to the relevant academic work.

Summing up, *Sir Alec Cairncross* argued that the importance of economic advisers was that they were the essential link between the theorists and the policy makers. The particular merit of economists, he said, was that they were 'rather good at other people's business'. They had a talent for listening to what two sets of people with entirely different backgrounds might be saying, and merging it together. The training of economists helped them to see that a number of disconnected points might fit together in a common framework. They had, as Dr Giersch implied, a gift as conciliators and arbitrators; and indeed as managers, for the job of managers was often to reconcile a lot of people with different points of view to working together as a team. In policy making, the economist's great merit was to master issues which were not his particular speciality to a sufficient extent to be able to illuminate what the choices were which had to be made. The economist was often rather better at this than people trained in other disciplines. Economics was a good discipline for training people to manage. It taught you, he said, to be more aware of your own ignorance and of the uncertainty of the world.

Turning to the question of whether there were too many economists inside the government machine, Sir Alec argued that the important thing was to have enough people in Whitehall to deal with the issues which mattered. If there were a lot of important economic issues, then the Government needed a lot of people trained in economics. But he felt that there was too great a tendency to take economists into Whitehall and make them think that was where their future career lay. It did not matter if the Treasury and the Bank of England took on a lot of economists, as long as they pushed some of them out again. There was no career for most of the economists who went into the Treasury, simply because in peacetime there were very few decisions which had to be taken there. It was very bad for morale if there were too many young people and too little for them to do that really mattered, and if as a result people were pushed into simply doing research. It was always healthy for young people to move around and change jobs from time to time, whether they were economists or not.

He agreed with Professor Erik Lundberg that one of the most difficult things in life was to know how far to accept propositions as absolutely indestructible, and how far to bend. If you bent too much, he said, you had no sense of commitment, and other people would not take you seriously. If you bent too little, then you might do real harm. As an adviser, he had always found it hard to decide where the sticking points should be, and where to accept that politicians were bound by electoral constraints. It was important that economists did not come to believe that they were deciding policy. That was the job of Ministers. Economists sometimes simply had to accept that in a democracy, public opinion might prevent their advice from being implemented.

The discussion had only touched briefly on the issue of how far economics was really about a society in course of change, where problems constantly altered. Economists were always passionate in the pursuit of the truth. But they had to accept that economic problems changed so rapidly that by the time the economist found an answer, a different set of problems had arisen. One of the differences between economics and the natural sciences was that economics dealt with a constantly changing world. By the time an economist had written his textbook, it might well be out of date. So economists must always have an experimental attitude.

2

The development of demand management

SIR BRYAN HOPKIN

THE ORIGINS OF 'DEMAND MANAGEMENT'

The origins of post-1945 demand management policy are to be found in the experience and economic thinking of the inter-war period 1918–39.

That period was characterized in Britain by a generally high level of unemployment which at its peak in 1932 amounted to 2.8 m., 22 per cent of the then insured labour force, and which even in good years like 1929 and 1937 did not fall below 10 per cent. Other industrialized countries also suffered heavily from unemployment in the years of cyclical recession, though for the most part they enjoyed higher levels of employment than Britain in the better years. Britain had in some degree a problem of her own.

The economic and social damage done by unemployment on this scale was undoubtedly substantial. A lot of productive potential went unused. Unemployment was the principal cause of poverty in the inter-war period. Life on the dole was straitened and demoralizing. For many years, however, the prevailing view (though not among economists) was that unemployment had to be accepted as the unavoidable result of economic forces. In particular, the principles of sound finance, adhered to by at least the two major political parties and by most influential economic commentators, ruled out the deliberate recourse to an unbalanced budget in order to create more demand.

During the 1930s opinion began to change. Inside the Treasury leading officials were influenced in their attitudes (especially to monetary policy) by the desire to promote employment. Outside, J. M. Keynes (who in 1929 had joined with Hubert Henderson to support a Liberal Party plan for a public works programme) overthrew the intellectual basis of the 'sound finance' attitude to economic policy. The *General Theory of Employment Interest and Money* (1936) argued that the economy contained no reliable mechanism for ensuring a flow of demand sufficient to secure or maintain an adequate level of employment, and that, if an insufficient strength of the spending propensities of the private sector was the cause of the situation, a remedy could and should be found through the use of public spending power. These ideas did not immediately take over the direction of government policies, but they soon became powerful in the thinking of economists both in Britain and abroad, and this paved the way to their later conquest of the citadels of economic policy.

In the light of subsequent events it is important to recall the relative lack of urgency during most of the inter-war period of the problems of the balance of payments and of inflation. Britain's balance of payments was sustained throughout the inter-war period by a large net inflow of investment income and, after 1929, by low import prices incidental to the depression in world commodity markets. And in the depressed trading conditions, the trade unions – given their strength at the time – were not able to secure any considerable advances in money wages. Retail prices were roughly stable in the late 1920s and actually fell in the recession years 1929–33. In 1939 the cost of living index was lower than it had been in 1922.

During the Second World War several factors combined to speed up the change in ideas about policy. The rapid disappearance of unemployment demonstrated the overwhelming importance of demand as a determinant of economic activity. As the war moved towards its end, and minds turned with hope to the task of working out plans for a better world to follow it, the theme emerged powerfully that a return to mass unemployment could and should be avoided. Beveridge's book *Full Employment in a Free Society*[1] both embodied and reinforced this demand, and the prevailing opinions both of economists and of the wider circle of people interested in economic policy were on his side. In this movement of ideas the influence of Keynes was undoubtedly very great. The government White Paper (1944) on Employment Policy (Cmnd. 6527; published *before* Beveridge) showed the progress of ideas above all in its first sentence: 'the Government accept as one of its main aims and responsibilities the maintenance of a high and stable level of employment after the war'. What *followed* this ringing declaration in the way of policy specification was somewhat confused and contradictory. It lacked the force and clarity of Beveridge. But the statement of aim was vitally important and already established a great break with the policy attitude of the inter-war period.

In the course of a few years following the end of the Second World War in 1945, it became an unchallenged fact that the Government had accepted responsibility for controlling the level of aggregate demand for goods and services in the economy. In other Western countries policy attitudes were developing on broadly similar lines, though the concept and Keynesian origin of the policy was perhaps somewhat more explicit in Britain than elsewhere.

During that period, the standard formulation of the objectives of macroeconomic policy was given as the following four-part statement:

  i full employment (or high and stable employment),
 ii balance of payments equilibrium,
iii 'reasonable' stability of prices,
 iv a satisfactory rate of economic growth.

These expression, as they stand, are somewhat vague and they beg several questions, but they are not beyond reasonably precise definition. They provide an initial basis for appraising the achievement of demand management policy.

The level of aggregate demand, and its rate of increase, have a clear and strong bearing on each of these four objectives: and it is from this fact that its importance in macroeconomic policy derives. Indeed, it would be true to say that so far as *short-term* policy variation is concerned, demand management was substantially the *sole* method by which the government sought to realize these objectives. This statement may encounter the logical objection that one instrument cannot promote four objectives unless there is no possibility of conflict between the objectives. If the objectives are genuinely independent you need four instruments for complete success.

There were, indeed, other relevant instruments of policy. The exchange rate, and to a lesser degree the system of tariffs, import restrictions and payments controls, constituted methods of influencing the balance of payments. But these were instruments which under Bretton Woods, the IMF and GATT were essentially a long-term framework in which the flows of trade and payments developed: they did not normally provide a means for *short-term* adjustment.

As regards inflation, in the long periods in which incomes were determined on a basis of free collective bargaining, demand management provided the only short-term method for influencing (directly or indirectly) the trend of prices.

As an explicit objective of macroeconomic policy, a high rate of economic growth can hardly be said to have been clearly recognized until about 1960. Then and later a strong and steady rate of growth of demand would have been thought the principal way in which short-term macroeconomic policy could be helpful in this context: other policies – investment incentives, indicative planning – were, again, long-term policies setting the 'framework'.

The dominance of demand management in macroeconomic policy reached its peak about 1960, when the last features of the system of direct controls inherited from the war (apart from exchange controls on capital flows) had been abolished. Around that time, it would not have been untrue to say that the presentation and discussion of economic policy seemed to presuppose the truth of the following four propositions:

i The level of aggregate demand was the main – almost the sole – short-term determinant of the level of employment (*given* the available labour force).

ii The level of aggregate demand had important repercussions on the balance of payments, the rate of price inflation, and the rate of economic growth.

iii Effective means of controlling the level of aggregate demand were available to the government through fiscal and monetary policy.

iv Though there could be a conflict of objectives – for in some circumstances an increase in demand which would be helpful from the point of view of employment and economic growth could have damaging effects on inflation and the balance of payments – in normal times it should be possible, by skilful diagnosis and timely choice of measures, for the government so to

36

regulate demand as to achieve a reasonable outcome in terms of *all* the objectives.

These statements did not appear anywhere as an accepted and explicit doctrine, but they were inherent in many of the statements both of the makers of demand policy and of their critics. In at least the short-term management of the economy, the control of demand was dominant.

The control of demand was operated, over most of the period in question, through both fiscal and monetary policy, but fiscal policy was regarded as much the senior partner. Fiscal policy, it was believed, could affect demand powerfully and fairly predictably, though with a time lag – partly through varying government expenditure, and partly through taxation which varied real purchasing power and thus (in the main) consumption.

Monetary policy could also be used to affect the level of demand. According to the prevailing philosophy (well represented by the Radcliffe Committee Report of 1959), the main vehicle of monetary policy was interest rates (the quantity of money was of no special importance, as the velocity of circulation might vary within wide limits and the banks formed only one part of a very large system for generating credit). But the influence of interest rates on demand for goods and services was not very powerful; and though the direct control of access to credit (bank advances, hire purchase) could affect spending, the use of such control could be unfair and disruptive of industry. The power of monetary policy to affect the economy was accordingly, in practice, rather limited. In one important department of monetary policy, namely interest rates, the major concerns of the authorities were to safeguard the capital account of the balance of payments, on the one hand, and to promote the sales of government stock, on the other, rather than to support any particular objective in the way of demand policy.

Because of the dominant role of fiscal policy, the annual Budget came to play a very conspicuous part in the presentation and discussion of macroeconomic policy. And because all measures of demand control take time before they show their full effect, there was a great development of short-term economic forecasting to provide a basis for policy. For many years this was an activity carried out (in the UK) solely within the government machine, and typically only the barest indication of its results was published. As time went on outside bodies in the academic and business worlds got into the forecasting business. Associated intellectually with the development of forecasting and the use of economic models to 'simulate' policy operations was a tendency, evident from time to time if not continuously, for the government to engage in 'fine-tuning', i.e. the attempt by frequent and small adjustments of policy to achieve a close correspondence between the state of the economy and official objectives for the level of activity and other key elements. In line with this objective was the institution (1961) of the 'Regulator' powers which enabled the Chancellor of the Exchequer, at times other than that of the Budget, to vary the level of indirect taxes, within limits, for stabilization purposes by a procedure much less cumbrous than that of a normal Finance Bill.

The account of macroeconomic policy which has been given above is applicable in a broad way to Britain between 1945 and about 1974. In trying to evaluate the experience, it is convenient first to limit ourselves to that period and to the four objectives which, as set out at the beginning of this section, can be said to have been the ones that were being aimed at. We begin with a brief record of the degree of success with each one.

i *High and stable employment:* broadly, high employment *was* achieved, the level of unemployment being on average less than 2 per cent, a great improvement on the inter-war period or even on pre-1914. The experience of other Western industrial countries in the same period was roughly similar. It has been argued that the immediate causes of high employment lay in strong spending propensities of the private sector rather than in the governments' fiscal policies: but at least the policies were such as to take advantage of the opportunity presented. Even so, there are some qualifications. There was some instability in employment, though on nothing like the pre-war scale: unemployment was above 2 per cent in five (separated) years between 1946 and 1966 and in *every* year after 1967. Further, the 'trend' level of unemployment, measured by the average of periods of four or five years, rose fairly steadily.

Studies by J. C. R. Dow[2] and Bent Hansen[3] suggested that demand policy in this country was itself a principal cause of the instability in the economy. There had been a tendency to act too late, when the economy was moving towards a situation either of excess demand (with inflationary pressure and balance of payments weakness) or insufficient demand (with an 'unacceptable' level of unemployment). Then when the action was taken, insufficient allowance was made for time lags and the condition of the economy was over-corrected. Even if we may be sceptical of any implication that the economy would have been more stable without any deliberate demand management (for the modern industrial economy has its own power to generate cyclical fluctuation), it is clear that the achievements of demand policy in post-war Britain fell some way short of the ideal of steady growth at an 'appropriate' employment level.

ii *Balance of payments equilibrium:* here the record was distinctly less good than on employment. Over a sizeable proportion of the post-war period there was an actual deficit on current and long-term capital account taken together, or a *tendency* to deficit held in check by various measures disagreeable in their side effects on our own society, or on other countries, or on both. From time to time this underlying trouble erupted in crises (in nine years between 1947 and 1972) damaging to internal confidence, to the country's international position, and to the international monetary system. Other countries on the whole did much less badly than Britain in this sphere.

iii *Stability of prices:* here the record was thoroughly depressing. The general price index rose in almost every year: the average for the period was about 4 per cent a year, and what was worse was that the rate of rise was accelerating, especially in the last ten years of the period. Other Western countries also suffered continuing inflation, the average rate being a little lower than Britain's.

It has, indeed, been argued that the policy of maintaining a high level of demand through thick and thin in the interests of full employment had the effect of 'validating' inflationary behaviour in the fields of wages and prices. In a situation in which the experience of inflation had a powerful effect on the scale of wage settlements, there was a ratchet effect in the inflationary process which was for a long time insufficiently recognized.

iv *Economic growth:* the trend rate of growth of the real national product per head in the post-war period to 1974 seems to have remained between 2½ per cent and 3 per cent a year. This was a good deal higher than our pre-war norm of about 1½ per cent: but it was a good deal less than the rate achieved in most other Western countries. As a result we lost the position we formerly enjoyed among the leaders of the nations in regard to real income per head and fell quite a long way down the list.

The question now arises: what contribution was made to this rather mixed record of economic success/failure by the control of demand? In trying to answer this question we may distinguish two levels at which demand policy can be evaluated. The first level is one which accepts the general aims and nature of the policy and seeks to appraise the detailed quality, or efficiency, of its execution. The second and more fundamental asks whether the whole conception of the policy was wrong in some basic way.

On the first of these two levels, that of the efficiency with which the policy was executed, the Dow/Hansen studies (and others) make it clear that in retrospect the efficiency was a good deal less than perfect. A fairly small part of this inefficiency seems to have been due to wrong economic forecasts. On at least three occasions (1959, 1962 and 1970) the forecasts pointed in a materially wrong direction and pretty certainly contributed to what afterwards appeared substantial errors in policy. Much more often, the policies seem to have been aimed at the wrong targets in spite of being based on broadly correct forecasts. A general feature of these policy errors was the tendency referred to earlier, to leave action too late and then overdo it − 'too much too late'. It is natural for policy makers to wait until they can be *sure* of the need for action; but it represents a failure to realize the implications of the long lags in the effects of policy.

Demand policy was thus somewhat inefficient; nevertheless it achieved a good average result in terms of what must be regarded as its principal objective, the level of employment. The more serious and fundamental doubts, affecting the shape and pattern of policy rather than its execution, arise in examining the record in other departments than employment.

Demand control as envisaged and practised in and around 1960 plainly proved incapable of safeguarding the balance of payments. Other policies, notably devaluations in 1949 and 1967 and the abandonment of the fixed rate in 1972, had to be resorted to in dealing with successive balance of payments crises − to say nothing of special measures from time to time like the surcharge of 1964. Even so, the underlying balance of payments position was probably rather worse at the end of the period than twenty years before. Kaldor has argued that demand policy as practised in Britain meant that the economy was 'consumption led' when it would have been better for economic growth if it had been 'export led'. The economists who form the Cambridge Economic Policy Group have taken this argument a stage further, arguing that macroeconomic policy failed to come to grips with a long-term trend in Britain's economic structure. This was manifested in a trend divergence between the volume rates of growth of our exports and of our imports of manufactures and this led eventually to a decline in *net* exports. It is difficult to deny that in comparative international terms British industry has shown a lack of dynamism − of the ability to identify and grasp opportunities for the exploitation of new technologies and new or expanding markets. Whatever the causes of this deficiency, it was clear that demand management did not and could not provide a remedy for it.

It is also clear that demand policy as practised was unable to prevent the acceleration during the 1960s of price inflation. Faced with the problem of cost inflation − i.e. inflation continuing at times when demand was clearly not excessive, whose proximate cause was normally to be found in the scale of wage and salary increases − successive governments attempted direct restraint on the cost-inflationary process by means of 'incomes policy'. The final balance sheet of these attempts is a matter of much debate. In several cases the immediate effect of the policy on the rates of increase of wages and prices was clear and strong: but each successive attempt was eventually abandoned and normally followed by a period of unusually large increases in both pay and prices. There is no doubt that at the end of the period the underlying inflationary pressures were stronger than at the beginning. This was one problem to which macroeconomic demand policy seemed to have no answer, and it was not certain that there was any other satisfactory answer available.

From time to time during the period under review (e.g. 1962/3, 1972/3), the desire to increase the rate of economic growth has been one motive for policies aimed at large increases in demand. There was also one fairly serious attempt to use the technique of 'indicative planning' to improve the supply side determinants of growth. The rate of underlying growth in productive capacity is difficult to measure with any confidence. Between about 1950 and about 1960 there is some suggestion of an acceleration but this does not seem to have continued. Here again demand policy had not proved to have any answer to the problem, and answers of any other kind were proving elusive.

By the end of the period, active demand management policy had lost a good deal of the glamour which had once invested it. It did not seem to have answers to the problem of the balance of payments or to that of inflation: other policies had had to be used to deal with those problems, which nevertheless remained serious. However, as late as 1974 the use of fiscal policy to sustain employment – a typical exercise in demand policy – played a large role in the macroeconomic policies of the year.

THE CHALLENGE TO KEYNESIAN POLICY IN THE 1970s

The challenge from events. Into a few years of the early 1970s were crowded a series of events which demonstrated that the economic environment had changed in ways which created great difficulties for demand management as practised in Britain up to that time.

First, there was the world commodity price boom of 1972–3 and the oil price rises of 1973–4. The first of these represented something more than a rather vigorous trade cycle effect, since over the twenty previous years commodity prices had shown no long-term trend. The second was even more of a break with the past. The oil price rise also had the special characteristic that it transferred purchasing power on an enormous scale to countries which were not able to use it immediately. It exercised a strong contractionary effect on world demand, while at the same time exercising a powerful inflationary effect on prices everywhere. It thus propelled the world economy into recession while inhibiting in governments any tendency which they might otherwise have shown to take counter action that would increase demand.

A second development was the collapse of the Bretton Woods international monetary system (1971–3). This made for a much more disturbed set of international trade and financial relations, with possibilities of large and unpredictable changes in exchange rates and in capital flows across the exchanges.

Thirdly, the inflationary potential of the wage and salary bargaining system was revealed strikingly in the events of 1974–5. This was the result of certain special factors (the system of threshold increases, the replacement of the Heath by the Wilson government) superimposed on a trend towards increasing strength and confidence among the organized workers which had been in progress for many years. 'Real wage resistance', i.e. the attempt to defend real earnings against the impoverishing effect of extraneous forces (such as the oil price rise) by seeking correspondingly large rises in money wages and salaries, emerged as a major contributor to the inflationary process.

These three factors together produced a sharp increase in the strength of the forces making for inflation in the economy, and added greatly to the uncertainty of all economic calculations. The experience of much faster inflation undoubtedly lessened the strength of private sector spending propensities. Consumers in Britain reacted to the situation with a sharp rise in their collective personal saving rate, for reasons which are not entirely clear but may represent a reaction to the depletion by inflation of the real value of their money-denominated wealth holdings (bank deposits, building society shares, etc.). Business investment was discouraged both by low consumption and by the prevailing atmosphere of insecurity.

The logical reaction of Keynesian demand management policy to weak private sector spending propensities would be to change fiscal and monetary policy in an expansionary direction, and this *should* have been made easier after 1972 by the fact that the exchange rate was floating. The *initial* response of British economic policy to the new situation, in 1974, could be regarded as following in this tradition though perhaps it was not a fully conscious and deliberate decision so to act. Later on, policy was conspicuously different.

Before, however, we come to examine policy reactions, a fourth development must be mentioned, this one, unlike the others, bringing gain rather than loss to the British economy: the exploitation of North Sea oil. Starting in 1976, over four years the British economy became self-sufficient in oil, with substantial gains to real national income and a gradual strengthening of the balance of payments. However, this good fortune also brought with it some quite serious problems.

The challenge from monetarist thinking. During the 1970s the discussion and practice of economic policy in Britain as in other countries have shown the influence of ideas which are directly or by implication inconsistent with the thinking which underlay the Keynesian demand management policy described above. Far the most influential of these ideas has been what is called monetarism.

From a practical point of view the chief feature of monetarism is the central importance it gives to the growth of the quantity of money as an element of economic policy. Also important, however, is that as a matter of underlying philosophy the monetarists give little credence to the dangers to the economy from instability in the private sector and/or the weakness of the natural mechanisms of adjustment to any such instability. Conversely, they take a low view of the ability and will of governments to foresee and accurately to compensate for fluctuations through one or other of the instruments of demand management.

The importance given to the rate of growth of the money supply depends on the belief that the velocity of circulation can usually be depended upon to be stable, or at least predictable, because its determinants are *either* themselves slow to change (private wealth; 'normal' income) or rather weak in their influence (interest rates). Thus the growth of money national income can reasonably well be determined from the rate of growth of the money stock. When, under the influence of a change in the rate of growth of the money supply, there is a change in the growth of money national income, the initial effect will be a quantity (or real) effect: the *volume* of production will change. But soon after this the effect will be shown in the trend of prices and before long this will take up the whole of the increased money supply: the volume of production will revert to the level it would otherwise have had. Experience, as read by the monetarists, suggests that the period after which the rate of growth of the money supply is fully reflected in the price trend is about two years, though this is subject to a margin of error. Fiscal policy *per se* is relatively powerless to affect demand and activity, except in the short run. If a change in fiscal policy is associated with a change in the rate of growth of the money supply, then there will be an effect on demand and for a time on activity, but in the long run the effect will be on prices. If the change in fiscal policy takes place without any change in the trend of money supply, the effect of the policy change, first on demand but soon on prices too, will 'crowd out' an equal amount of private sector demand through the effects of increasing demand for money on interest rates.

It follows from the argument so far that the central element in economic policy is and must be the rate of growth of the money supply. But the control of this key element is not to be used in a discretionary way to offset year to year changes in private sector spending: for the lags in the influence of money on the economy are long and variable, and governments are not to be trusted in prognosis or policy adjustment. What is wanted is adherence to a long term steady course of monetary growth, set in advance and *published* in order to reduce uncertainty and give the maximum of advance knowledge to the private sector.

In its account of the labour market, the key concept of monetarist doctrine is the 'natural rate of unemployment'. At this level of unemployment, which is set by the institutional framework and modes of working of the labour market, and which changes only slowly if at all, there will be a constant rate of inflation. A lower level of unemployment than this natural level can be achieved only at the cost of *steadily accelerating* inflation. It is, indeed, this accelerating inflation which is the *cause* of the low unemployment: it works by causing the workers to overestimate their future real wage level and therefore to find employment more attractive. Conversely, a deceleration of the inflation has the opposite affect on workers' expectations and so produces unemployment above the natural level. When actual inflation and expectations of inflation are brought into line, unemployment will be at its natural level. All unemployment above the natural level arises from the unwillingness of workers to accept employment at the real wages they *believe* they are being offered, therefore it is said to be voluntary. Unemployment is not caused simply by deficient demand, but arises out of the interplay of actual prices (which may be influenced by demand) and expected prices.

It is a mistake to think that monetary expansion can bring about a lowering of interest rates, except in the very short run. Once the effects of the expansion on prices have been appreciated, the rise in inflationary expectations will force interest rates up to compensate.

Finally, monetarism sees the balance of payments (taking the current and capital accounts together) as the difference between the growth of the country's *demand* for money and the supply of money from *domestic* sources (domestic credit expansion). A balance of payments deficit is always the result of an excessive level of domestic credit expansion. With a freely floating exchange rate and a proper restraint in domestic credit expansion, there would be no balance of payments problem.

Changes in the priorities and instruments of economic policy in the 1970s. The changes in the economic environment, and in economic thinking, which have been summarized above, had − in Britain as in other countries − a substantial impact on economic policy, both in its priorities and in its methods. Everywhere, resistance to inflation became more and more important as an objective of policy relative to the maintenance of employment. In Britain, an additional factor was that for several critical years after 1973 the maintenance of the country's international credit-worthiness became a vital objective, in order to assure finance for very heavy balance of payments deficits; and for this reason too the relative priority given to the maintenance of employment had to be reduced.

Accompanying these changes in priorities were certain changes in the nature and relative weight of different methods of influencing the economy. The most striking of these was the adoption of targets for monetary growth and their gradual rise to a central position in macroeconomic policy. Fiscal policy became less important and from being the senior partner came to be thought of largely from the special point of view of its effect on the financial markets and through them on the growth of money supply.

The relation of policy to the balance of payments was changed considerably by the collapse of the Bretton Woods system between 1971 and 1973. Britain floated the exchange rate in June 1972; in the following years the system could be described as one of 'managed' floating though the degree of the authorities' control was never very complete and as time went on its limitations were more and more clearly recognized.

The anxiety about inflation generated two substantial experiments in incomes policy during the 1970s, one under the Conservatives in 1972−4 and one under Labour in 1975−9. Each had a period of apparent success but eventually ran into problems which proved (or at least seemed) insurmountable. The extreme need to find a solution to the inflation problem which does *not* rely on deliberately created recession and unemployment must presumably explain why in spite of past failures governments have repeatedly turned to incomes policy after saying forcibly that they would not do so. We have probably not seen the last of such occasions.

In sum, therefore, as the 1970s went on, the management of demand for purposes of employment maintenance became a less and less dominating objective. Already in 1975 there was the landmark of a Labour government, faced with the prospect of a substantial increase of unemployment, deliberately choosing a fiscal policy which did nothing to prevent that outcome. In 1976 a monetary growth target was instituted and at the same time fiscal policy was moved strongly in a contractionary direction. In 1978 there was a fiscal relaxation which could perhaps be regarded as the last dying kick (for the time being at least) of Keynesian demand management; for in 1979 with the election and coming to power of the Conservative government a full blooded monetarist policy was adopted, and demand management was entirely abandoned. The essential feature of present policy is a published target (stated as a range) for the growth rate of the money supply (£M3): this was fixed ahead for four years on a year-by-year falling scale. The overriding aim of policy is to reduce the rate of price inflation and the reduction of the rate of growth of £M3 was seen as the necessary and sufficient condition – incomes policy being anathema – for achieving this aim.

An important but subsidiary element in policy is the size of the Public Sector Borrowing Requirement (PSBR), which is seen as indirectly controlling the level to which interest rates have to be pushed in the course of controlling the growth of £M3 to the announced target. For this also there is a medium-term programme which involves a step-by-step reduction over the same four years: this is a much less precise commitment than the £M3 target. To make this reduction possible, while simultaneously allowing a reduction in taxation, the government is seeking to exercise a very severe restraint on public expenditure.

A third principal element in the present structure of macro-econonomic policy is a high external value for the pound. This is to a large extent a resultant of North Sea oil and the high interest rates which have proved (as things have turned out) to be a necessary accompaniment to the government's monetary policy: but it has been accepted because it helps to keep prices down and so contributes to the objective of reducing inflation.

In line with monetarist thinking generally, a large role is given in this policy outlook to the public's *expectations* of future inflation. One element of this thinking is that the mere *announcement* of firm (and medium-term) targets for monetary growth will of itself lower inflationary expectations and so affect actions, e.g. in regard to wages, in ways which will reduce price inflation. But even if this effect fails, there will still be effects on demand via fiscal policy or via interest rates which will slow down the rise in (wage) costs and *possibly* also reduce profit margins. Once inflationary expectations have been largely or completely destroyed, the continued maintenance of the target money growth will permit a faster growth of *real* demand and in this way unemployment can be expected to fall to or towards its 'natural' level. During the transitional period there will have been some unemployment which will have been caused essentially by a systematic error in the workers' apprehension of the future real wage level. That is, the workers expect more inflation than there will be, underestimate the future real wage, and in consequence there is an increase in (voluntary) unemployment.

THE FUTURE

At the time of this conference, the chances of success of the present monetarist experiment do not seem to me to be high.

First, it is quite plain that the technical difficulties of controlling the growth of money supply to a pre-set target figure were grossly underestimated. This is partly because monetarist economics has always failed to recognize the extent to which the money supply is endogenous to the system of production and trade. A good deal of the observed relation between the money supply and the money national income has been due to the fact that monetary systems typically respond to changes in the rate of expansion of the economy with changes in the rate of increase of the money supply. The public and the private elements of the monetary system have each made their own independent contributions to this result. It has proved and is proving extremely difficult, given these tendencies, to turn the money supply into a control variable.

Secondly, and partly for the same reason, there are grave doubts about the asserted relationship between the growth of money supply on the one hand and the growth of nominal income and the price level on the other. In the statistical relation observed in the past, the direction of causation has not been, or not only been, from money to national income but also from national income to money; and we are not entitled to infer from the statistical record of the past any definite conclusion about the strength of the *causal* influence of money on income.

Thirdly, there are doubts about the mechanism linking the money flow with prices. The relationship between money supply lagged about two years, and the price index is, in my view, impressive only to those who look at it with the eye of faith. Nor is this surprising given the absence of any identifiable and reliable mechanism linking the two. With 'normal cost' pricing as the dominant element in the formation of prices in Britain, the most plausible *modus operandi* of monetary restriction runs *via* wages/salaries and labour unit cost. This *modus operandi* depends on the effect of unemployment in bringing down the size of negotiated pay settlements. We have no reason to expect this to be anything but slow, at best. Thus the slowing down in the growth of money national income brought about by restriction of monetary growth will for a long time take the form of falling activity and not of lower price inflation.

Fourthly, the monetarist account of the labour market is deeply unconvincing. We are asked to believe that all unemployment above a normal or 'natural' level of unemployment arises from wrong forecasting by the workers. Thus the huge increase in unemployment between 1973 and 1976, and again from 1979 to 1981, must be made up of two elements:

i an increase in the natural level of unemployment
ii an increase in the amount of unemployment attributable to workers' wrong forecasts of prices

There is nothing remotely plausible which could have generated the first effect on the scale of the recorded increases in unemployment in such a short time, and it is even less plausible that − as a *continuing* phenomenon − they could be accounted for by effect ii. There is thus something basically unconvincing about the monetarist explanation of unemployment as we are suffering it.

Fifthly, the argument that any attempt to secure expansion by fiscal policy would necessarily 'crowd out' an equivalent amount of private sector demand is unconvincing when applied to situations of heavy unemployment and general unused capacity. In such situations, where the economy is physically capable of meeting a substantial increase in demand by bringing its productive capacity more fully into use, it is difficult to see why there should be any overriding difficulty on the side of finance. Savings are not fixed, but will expand with the rise in national income: only on very extreme assumptions would the resulting rise (with fixed money stock) in interest rates have such an effect on demand as to offset the original fiscal stimulus completely. And on a wider view, in which fiscal and monetary policy are viewed as complementary there must be some way in which the asset-preferences of the private sector could be satisfied without any damaging increase in interest rates. Only *idées fixes* of an extreme and unjustifiable kind about the rate of growth of the money supply could provide an apparent rationale for this chimera.

If then, the monetarist answers to the problems of macroeconomic policy are so unsatisfactory, it is natural to ask why the doctrine has made so many converts and why it has taken over the direction of British policy. The answer may be that it seemed to provide an answer to the frustration created by the apparently invincible combination of inflation with unemployment from which we and other countries have been suffering in recent years. A simple explanation of inflation, and a simple, available and clear-cut remedy for it which holds out the promise, at least in the long run, of returning to something nearer full employment, had many attractions. It is an interesting fact that this doctrine of somewhat abstract economics has won more converts among practical men in the city, financial journalism and politics than it has among academic economists. The protest against monetarist policy by the 364 university economists can reasonably be regarded as expressing a consensus view among the academics.

These arguments do not show, and are not intended to show, that the rate of inflation will not, in the end, be reduced by fiscal and money policies which reduce demand, assuming that they are steadily maintained for as long as it provides necessary (nor would this ever have been denied by most non-monetarist economists). What they tend to show is first, that the length of time required, and the losses on the way, are likely to be much greater than the monetarist doctrines suggest; and secondly, that there is no reason to believe that these policies on their own will prevent a re-acceleration of inflation if and when activity increases again or there is some shock to the system from, e.g. import prices or trade union militancy. A very high price is being paid for what is likely to turn out − on present policies − a rather meagre achievement. What is more, the policy at no point comes to grips with the problem of international competitiveness and the inadequate performance of British manufacturing industry. Indeed, in at least one respect − the exchange rate − the present policy is actively promoting the destructive trend from which the economy is suffering. It is natural therefore to look at alternative policies, if only in barest outline, and to ask what role these might allocate to 'demand management'.

Can we envisage a future in which the level of demand, and the rate of unemployment, are once again elements in the set of objectives at which policy is aimed? Possibly, but clearly it will not be possible to set high targets for demand and employment except within a broader framework of policy which effectively constrains the rate of inflation, preserves international competitiveness and provides a remedy to the problem of industrial failure.

Such a policy might contain three elements:

i some kind of 'incomes policy'
ii a policy for international competitiveness
iii a policy for home demand.

Ideally, the list would have included a direct attack on the causes of the industrial weakness instead of, or along with, item ii. But for this, at the present, the necessary knowledge cannot be said to exist.

As regards item i, no formula can be laid down since so much depends on the states of mind of the parties to the income determination process. Until an attempt is made by a government which believes in the objective it will not be possible to say anything very definite about the detailed forms and targets of the policy.

Take first an optimistic hypothesis about the results of such an initiative. This would open up the way to a policy of improving international competitiveness, and this must involve getting the exchange rate down. Once the monetarist shibboleths are abandoned, the means for achieving this will certainly exist though there may be some technical problems in getting the scale and timing right. The main danger on this side, however, is that of setting off, via the cost of living and 'real wage resistance', a compulsory movement in domestic incomes and costs which would in no long time erode the desired improvement in international competitiveness. This is where incomes policy could make an essential contribution.

In the optimistic scenario in which these policies are successful, it will be possible to return to 'demand management' and aim fiscal and monetary policy once again at a return towards full employment. In such a scenario there might well be a place for an element of announced targetry so far as nominal GNP or the total of nominal domestic expenditure is concerned, but the PSBR and the growth of the money supply should have the status of interesting by-products of the economic forecast, not of policy targets and over-riding constraints.

If optimism about the chances of a consensus incomes policy proves unjustified we shall face an altogether harsher world. It is difficult, and perhaps unnecessary, to try to guess what policies would recommend themselves in such a situation. We may find ourselves having to face such painful measures as a statutory incomes policy operated against trade union non-cooperation, or a protectionist policy operated against international opposition, simply because the results of the alternative policies for inflation, industrial performance, and employment are too bad to tolerate.

NOTES

1   W. H. Beveridge, *Full Employment in a Free Society,* London: George Allen & Unwin, 1944.
2   J. C. R. Dow, *The Management of the British Economy, 1945–1960,* Cambridge: Cambridge University Press, 1964.
3   Bent Hansen (with W. W. Snyder), *Fiscal Policy in Seven Countries,* OECD, 1969.

Comments by
Alan Budd

I should perhaps begin my comments by saying that I did not meet Sir Alec Cairncross until he had left the Treasury.[1] I have however had the pleasure of meeting him on many occasions since and I am delighted to be able to celebrate his seventieth birthday. On the other hand I did work under Sir Bryan Hopkin at the Treasury and I regard that experience as one of the most fruitful and enjoyable periods of my career. Sir Bryan has written an account of post-war economic policy which I suspect will be warmly endorsed by Sir Alec and by most if not all of the distinguished economists and administrators who are here at this conference. It is only therefore, with considerable reluctance, that I take issue with some of the points he makes.

There is first the account of the role of demand management in the post-war years with its apparent success followed by disillusion and finally rejection. That account can, I think, be described as 'Keynesian history'. It is written from the standpoint of one who believes that Keynesian demand management policies are correct, that their failure was due to external events, and that their replacement by monetarist policies was a mistaken response to those failures. The events are described in Keynesian terms. Within such a framework one is likely to reach conclusions which are favourable to traditional demand management, albeit with the addition of an incomes policy of some sort. Sir Bryan does provide an account of monetarism but he does not relate it to the events of economic history.

Let me try to redress the balance. Sir Bryan describes the abandonment of demand management in terms of external events − the breakdown of Bretton Woods, the commodity price boom, the oil price increase, the wage explosion of 1974−5, etc. To this list can be added another external event − the adoption of monetarist policies. There is an alternative version which could be described as 'monetarist history'. Its main feature would be as follows. The success in achieving rapid growth was part of a world-wide experience of post-war reconstruction, innovation and expanding trade. Success, such as it was, in controlling inflation was due to the constraints of a fixed exchange rate. (It is also possible that Britain enjoyed exceptionally favourable competitive conditions after the devaluation of 1949). During this period the natural rate of unemployment was rising as a result of institutional changes including higher unemployment pay, loss of the private rented sector in housing, increased provision of council housing and increased strength, in terms of numbers and legal position, of trade unions. Governments tried to maintain the low levels of unemployment achieved in the early post-war years but their attempts to do so led to recurrent balance of payments crises. These crises caused the expansionary policies to be reversed although there was enough flexibility in the system for the UK to have an excessive rate of inflation and to lose competitiveness progressively.

The collapse of the Bretton Woods system and the increase in commodity prices in 1973 was due at least in part to the policies of the United States which expanded credit excessively from the mid-1960s onwards. (At its worst it was simultaneously expanding demand at home and fighting the Vietnam War). The oil price increase of 1973−4 can be counted as a genuinely exogenous supply side shock. In Britain demand management had its final glorious phase with the Budgets of 1972 and 1973. They were accompanied (after *Competition and Credit Control*) with a rapid increase in the money supply. The immediate results were indeed a rapid growth of output. The floating of the exchange rate in 1972 also removed the constraint of reserve management. The exchange rate fell rapidly but the policy makers did not appreciate the significance of this.

The pay explosion of 1974–5 was certainly made worse by the thresholds system but it also reflected the monetary growth and exchange rate falls of earlier years. The effect was postponed by the incomes policies of 1972–4. Similarly the price effect was postponed by price controls and by tax and subsidy changes in 1974. The economy is still adjusting towards equilibrium from the policy shocks of 1970–4 and from the oil price shocks of 1973–4 and 1979–80. Some success in reducing inflation was achieved after 1976; but the success was reversed by the monetary and fiscal expansion of 1978.

The revival of the monetarist approach to policy was a reaction to the events of the 1970s. Monetarism, in its many forms, seemed to offer an adequate explanation both for the apparent policy successes of the 1950s and 1960s and the policy failures of the 1970s. It was therefore preferable to the Keynesian explanation which had to rely on exogenous factors, in terms, for example of wage behaviour, for the breakdown of the policies.

I merely offer that as an alternative account. I am not necessarily asserting that it is correct (although I believe it is). I suggest that the discussion could attempt to evaluate the two accounts and to see what could be usefully preserved from each of them.

I have offered an alternative account to Sir Bryan's 'Keynesian' history. The 'monetarist' view is derived from a set of theories which imply *inter alia* that control of inflation requires control of the money supply and that the level of unemployment cannot be altered permanently by monetary or fiscal policy. (A stronger version would question the feasibility or wisdom of attempting to control unemployment in the short term). The fact that there are these two distinct views of history and of policy leads me to two important and related questions suggested by Sir Bryan's paper. First, why has there been a breakdown in the consensus of macroeconomics? Second, why has government policy shifted so markedly from the previous tradition?

The development of demand management

It is surely remarkable that this distinguished gathering of economists and policy makers should be virtually unanimous in condemning the current direction of economic policy. This is an extremely enjoyable birthday party but it should be noted that it is being held in exile. The participants fully recognize that this has happened but I am not sure that we have adequately attempted to understand why it has happened.

I have some tentative answers. The first is that the economic performance of the mid-1970s, and later, was so bad that whatever policy views were in operation at that time would have been rejected. The traditional methods of demand management, and those who practised them, have been made scapegoats for events that were beyond anyone's control. The second possible answer is that the change in the policies was a side effect of the struggle for leadership within the Conservative Party. The contest between Mrs Thatcher and Mr Heath was presented as a contest between different views of Conservatism. The victorious group was associated with economic liberalism and monetarism and the change in leadership has been marked by a change in policies. A third possible answer is that the barbarians have taken over and that all reason has fled.

A fourth possibility is that the policies supported by this distinguished group were actually mistaken and that the exile is well deserved. In general, the whole idea of demand management may have been wrong or at least grossly oversold; in particular, policies were disastrous in the period 1971–4.

I would argue that each of those answers contains at least some truth. I can recognize that the explanation that the barbarians have taken over is the most comforting but I think the complacency would be mistaken. Further it allows one to raise the following question: if the barbarians have taken over, why were the defences so weak?

Certainly the consensus was shattered by the combination of rapid inflation with high unemployment during the 1970s. That in turn was a result of the great shocks of the late 1960s and early 1970s: the change in the price of the oil and the policy shocks in the United States and Britain. I have a crude theory of the way in which opinions have divided among those involved with policy. It is the theory of the 'searing experience'. For those who have been responsible at the highest level for policy making since the War the searing experience was the unemployment of the 1930s. They have resolved

55

that the policies followed then must never be adopted again. For a younger generation the searing experience was the inflation of the 1970s. They too have decided that the policies followed then must never be adopted again. I realize my theory is incomplete. Views do not divide neatly between the generations. One reason for this — and I believe it is perhaps the most alarming development of all — is that views on macroeconomics have became, as never before since the War, a matter of party politics. Whoever is right, it must be wrong to subject the economy to the kinds of policy swings threatened by the current polarity of views.

As a final question, we can ask whether a consensus will be restored. I believe it will. Keynesianism will never be the same again after the experiences of the mid-1970s; monetarism will never be the same again after the experiences of the early 1980s; but I do not attempt to predict where the middle ground will be found.

NOTES

1 These comments differ somewhat from the version used at the Conference. I have omitted a summary of Sir Bryan Hopkin's paper and I have added some points I wished to make at the Conference but could not do through shortage of time.

Discussion

The theme developed by Dr Alan Budd of the rise and fall of demand management was taken up by other speakers. The fundamental question was whether it *ought* to have 'fallen'. *Mr Christopher Dow* agreed that there were good reasons why it had 'come a cropper' but they were not theoretical reasons. The criticism he had made in his *Management of the British Economy* of policy in the 1950s — that fitful intervention had increased the instability of the economy — seemed to him now, in the light of later events, an entirely trivial criticism. It was very difficult to run an economy without a stock recession now and again, basically because of time lags. The upsets usually quickly corrected themselves. Policy interventions, similarly, were quite likely to be on the late side and so exaggerate or prolong the swings or at least not be exactly right. Most other countries had had much the same experience with minor cycles. There was nothing peculiarly British nor particularly associated with fiscal policy in that experience. In any event what prescription could be offered by way of a remedy? There was no rule of thumb that would ensure that governments would do better: merely an injunction that they should be cleverer, or be more wary of intervening.

The truth was that governments had been rather too ambitious. But monetarism, which was sometimes recommended in reaction against ambitious government policies, was also in principle ambitious. It hoped to achieve great results by means of a certain manipulation of monetary variables − namely, to stop or slow down inflation. That, however, was not at all easy. If policy appeared to have failed it was because the problem of inflation had clearly got very much worse. That that would happen should have been foreseen − indeed it was foreseen. The barriers protecting us against inflation were always likely gradually to break down. The inflationary time-bomb had been ticking away all through the post-war period.

Mr Dow took the view that the problem was beyond economics. This did not mean that it did not concern economists but that it was not capable of being dealt with by equilibrium theory. The strength of inflationary forces had much to do with the working of labour market institutions. Those in the United Kingdom were perhaps the worst in the world from this point of view, and seemed designed to ensure that inflation would take place. One ought to be able to learn how to make inflation less likely from an international study of labour market institutions. In dealing with something so fundamental, however, the political forces embedded against change were bound to be very strong in relation to the political coherence of a government attempting to introduce reforms − and it would be unwise to be starry-eyed about what could be done. The lack of growth in productivity had been another powerful impediment to the success of policy − and was also due to deep-seated reasons. Some economies were relatively prosperous and others relatively unsuccessful, and there was no satisfactory explanation why this should be. Our failure to cope with these problems was in his view the searing experience with which we had to cope in the 1980s.

The view that government policy had been too ambitious was endorsed by *Lord Roberthall,* who found himself in close agreement with the paper by Sir Bryan Hopkin. In the early days of demand management, when little was known about it and the government was very ready to take advice, the Economic Section had not given enough thought to what was meant by full employment. Apart from Beveridge's suggested 3 per cent, little work had been done to give substance to the idea. As a result the economy was run under too great pressure and this showed up in balance of payments difficulties. Sterling balances in London were also a highly unstable feature and their withdrawal exaggerated the balance of payments fluctuations associated with changes in the pressure of demand. It was noticeable in 1958, when the economy was contracting, how rapidly the balance of payments appeared to recover. The experience of that year also showed how the management of policy might be thrown out by bad statistics. At first a very large surplus appeared to be on the way and expansionary action was taken; later revisions showed only a modest surplus but the damage was done.

The second failure throughout the period was summed up in the phrase: 'too much, too late'. The reasons for this failure lay largely in bad statistics, particularly in the statistics of government expenditure. One might suppose that the government knew what was going on in the public sector even if it was less well posted on the private sector; but this was the reverse of the truth. Government figures of expenditure were very unreliable and one could also put little faith in what it said it would spend. If the recommendations of the Plowden Committee[1] had been implemented this would have helped to reduce the amplitude of the swings in activity. But 'politics being what they are' it was not possible to get the government to behave in a way that would stabilize the economy. The most interesting experience had been in the late sixties when Mr Roy Jenkins set the economy on a course that left a sustainable margin of unemployment in the sense that the pressure on resources was not so great that it opened the way to damaging import penetration and balance of payments difficulties. It would have been valuable to have had this experiment continued to a further period but the incoming Conservative government were incipient monetarists and changed course. They carried their policy too far, got into a panic, and then set going in 1973–4 the most disastrous boom of the post-war period.

Demand management could, in Lord Roberthall's view, have been more successful but only if the movement of wages had been controlled. As early as the 1944 White Paper it had been stated that full employment was contingent on wage restraint; and this strand of thought ran through a long succession of White Papers from 1948 onwards. He personally had believed in an incomes policy all along but it was only after (just after) he left the Treasury that the government had adopted one. The inflationary troubles of the subsequent period bore out the view that it was not possible to have full employment without some sort of incomes policy.

Broadly speaking therefore demand management had been fairly successful. Had we learned more quickly to avoid over-full employment, and had it been possible to get the government to implement the Plowden Committee recommendations, the first two mistakes would have been avoided. But the inflationary problem would have remained. Since this had been for much of the time a problem of cost push, demand management was not the right way to secure price stability and some other method of dealing with inflationary difficulties was necessary.

Since some of the discussion appeared to imply that inflation had only become a problem in the 1970s the chairman, *Professor Robin Matthews,* drew attention to the fact that there was no peace-time parallel to the great price increase in the 1960s and 1970s for over 300 years. There had been no comparable period of prolonged inflation since the beginning of the seventeenth century.

Mr Andrea Boltho reverted to Mr Christopher Dow's comments on the supposed destabilizing effect of government intervention in the 1950s and 1960s. His own research into the period made him doubtful whether Bent Hansen was right in describing policy as destabilizing but that was neither here nor there. What mattered to the behaviour of businessmen was not the *ex post* findings of academic economists but their expectations of how the government would behave. Long-run expectations had been based on the commitment of the government, if it proved necessary, to intervene to rescue the private sector from a recession. This provided an incentive for investment which carried the economy forward at full employment for a prolonged period. Once the public sector was seen not to be able to rescue the economy, however, expectations were broken, the process was reversed and growth began to falter.

Dr Alan Budd had opposed a monetarist interpretation of recent history to a Keynesian. But there could also be a Marxist interpretation. For example, it could be argued that the prosperity of the earlier post-war decades had tightened the labour market and strengthened the power of labour in the Marxist sense, so making the development of inflationary pressures virtually inevitable. Demand management from this point of view represented the upward phase of long-run capitalist cycles while monetarism was the inescapable consequence of a downward phase: not just a radical way of getting rid of inflationary expectations but a more concerted attempt at breaking the power of the labour movement.

American experience was cited by *Dr Joseph Pechman*. There had been a fleeting moment in the early 1960s when demand management had scored a notable success: unemployment was low, productivity was rising satisfactorily, prices were rising by about 1 per cent a year, and an incomes policy was in operation. There had been no opportunity to repeat the experiment until President Carter came to power. Arthur Okun warned him that if he let the economy expand without an incomes policy the rate of inflation would increase from 6 per cent to 10 per cent by the time he presented himself for re-election. The President equivocated for two years and then introduced an incomes policy which was completely ineffective. The danger was that, in the absence of an incomes policy, tight fiscal and monetary policies would generate a long period of slow growth and high unemployment, which would be bound to create widespread social unrest. Were there any alternative ways of securing wage restraint? There was no mention in any of the papers of the favourite prescription of American economists: a tax-based incomes policy. Such a policy would, in his view, be extremely difficult to implement and would require a great deal of highly complex administrative regulation. His conclusion was that some method was needed of co-ordinating policy in the private and public sectors and that if there were no incomes policy at all, the economy would have to be a great deal less buoyant.

Mr John Wright sought to inject a note of non-monetarist scepticism into the discussion of demand management in the 1950s and 1960s. If one compared that period with the previous hundred years in British history it was clear that there had been no serious export instability to cope with and one wondered how well the managers of demand would have succeeded had they encountered the large export fluctuations of former times. In addition, the British economy had emerged from the war structurally very well adapted to the pattern of demand. Rearmament before the war and the requirements of the war itself had brought 1–1½ m. workers into the engineering industries which were therefore in a good position to meet the very high level of export demand when the war was over. The rest of the world had continued to grow rapidly and it was not surprising that this pulled the British economy along.

He also took a more agnostic view of the relationship between full employment and growth. It was taken for granted in the conference papers that there was no conflict between the two. But did this remain true when demand was excessive and put no pressure on business to adapt, as in the 1950s and 1960s? We were often told that devaluation in 1967 was necessary because of the low margins on exports but if this was so, the profitability of the home market implied by the profits of firms in the early 1960s was enormous. Companies making such profits were under no real pressure to develop exports and the fact that this was so might help to account for the comparatively slow growth of the British economy.

The discussion was taken back to incomes policy by *Sir Fred Atkinson* who saw no likelihood of such a policy in the near future. It was no doubt right to expect a continuing decline in economic activity for the next year or so with a modest revival in due course. This might fall short of expectations so that inflation continued at 5–10 per cent and unemployment at about 3m. The practical possibilities in such a situation needed thought. If one could introduce an effective incomes policy no doubt recovery could be engineered. But there was no general acceptance of the need for an incomes policy, much less an inclination to accept the settlements in individual cases that a successful policy would imply. There was no alternative, therefore, but to acquiesce in a very high level of unemployment to prevent inflation from getting out of hand; and without an incomes policy it might be necessary to put up with high levels of unemployment for an indefinite period.

Before returning to this line of argument, *Mr Maurice Scott* said that it was unsatisfactory just to assert, as Dr Alan Budd had done, that fixed exchange rates in the 1950s and 1960s had moderated inflation. One had to ask why they had done so. Perhaps the explanation was, as Roberthall had said, that the government, with no very definite views on what constituted full employment, had felt it necessary to deflate when the balance of payments weakened. But the more fundamental explanation lay, as Christopher Dow had suggested, in the behaviour of the labour market. There had been sufficient wage moderation, despite the very low levels of unemployment, to keep inflation moderate and enable the exchange rate to remain fixed. Was this because it had been possible to frighten the unions by pointing to the loss of reserves, as if the country were running out of money and facing some unspecified disaster — national bankruptcy? This could no longer be threatened when there was a floating exchange rate. The real danger was, and always had been, that of inflation, and it would have been better had that always been made clear.

Mr Chris Allsopp took up Dr Alan Budd's contention that one's conclusions depended on the way one read the history books. If one were a Keynesian looking back on the inter-war period, the world could be seen as being in major disequilibrium and this would seem the natural state of capitalism under conditions of laissez-faire. Looking back on the post-war period, the world would be seen as having enjoyed rather a rapid and stable growth for rather complex reasons of the kind Mr Andrea Boltho had suggested. Once the expectation developed that national governments would remain in the business of maintaining employment and growth — and they had really had no option politically — the whole climate of business expectations was transformed and a long period of rapid growth followed.

The puzzling question for a Keynesian was not what part demand management played in contributing directly or (more significantly) indirectly to that growth but why there had been no earlier break-down. The basis of growth had been fragile so long as it rested on nothing stronger than expectations of growth. It had not been thought in the early stages of demand management that it would be the be-all and end-all of economic policy as it appeared to have become by the early 1960s.

After the war — with the problems of the inter-war period fresh in their minds — many economists had expected really serious difficulties to arise in the international economy from recurrent balance of payments crises. It also appeared likely that the problem of cost-push inflation would become acute if high growth and low unemployment were achieved. In the event the difficulties were, for many years, much smaller than expected, and so the idea could gain ground that demand management was, by itself, enough. Given that policies to ensure international balance and against inflation were so weak, a Keynesian might well feel that the really interesting question is what it was that allowed demand management to seem such a success in the 1950s and 1960s. What was it that led to the postponement of the expected difficulties to the 1970s?

If one took a monetarist view, the record looked very different. A monetarist would dismiss the 1930s as 'a policy cock-up' and regard the 1950s and 1960s as the natural state of capitalism left to itself. It would be extremely difficult to devise tests that would allow one to judge between the two conflicting views. Ultimately the issue seemed to be whether unrestrained laissez-faire capitalism would generate steady growth or not.

But whatever view one took of the way markets behaved there was a quite different issue as to the *theoretical* basis of the monetarist revolution. Did general equilibrium analysis or something like it ever justify monetarist theory? In elementary economics there was always a long list of conditions attached to equilibrium analysis governing its application in practice and these made the analysis somewhat academic. Monetarism did not fit neatly into economic theory.

The fact of the matter was that the roots of monetarism did not lie in the economics profession but in the political sphere: in disillusionment with attempts to control inflation by other means. This had revived some extremely old-fashioned ideas which appeared in the political arena before monetarism had much of a following among academics, and it did not seem likely to have such a following for very long.

There were two types of monetarist. One was a very optimistic view that, by controlling a couple of numbers it was possible to deal with something of such major social importance as inflation. The type of monetarism common in Britain fell into this trap of regarding control as relatively easy. The other type was pessimistic and took the view that it would be necessary to be tough in the face of a difficult labour market situation. Was there much practical difference between a tough monetarist and a tough Keynesian? Both were relying in the end on the manipulation of aggregate demand and employment, i.e. on demand management.

Was there then so much disagreement after all? The dispute about the use of monetary or fiscal instruments did not seem to him very important. Indeed he would say that present British policy was more fiscalist than monetarist. One thing it certainly embraced was demand management. In the past demand management had enjoyed a great deal of luck in escaping international constraints when it aimed at full employment. Now what was happening was that it had been redirected to the control of inflation with less good luck and less success.

Professor Erik Lundberg pointed out that there were important interactions between demand and supply. In a depression there was a check to investment and the creation of new capacity on the one hand and to the training of labour in new skills on the other. This would impose ceilings on recovery when it came and create bottlenecks and inflexibilities, limiting growth and renewing inflationary pressure.

There was a time when he would have hesitated to refer to Swedish experience. Sweden had been held up so often as a model of the welfare state, the use of incomes policy and so on that his audiences tended to show some irritation when it was again paraded. Now that Sweden was interesting for the contrary reasons he felt less embarrassment. There had been renewed interest there in supply side responses: in maintaining a competitive economy and ensuring profitability above all, but with workers sharing the profits. A radical scheme for the private sector made it a condition of reasonable profits that the workers would always enjoy collective ownership of a majority of the shares through a kind of wage fund. It was a condition of incomes policy under this scheme of things that it should include co-ownership and control and a share in profits. To transfer to such a system was a radical shift and would prove very difficult: for example, how were new firms to be established and with what incentives? No doubt ideas of this kind existed in Britain too. But Sweden was closer to experimenting with them so that from the point of view of economic research it would continue to be an interesting country.

Professor Tom Wilson went back to Dr Alan Budd's comment that Keynes had been very unlike a neo-Keynesian. The lowest level of unemployment that he had been prepared to consider was 5 per cent. He might have been prepared to reduce this a little in the light of experience but there is no reason to suppose that he would have regarded a figure in the region of 2 per cent as being compatible with the avoidance of inflation. His cautious interpretation of full employment has also a bearing on the much debated point about the feasibility of 'fine-tuning'. How fine? In the neo-Keynesian phase about as much weight was being given to a change of 0.1 per cent in unemployment as Keynes might have given to a 1.0 per cent change.

A serious error of the post-war period had been to accord little importance to the control of the money supply. To take the view that its control was important did not commit one to all the other propositions of monetarism including an exclusive concentration of attention on short-run monetary targets.

Attention needed to be directed to the ambiguity of the monetarist interpretation of a quite fundamental concept: the 'natural rate of unemployment'. This was defined in some places as the frictional and structural minimum but it was also defined as the level of unemployment at which expected inflation would be equal to actual inflation.

Now it could *not* be assumed that these two 'natural rates' would coincide. A very high level of unemployment − say 3 million − might be needed to ensure that expected inflation was not exceeded − far above the frictional and structural minimum. How would the excess unemployment above the frictional and structural minimum ever be absorbed with the money supply rising thereafter only in line with the trend growth of output, as monetarists prescribe, and with velocity roughly constant as monetarists assume? Presumably *downward* flexibility of money wages would be required − and that was scarcely realistic?

The government had not yet explained how recovery could be achieved without a resurgence of inflation as the demand for labour increased. In other quarters an incomes policy was often recommended, but it was hard to get it accepted by the unions − apart from the scepticism of the present government. One reason for the reluctance of the unions might be that when, under an incomes policy, the amount available for disbursement came to be considered, this would blow sky-high the Marxist myth, dear even to some who are not strictly Marxists, that the basic conflict was between labour and capital. With dividends at less than 3 per cent of personal income before tax, it would then become clear that the conflict was primarily between different groups of the employed population − indeed between different unions, especially after the widespread unionization of salaried workers.

The role of fixed exchange rates in limiting the rate of inflation, discussed earlier by Mr Maurice Scott, was raised again by *Dr Walter Salant*. It was true that a fall in the exchange rate raised the price of tradeable goods whereas if the rate were held steady the consequent loss of reserves brought into operation a counter-inflationary effect on demand. But these effects rested primarily on policy action and there might be just as big, or indeed a bigger, inducement to take policy action if the exchange rate began to slide. Most governments were more embarrassed by a fall in the rate commanded by their currency than by a loss in reserves. They would respond more vigorously, in his view, to the first than to the second.

He agreed with Dr Alan Budd that the 'searing experience' of unemployment had faded by the 1970s and given way to the 'searing experience' of inflation. A large proportion of the adult population had experienced nothing but inflation. If it took them as long to get over that experience as it had taken the previous generation to get over the depression, it would be a long time before inflation ceased to be the normal expectation. Why did these expectations take root when, as the chairman had said, there had been no parallel to the protracted experience of inflation in the previous three hundred years? Mr Allsopp had drawn attention to the development of firm expectations that full employment would be maintained and the consequences of this for investment and growth. But there was another side to the matter. When confidence spread that any depression would not be long-lasting and that no fundamental adjustments need be made to any check to activity, this confidence in the commitment to full employment was shared by workers' organizations and communicated itself to wage negotiations, enhancing the downward inflexibility of wages. The searing experience of inflation was thus a reflection of the success of demand management in the past and not a demonstration that it had been fundamentally wrong. It was one more case in which the solution of one problem gave rise to another.

Sir Bryan Hopkin, looking back at the contrasting interpretations of history put forward by Dr Alan Budd, thought that there was much less in dispute than he had implied. He had not intended in his paper to represent demand management as having exercised a very powerful influence over the course of events and conferred enormous benefits. His attitude was rather it was simply not possible to avoid having some attitude to the level of demand at any time and it was necessary to decide what that attitude should be. The most he would claim for demand management was that it did, over a considerable period, create the kind of confidence in the future to which Mr Boltho and Mr Allsopp had referred and he agreed with their diagnosis of the benefit received from it. He would not want to deny that many things went on in the world that were exogenous to the economic system and these included such things as the growing confidence and power of the labour movement – the various factors that had made for an increase in the 'maintainable rate of unemployment'. He would also not deny that the fixed exchange rate system had probably helped to moderate inflation. On the other hand, what he had said towards the end of his paper in a positive and critical way had been left aside by Dr Alan Budd and he was left not knowing what answers he would give in response to the paper's diagnosis of the fatal weaknesses of the monetarist pattern of thought underlying current policy.

Sir Fred Atkinson had been even more pessimistic than he (Sir Bryan) had been and had suggested that we would fail to get back even to 5 per cent unemployment. Did that mean that it was inconceivable that we could recover the position when the present government took over, i.e. a level of unemployment of 1¼m. and a rate of inflation about the same as now? Could we not have carried on as we were? He would agree that it was necessary to hasten slowly in expanding the economy for a variety of reasons, largely connected with confidence.

In November when drafting his paper he had not thought the chances of success for the present policy were high. They were now distinctly lower. He confessed to some surprise at the reaffirmation of monetary targets in the Budget: he had supposed that they had been discredited by the experience of the past year and could not be restored to a central role in policy.

Finally, he agreed with Professor Lundberg that if enough unemployment were created for long enough it would damage the growth of productive potential. The small fluctuations in demand in the 1950s and 1960s might not have impinged on the underlying rate of growth. But this was no longer true in a deep and continuing recession. When recovery began, the lack of new capacity and trained labour would make it impossible to regain full employment or climb back on to the previous trend of growth. This was one of the disadvantages of following a policy of deep recession as a remedy for inflation.

NOTE

1 *Control of Public Expenditure*, Cmnd. 1432, July 1961.

3

Labour market policy

SIR HENRY PHELPS BROWN

1911: THE STAGE IS SET

The perspective of seventy years takes us back to 1911.[1] In the August of that year of burning sun and mounting conflict, many people thought themselves confronted with the imminent prospect of revolution. As the overture to an opera introduces the themes of the ensuing drama, so those troubled times present the main factors that were to operate in the labour market in the years to come.

First and foremost there were the trade unions. They carried passports issued to them by Victorian society, but after those passports were issued the unions had greatly changed their type and tendency. Two Royal Commissions, in 1867–9 and 1891–4, had been led to report favourably on the moral influence of the trade union on its members, and its steadying role in wage negotiation. These Commissions had had before them the craft union and the unions of the textile workers and the miners. The leaders of these unions were men of the utmost respectability, many of them local preachers. By the time of the later Commission a number of employers were testifying to the usefulness of the unions. The Report of 1894 found that industrial relations were at their best when organization was strong on both sides. Two riders were attached for the labour market. One was that the trade unions were acceptable and healthy institutions, and an integral part of society, whose ability to perform their functions must be safeguarded. The other was that wage negotiations, like other elements of industrial relations, were best treated as a matter of direct voluntary transaction between the parties, free from administrative intervention or legal regulation.

But while these conclusions were being reached, trade unionism itself was changing. The upheavals of 1911 marked a second wave of the New Unionism whose first uprising had been signalled by the

68

London dock strike of 1889. This New Unionism arose out of the new-found ability of the unskilled worker to sustain a strike and support a union, but it had also brought militancy among the older unionists. The rank and file were more likely to take up issues on their own. The great transport strike of August 1911 began with a spontaneous stoppage by the railwaymen of Liverpool. There were shop stewards in the engineering works. Control by the national and local officers of the unions was becoming more difficult. And much more than this, the ability of the miners, the transport workers, and now the railwaymen, to maintain a stoppage throughout the country put their thumb on its windpipe: the sanction behind their claims was no longer simply the loss they might inflict on their own employers, but the disruption of the national economy. This was not one of the potentialities of voluntary collective bargaining envisaged by those who had endorsed it. But the endorsement remained, and trade unions whose powers differed radically from those of the unions that had gained Victorian approval continued to enjoy the status which that approval warranted.

Only five years before, Parliament had had to determine whether that should be so. The Taff Vale decision of the House of Lords in 1901 had rendered trade unions liable to be sued in tort, and by previous decisions of the courts the torts for which they might be sued now included civil conspiracy: the effect was that any strike was liable in practice to involve a union in heavy damages. For a number of years, while inquiry proceeded, the unions had had to lie very low. It was agreed that the law must be changed, but how? The weight of informed opinion, including that of Sidney Webb, was wholly against restoring the old freedom to strike, and inflict losses indiscriminately with immunity, to unions whose power and militancy were much more formidable than of old. In one way or another these advisers wished to see a positive code of regulation. Trade union action should enjoy immunities, but only when it observed certain rules, which distinguished acceptable from unacceptable practices. But the trade unions themselves demanded the outright restoration of the status quo, in which they conducted their affairs largely outside the purview of the courts. In a fateful moment, Campbell-Bannerman had swung round to their view. Thereby he set British industrial relations on their distinctive course of 'voluntarism', not to be interrupted until 1971.

In the interval when the law was on their side, not many employers had actually been disposed to take advantage of it. On an international comparison British employers appear as unwilling either to compete or to combine. An early technical lead had saved many manufacturers from the pressures of price competition; others in later years were saved from it by the absence of standardization and mass production, and a tacit willingness among themselves to live and let live. But at the same time employers generally valued their independence, and it was difficult to get them to combine, even for defence against trade union pressure. At the first onset of unionism they had sometimes combined, and turned on the incipient union and crushed it. But more often when an employers' association was formed it was for the purpose of collective bargaining: as such, it only relieved the individual employer of the task of negotiation, and there was no question of its executive exercising any authority over the members. Multi-employer negotiation is the procedure readily adopted when the employers have no positive policy towards wages and merely react to the pressures of the day: the negotiation covering all the firms of the industry in the region, or the country, ensures that they will be treated alike, but respects their independence. We owe it to the type of the British employer that this method of wage regulation became predominant. It carried two shortcomings. One was the neglect of wage structure within the firm. The other, which appears by contrast with Sweden, Germany and the United States, was the lack of pressure on the trade unions to reform their own patchwork structure, either to oppose strength to strength, or to meet the refusal of individual employers to negotiate with a plurality of unions.

But it is necessary to distinguish. Not all employers were sheltered from price competition – there were coalfields, and sections of the iron and steel industry, whose markets were international; or again there were the railway companies, caught from the turn of the century between rising costs of fuel and materials, and charges held down by Act of Parliament. Where prices were out of the employers' control it was no easy matter to reach agreement with the unions, and from time to time the employers had to demand cuts; the unions consequently became militant. This was not a world where good relations could be maintained by agreements covered, if necessary, by price rises that the customer would bear. The distinction between the employers whom – according to conventional standards – we should approve of as enlightened and conciliatory, and those we regard as reactionary and aggressive, may lie not so much in differences of their personal outlook, as in the former being sheltered from and the latter exposed to price competition.

The movement of wages depended largely on the trade cycle. In 1911 itself, the outburst of strikes by the transport workers was a response to the rising phase of the 8-year cycle which already for nearly a hundred years had dominated the year-to-year movements of the labour market. In 1958 these movements were to be displayed graphically as forming a loop: when recession set in and unemployment (entered along the horizontal axis) increased, the rise of wage rates (entered on the vertical axis) declined and might even become negative; with recovery and lower unemployment the rise of wage rates itself rose again, but on a path higher than it had previously fallen along, so that, when unemployment was say 4 per cent and falling, wage rates rose more than when it was 4 per cent and rising. This loop, collapsed into the Phillips curve,[2] looked like a straightforward market relationship between the supply of and demand for labour whose changing balance was expressed by the rate of unemployment. As such it was seized on by economists who were unacquainted with the actual processes and events by which the movements of Phillips's series had been brought about. These economists, not being historians, thought in effect that they could reduce the course of history to the solution of an equation: the movement of wage rates was determined by the level of unemployment. For the purpose of public policy, it then appeared that control of the level of activity, through whatever fiscal and monetary constraints were available to maintain a certain margin of unused resources, would of itself exert a restraint on pay claims sufficient to prevent cost inflation. But this is to anticipate.

What was actually happening in the course of the trade cycle was that moods of confidence and apprehension succeeded each other among the working population as the state of industry changed. That there was a cycle at all was very likely not apprehended. The changes brought by each year seemed, like those of the weather at harvest, to compose no pattern, and to be beyond men's power to control or resist. But while they lasted, they deeply affected the mood in which employers and employed approached negotiations about wages. In particular, the willingness of particular workmen to take the lead in raising claims, and of their comrades to back them by striking, depended on their sense of the current balance of power. This sense in turn depended on the relative difficulty that employers were experiencing in filling jobs and men in finding them. To that extent there was a factor of supply and demand at the origin. But there is no presumption that the outcome was a price that cleared the market, or even a movement towards such a price. The essential consequence of the shift in the balance of supply and demand was a change of attitudes. These determined what claims if any would be raised, and the vigour with which they would be pressed. Besides their cyclical variation, they underwent other changes from time to time: there were waves of militancy that animated wide sectors of the labour force for a number of years and then receded, and there were seemingly non-reversible shifts due to the change in the predominant outlook of the labour force in the course of the turnover of generations. But this again is to anticipate.

One influence on attitudes in 1911, especially those of the lowest paid, was a rise in the cost of living. There was no official index to confirm this at the time, but in 1913 a report of the Board of Trade was to put the rise at nearly 14 per cent over the preceding seven years. Money wages had been rising, but would not catch up till 1914, and even then real wages would be no higher than they had been in 1895. Underlying these nearly twenty years of stagnation and rising prices were two factors. One was the declining productivity of the British economy: from 1900 down to the First World War there seems to have been virtually no rise in output per head at all. The other factor was the terms of trade: the standard of living of the British wage earner evidently depended not only on the productivity of domestic industry but on how much wheat, meat, sugar and cotton he could obtain in world markets in exchange for a unit of domestic produce. About 1896 the terms of trade had reached the turning point of one of their long swings, and from then until the war they were less favourable to the British worker. In the years to come much of the variation of pressure in the labour market was to depend on these factors of productivity and the terms of trade.

The conjunction in 1911 of wage rises with social tension reminds us that in a traditional and stratified society men do not see wage fixing simply as a market matter. Despite substantial social mobility, most wage earners are bound to see themselves as born into a particular status and obliged to accept the relative remuneration that society assigns to the jobs accessible to that status. This may be taken for granted, or resented as class exploitation. But in either case wage earners have been slow to accept the economics of wages – in particular, the significance of labour costs, and the functions of profits. They have seen their wages rather as the allocation of a low standard of living to persons deemed to be of a low status in the community;[3] and in pressing wage claims they have seen themselves not as taking advantage of a seller's market for labour so much as rising with the heightened morale of the labour movement to demand fairer shares.

Major wage movements have accordingly been associated with waves of working-class assertion and cohesion. In 1911 a great expansion of trade unionism was going on: between 1910 and 1913 membership rose by two-thirds. That was, immediately, the effect of Lloyd George's provision by which the trade unions became approved societies administering National Insurance; but the abrupt rise on that account fell within an expansion of membership for more general causes lying within an organic change in society. Between 1888 and 1914 it more than quadrupled the number of British trade unionists. A similar expansion occurred internationally: over much the same span the number of trade unionists was multiplied sevenfold in France and the United States and ninefold in Germany, while in Sweden, from small beginnings, it rose to a greater density in the industrial population than in any of the other countries. That movements of this kind occur at the same time in a number of Western countries is an important characteristic of the labour market that we shall meet again.

It was the imminence of conflict and disruption that shaped the policy of the government towards disputes in the labour market. These appeared as signs of social tension and likely sources of public disorder. Protracted strikes and lockouts brought great hardship to the workers and their families and the communities around them. There could now be stoppages of vital supplies and services that would bring the whole economy to a standstill. On these grounds the government was moved to seek a settlement. But because it had been agreed that industrial relations were best conducted informally, the government was armed with no more powers than an Act of 1896 had given it by authorizing the President of the Board of Trade to use his good offices in conciliation. In the adroit hands of Lloyd George, however, those good offices became coercive of the employers. Not responsible as trade union leaders were to great numbers of constituents, and individually more open to the threats or blandishments that a skilful Minister could wield, the employers were the party that could the more easily be induced to come to terms. It was by conciliation and concession that the disputes of 1911 were settled. But in the early months of 1912 a dispute arose in coal mining in which the employers were obdurate. A continuance of the stoppage would have brought the economy to a standstill. The government rushed through legislation giving the miners part but not all of what they had been standing out for and the employers had been refusing. This is the only time in our history in which the settlement of an industrial dispute has been attempted by Act of Parliament. As the Bill went through the House, Members asked 'What will happen if the miners still won't go back?' By a narrow majority they voted to stay out; but their executive took them back.

For the rest, the government saw 'the claims of labour' as part of 'the condition of England question'. In 1909 it had taken a major step in principle, albeit a small one in practice, by Winston Churchill's Trade Boards Act, with its statutory enforcement of minimum wages. The first Labour Exchanges opened in 1910. In 1911 itself the National Insurance Act brought in health insurance that covered almost all wage earners, and the first scheme of unemployment insurance that covered about one in six. In this branch of its policy the government was under the pressure of the labour voter, whether Members were Liberals dependent on labour support, or Lib-Labs, or Labour. Unemployment in the recession of 1908–9 was almost at the level of the dread year 1886. What was to be done about it remained the major issue that Labour kept before Parliament. The extension of 'outdoor relief to the able-bodied pauper' – that is, a dole, free of the workhouse test, to the unemployed – had merged with a limited provision of relief work by the local authorities. The Webbs advocated those works on the large scale, and Keynes later was chivalrously to acknowledge his indebtedness to their advocacy.[4] But it was no Keynesian light that these proposals were seen at the time. That they would involve borrowing, and putting borrowed money in circulation, counted not for but against them, and they were justified only as less demoralising than the outright dole.

For fifty years after 1911 in some basic respects the labour market changed very little. Public policy, it is true, accepted new responsibilities. The First World War confronted it not only with the task of mobilizing and allocating manpower but with the need to restrain the rise of labour costs. That need was renewed in the Second World War and persisted through the years of full employment that followed. Between the wars a great debate on the causes of general unemployment had led to the predominance of the Keynesian belief that the level of employment could be varied by the control of effective demand, and to the government in 1944 undertaking to use monetary and fiscal regulators to that end. But within the labour market itself the ways in which the parties behaved and wages were fixed were remarkably persistent. The economic circumstances of the country changed greatly from time to time, and the response of wages with them, but these were the effects of varied pressure on the same spring. If we look back from the crisis of sterling under Macmillan's government in the summer of 1961 to the crisis of the halting of the ports and railways under Asquith's government in the summer of 1911, what stands out is how little the institutions and procedures of the labour market and the attitudes of the parties had changed meanwhile.

The institutions had been affirmed and extended during the First World War. Some commentators have seen a significant step in the Treasury Agreement of March 1915, by which the trade union leaders in the munitions industries renounced the strike during the war, gave up restrictive practices on war work, and accepted compulsory arbitration, in return for commitments to restore customary practices after the war, and to restrict the profit of firms in which restrictions were relaxed. This significance, it has been said, is that the trade union leaders concerned stood this time in the presence of Ministers not as a respectful delegation, nor even as stubborn negotiators, but as the plenipotentiaries of a 'high contracting party': the trade unions had become an estate of the realm. It is true that the status and influence of leading trade unionists was transformed as they served in the wartime administration. But the relation of the leadership to government was transitory. In any case it was never a relation between two independent centres of power and sources of initiative. The unions had great power to obstruct and resist: when the government needed their co-operation, as it did for war work, then their consent to dismantle their barriers had its inherent price in the importance attached to them. But let the position be reversed, let them try to take the initiative and seek something of the government: what pressure could they bring to bear on it if it did not happen to be asking something of them at the time? Their lack of positive potential was to be made clear in the General Strike.

The extension of negotiating arrangements throughout the economy was more durable. Trade union officials and employers had worked together as never before in the wartime administration of industry. The total of four million trade union members in 1914 was doubled during the war. This broadened base was used to set up the arrangements of multi-employer collective bargaining, in the immediate interest of the control of wages during the war. The great conciliator Sir George Askwith was active in this: his major problem often was to get hold of the employers and bring them together. The Whitley Committee appointed to examine the causes of industrial unrest recommended that where 'the machinery' for collective bargaining had not been set up voluntarily, and organization needed a supporting hand, government should promote the formation of National Joint Industrial Councils, and at the end of the war this was done by the recently created Ministry of Labour. The recognized pattern of wage regulation, then, was that the wage rate actually applied to each person's job should be fixed in an agreement negotiated from time to time between trade unions and employers meeting for voluntary collective bargaining, or somewhat more formally but still voluntarily in a Joint Industrial Council: or the rate might be the legally enforceable minimum awarded by one of the Trade Boards, greatly increased in number at the end of the war. The movement of salaries was left to individual negotiation or to the graded structures of the public service and the larger concerns – few of the white-collared were unionized.

The counterpart to this design of 'the machinery' was a conception of the limited role of public policy. To the question 'How do you want wages to behave?' governments would reply 'So as to bring about agreement between the parties'. The terms that promised a lasting settlement, based on mutual respect and understanding, with provision for orderly adjustment of subsequent claims, were the best terms from the point of view of the Ministry of

Labour. Its own function was to help the parties to arrive at them. This function it discharged through its own staff of conciliators and through the appointment of committees or courts of inquiry to investigate and report on cases that had reached an impasse. But these good offices could be accepted only at the discretion of the parties. Acceptance depended not only on the Ministry and its representatives being even-handed as between employers and employed, but on their having no view of a wage they should aim at in the public interest.

It was possible for public policy to stand aside from wage movements for many years after the abandonment of laissez-faire elsewhere because those movements were largely restrained of themselves. The change in attitudes so marked in the New Unionism had not wholly overthrown the sway of custom: men continued to accept certain differentials and relativities as in the nature of things. We have seen how quantitative shifts in the balance of vacancies and applicants caused qualitative changes to run through face to face relations and the willingness of men to press for a rise. But it must have been by custom again that the rises for which they would settle in the boom were still seldom more than 5 per cent. If there had been a general tacit agreement to demand more, as in later years, would it not have been forthcoming? There was no market-clearing or equilibrating virtue about the rises actually agreed. In any case the booms did not last long. Then in recession and depression the trade unions had to meet employers' demands for cuts – indeed down to the Second World War it was usual to give the primary function of the trade union as defence. The elbow joint held, in that cuts were generally smaller than the preceding rises, but cuts there were. In the inter-war years, moreover, though two cycles of the old eight-year span ran through them, the persistence of structural unemployment exerted a constantly dampening effect on attitudes. Trade union membership had fallen away in the slump of 1921, and again after the General Strike. But the cost of living was kept down, and reduced sharply in the great depression of 1929–32 by the fall in import prices, so that some cut in money wages was consistent with a rise in real wages. In fact the secular rise of real wages that had been checked in the years down to 1914 was resumed in the inter-war years. But there was as yet no expectation of an 'annual improvement factor', so that one later source of pressure for wage rises was absent.

It might seem that the government would have been driven to a wage policy in the inter-war years by its concern with the external value of sterling. The appreciation of sterling which culminated in the return to gold in 1925 was hardly compatible with the level at which wages had settled in 1923, and the consequent pressure divided the economy and the labour market into sheltered and unsheltered sectors. It so divided coal mining, but the miners demanded a single wage structure covering both sectors and financed from a national pool. The coal owners, obstinately opposed to any such step towards nationalization, demanded such reductions in labour costs as would enable them to pay their way as they were. Baldwin and his colleagues treated the dispute as they would have approached the threat of any other stoppage that would disrupt the economy: their aim was a peaceful settlement, and they were willing to subsidize the industry while the Samuel Commission looked for a way out. In the event, they were not prepared to depart so far from the Conservative commitment to private enterprise as Samuel would have them do, and so they accepted the need to set a level of labour costs that would restore the profitability of the industry with its existing structure. On the collapse of the General Strike they left the intractable miners to be starved out. But this was seen as the only way out for a particular industry, and not as part of a national policy for wages.

It is true that there was some discussion of a general reduction in wages as a remedy for unemployment, and it persisted even after sterling left the Gold Standard in 1931, because unemployment continued to rise for some time. But this was a discussion among economists: to balance the Budget the government cut pay in the public sector, but elsewhere it could not conceivably by its own lights do other than leave pay to 'the machinery'. Where pay was being cut because collective bargaining was breaking down under pressures of surplus capacity and unemployment, as it was in cotton manufacturing, the government actually intervened to hold pay up: to stop firms that still observed the agreement being undersold by those who broke away, an Act of 1934[5] provided that the terms of the agreement should be legally binding on all firms in the industry. That the government should have felt itself able at this time to reinforce the accepted 'machinery' for 'putting a floor under competition' and holding up wages can be explained in part by the absence of any great concern about the balance of payments; and this in turn was due largely to the movement of the terms of trade, and the sharp fall in the prices of our imports of foodstuffs and raw materials.

The rationale of the 'machinery' implicity assumed that if the parties could not agree, the consequent stoppage, however regrettable, was at most a sectoral or regional matter, and not a national issue. But already before 1914 the obligation on the government to find a settlement was clear when the stoppage was broad enough to cut off vital supplies or services from the whole country. The unions that had seen their power demonstrated in that way had also seen that when one group of them struck, be it the dockers, the railwaymen, or the miners, the others would in practice find themselves out of work too. They were thus led to form a Triple Alliance under which they would act together in conflict, though they defined their mutual obligations only loosely. The question was how government could meet the national emergency such as the action of any one of them would create, when the threat of it impinged again after the war. Lloyd George's government armed itself by the Emergency Powers Act of 1920 with the authority 'to make regulations for securing the essentials of life to the community'. But the same Act provided 'that no such regulation shall make it an offence for any person or persons to take part in a strike, or peacefully to persuade any other person or persons' to do so. Nor was any special provision made at this time with intent to inhibit strikes of this kind or to provide a special procedure for their settlement: the principle of voluntarism, with its correlate that government must not apply legal constraints to industrial relations, was overriding. Underlying it was the right to strike, that must be kept free of encroachment by government or legislature, lest the balance of social equity be tilted against the wage earners.

That this position could be maintained through the ensuing years, in practice if not formally, was due to a train of dramatic events. In 1921 the miners did call upon their allies to strike in support of their resistance to the coal owners' demand for a cut in wages. No time could have been less propitious for quitting one's own job in another man's cause: the railwaymen demurred, and the Alliance broke up. It was in great part unwillingness to let the miners down a second time that led the General Council of the TUC into the General Strike. That strike collapsed because the majority of those who took part, leaders and followers, were far from having any revolutionary intent, and saw no purpose in protracting the strike when after the first week it clearly was not going to shake the determination of the government to terminate the subsidy to the miners. Two lessons were drawn from these events. One was that in matters of wages the trade unionists of each group or industry would have to fight their own battle. Sympathetic action might still be expected, and did occur, on issues of trade union principle – for example, if trade unionists were victimized, or proceeded against in the courts for what were regarded as proper activities; but the unity of 'the trade union movement' did not extend across a wages front. The second lesson was that the great industrial power wielded by the trade unions was a negative power to obstruct government but not a positive power to coerce it and prescribe policy to it. Unless a general strike is to deprive the strikers themselves of the essentials of existence, it leaves the government free to provide them, and strengthen the dependence of each and all upon it, while the idleness of the strikers becomes increasingly meaningless. But in any case the British trade unionists were devoid of the political thrust that must activate any serious intent to change government policy by threat of the strike. In the year after the General Strike Baldwin's government did proceed to outlaw strikes that were not simply concerned with a trade dispute in the strikers' industry and were 'designed or calculated to coerce the government either directly or by inflicting hardship upon the community'.[6] This remained on the statute book until the whole Act was repealed in 1946, but there was never any occasion to apply this part of it.

Thus the stance survived intact, of promoting voluntary agreement without regulation. But two problems of the labour market did demand intervention. One was unemployment. The other, subsequently, was the pressure exerted under full employment for even higher earnings.

Unemployment had been a driving issue in the rise of the Labour Party. The major extension of the franchise in 1884 had been followed by the the heavy unemployment in the depression of 1886. Unemployment was the theme to which Keir Hardie returned insistently. What could the government do about it? Labour members made two demands – that the workmen destitute for the time being through the fluctuations of industry should be spared the stigma of the Poor Law; and that relief works should be provided, less wasteful for society, less demoralizing to the man than 'outdoor relief'. Lloyd George met the first claim by a scheme of unemployment insurance, confined to occupations where the risk was great enough to warrant a contribution but calculable in the light of experience so as to promise a solvent fund. But after the war, with demobilization and in 1921 a deep depression, a 'dole' was provided for all 'genuinely seeking work'. As cyclical recovery proceeded, moreover, a residual mass of unemployment remained, the 'irreducible million' of the inter-war years, regionally concentrated. These were the victims of the worsened competitive position of the country in the world market, whose inroads had been felt already in the 1890s, only to be masked down to the war by an expansion of the demand for our old staple exports. Now in the inter-war years the regions that produced those exports became the Special Areas of high and long-term unemployment. Governments could aid them by various measures to help men move to jobs elsewhere, or bring in new industry. But both types of aid implied the creation of new jobs, and was it in the power of governments to do that? The debate revived the old question of relief works, but in an enlarged form, and with reference now not only to the number of men directly employed but to the employment that would be given by their wages when spent. A landmark here is the support given by Keynes and Henderson to Lloyd George's proposals in the General Election of 1929. On the other side was the Treasury view that for every job created by public works in one place a potential job was aborted in another. In fact rearmament was to come as a scheme of public works *de facto*.

We know how, after the government had accepted responsibility for maintaining a high and stable level of employment, for more than twenty post-war years employment did remain high, though with some minor fluctuations as a four-year cycle ran through the economy. The experience was common to a number of Western countries. Looking back on it now, and its termination, we may wonder whether it was in fact due to the application of Keynesian policy to the demand for labour, or whether it did but mark the response of this country to a particular conjuncture of the world market. This conjuncture enabled it to postpone – as another such conjuncture had done in 1900–14 – basic changes in the structure of its industry and deployment of its labour force, the need for which had been manifested already before the end of the nineteenth century.

The other great cause of intervention by government in the labour market was the progressive rise of unit labour costs under full employment. Governments had much cause for concern about this within the fifty years after 1911, for about half of these years were in fact times of full employment, in war and peace. Already in 1915 a Liberal government, having outlawed the strike, found itself committed to what would later have been called a national wages policy. But what happened then, and under the renewed pressures and restraints of the Second World War and the first fifteen years thereafter, opens up the central issue of public policy towards the labour market in the 1960s and 1970s, and this is a main subject of the next and last section.

THE PAST TWENTY YEARS

The years of full employment after the Second World War were gradually to erode the two basic principles of the labour market that we saw established at the outset of our perspective. In 1906 it had been decided that the trade unions should be allowed to conduct their affairs free from legal direction and constraint, and in particular should be endowed with the legal immunities needed to protect the right to strike. By the end of the First World War negotiations between an employers' association and the trade unions organizing their workers had been established as the standard machinery for the regulation of wage rates in a regime of voluntary and open-ended negotiations. Both these principles were now to be undermined by a change in attitudes at the place of work. The immunities enjoyed by trade unionists taking 'industrial action' were called in question when employees of particular firms increasingly took the initiative in striking on local issues without processing them through 'the machinery', and in the 1960s the tally of these unofficial strikes mounted alarmingly. This development was a mark of the shift of effective wage fixing from multi-employer negotiations to the firm or plant, and this in turn was associated with a cumulative annual rise in unit labour costs. Governments could no longer stand back and leave the movements of the wage level to the market. Their concern on this score had been lively since the end of the Second World War, and we will therefore deal with it first.

82

Labour market policy

The end of Lend-Lease in 1945 had confronted Whitehall dramatically with what was to be the dominating constraint on the economic policy of British governments henceforward — the weakness of the balance of payments and the external value of sterling. A rise of labour costs that worsened our international competitiveness, and an excess of purchasing power that spilled over into an increase of imports, were both of them mischievous, but under full employment both were continually tending to come about. Yet governments were reluctant to attempt any administrative control of the wage movements from which they arose.

For this reluctance there were several reasons. The Ministry of Labour carried down from the First World War the tradition that the statutory enforcement of wage regulation, which meant a ban on strikes and the substitution of compulsory arbitration, was impracticable in the last resort; above all the prosecution of strikers, to which a system of imposed control must come in the end, could only lead to humiliation for the judiciary and the government. On the other hand much could be done by persuasion, if the voluntary machinery were left intact and an appeal were made to the good sense and public spirit of the parties. That had been shown by the outstanding achievement of Ernest Bevin as Minister of Labour during the Second World War: though formally armed with a ban on strikes, he made virtually no use of it, but relied on two basic factors — keeping down the rise in the cost of living, and engaging the trust and loyalty of the workers. The support of trade union leaders had equally ensured that remarkable achievement under the Labour government after the war, when for more than two years from February 1948 to September 1950, no rises in wage rates were negotiated, and this at a time when they could have been negotiated readily. When the Conservatives came back in 1951 and were engaged in dismantling controls, they were certainly unlikely to devise a new one on wages. They were keenly aware that the inflation which was harassing the economy had its source in full employment. 'In order to maintain full employment', their White Paper of 1956 said,

> the Government must ensure that the level of demand for goods and services is high and rises steadily as productive capacity grows. This means a strong demand for labour, and good opportunities to sell goods and services profitably. In these conditions

it is open to employees to insist on large wage increases, and it is often possible for employers to grant them and pass the cost to the consumer, so maintaining their profit margin.[7]

But the inference could be only that all concerned should exercise self-restraint. The government would not contemplate controls. Nor would it even risk a clash between employers and the unions: when in 1957 the engineering employers made a stand against the latest wage claim, the government saw the prospect of a stoppage as more threatening to sterling than another round of pay rises would be, and pressed the employers to settle.

There was the less likelihood of governments applying direct restraints to pay, because there was no agreement among administrators and economists that any upward thrust on pay could arise in the absence of excess demand. Already when the maintenance of full employment was being projected during the war there had been some economists − Beveridge, Keynes, Joan Robinson, Worswick − who with the actual processes of bargaining before the mind's eye had foreseen an upward pressure on wages as the result of a change in attitudes. But the economists who viewed the labour market from a greater distance and thought of it like any other market naturally interpreted a rise in wages as the adjustment to an excess of demand over supply. 'Demand pull' fitted into the ready-made framework of economic analysis: 'cost push' did not. Those who contended for the reality of 'cost push' accepted a high level of employment as a necessary condition for it, but only as a blanket condition: unlike the believers in 'demand pull', they did not expect that variations in the level of employment − within wide limits − would be associated with variations in the rate of rise of pay. For practical purposes they held that at a given high level of employment there was a margin of discretion in the decisions of trade unionists and employers about the rate of rise of pay. That rate was not uniquely determined by market forces of supply and demand. Only gradually did the possibility that this was so come to be accepted. The Council on Prices, Productivity and Incomes − 'the Three Wise Men' − appointed in 1957 by Macmillan's government as a way of providing impartial and persuasive guidance for negotiators recommended in its first report that demand be restricted so that the economy be run at a somewhat higher level of unemployment. In the same year the Phillips curve appeared, and was readily accepted as showing that wages moved with the balance of demand and supply in the labour market. But the Council's fourth report – by this time the three members were all different – accepted the reality of cost push, and recommended a national forum to assess and adopt a projection of the course of national productivity, so that decisions about prices and incomes might be kept in line with it.

This last report appeared at the exact time in July 1961 when a renewed and more severe crisis of sterling was forcing a Conservative government to abandon its objections to intervention, order an immediate pay pause within its own jurisdiction as an employer, and call on all those concerned with pay elsewhere to follow the example. In the new year it set up the National Incomes Commission to which it could refer suspect claims or settlements for investigation and report. Though it did accept the need to trim demand by accompanying these provisions with fiscal and monetary restraints, it would not have availed itself of the provisions at all if it had not at least implicitly accepted the existence of a margin of discretion in decisions about pay and prices. This margin might have been created only by what the first report of the Three Wise Men gave as 'the main cause' of 'the rising trend of prices and incomes since the end of the War' – 'an abnormally high level of demand for goods and services in general, maintained for an abnormally long stretch of time'.[8] But once the margin was there, governments would try to make use of it to check the rise of costs and prices in an emergency. At the same time governments of either party remained until 1979 wholly unwilling to depart deliberately from a high level of employment. For purposes of practical policy the question whether 'cost push' or 'demand pull' was the source of inflation was therefore decided in favour of 'cost push'. Moreover those who were in touch with the shop floor were increasingly aware of the growth of attitudes and expectations that would now exert great pressure to carry the rise of pay on even in the presence of substantial unemployment: that is, of the reality of 'cost push' as a force independent, within limits, of the current state of demand in the labour market. From the July measures under Macmillan and Selwyn Lloyd in 1961 to the Social Contract under Callaghan and Healey in 1976–8, the forms of incomes policy have been outwardly various. But this variety has been due in part to incoming governments that had repudiated the policy and dismantled the apparatus of their predecessors being forced to bring the policy back albeit with a different appearance for the apparatus. A common element has been the prescription of a permissible general rate of rise, it might be after an initial standstill. In one instance, under the new Labour government of 1964, the general rule was supplemented by the statement of four cases in which greater rises were acceptable – a statement evidently copied from guidelines issued under President Kennedy. To allay the fear that holding wages back would only allow profits to expand, Labour governments linked wage restraint with price control and dividend restraint. Beginning with the Labour government in the July crisis of 1966, governments took statutory powers to halt all movement for a period, or suspend a proposed rise pending investigation. The statutory directives were never flouted where that would have been conspicuous, and there were no prosecutions under them. But there was no means of checking the drift of individual earnings at the place of work, or the change of pay in minor employments and short engagements; there were also forms of avoidance through non-pecuniary remuneration. Government could control the sector of tax-supported public employment directly and exercise influence, though not in the last resort control, over settlements elsewhere in the public sector. It had sanctions it could apply to firms in the private sector with which it had dealings. But beyond that, its statements of policy depended more on understanding and voluntary compliance than on any sanctions. One way in which the Labour government from 1965 onwards sought to combine the spread of understanding with the mild sanction of the deferment of a rise for some months, was investigation by the National Board for Prices and Incomes. Under the direction of the chairman, Aubrey Jones, the Board made a distinctive approach to the cases that the government referred to it, considering not merely whether a proposed rise in pay or prices was within the guidelines, but whether ways of raising productivity could be found so that higher earnings would not mean higher labour costs, or higher costs could be absorbed without raising prices. This form of consultation is likely to have had its instructive or cautionary effect on decisions taken elsewhere. But with this exception, remarkably little administrative support was provided for incomes policies.

Yet Labour governments had one means of administration that was not available to the Conservatives – the cooperation of the trade unions. Conservative governments sought this, and it was a principle of the TUC to deal freely with the government of the day according as the upholding of trade union interests required, whatever that government's political colour. But to the proposal that they accept and propound to their affiliates something so contrary to their inherent propensities as was wage restraint, the General Council was bound to react by bargaining: what could the government offer them by way of compensation? Conservative governments could not give them what they asked: Labour governments were more amenable. There were periods, moreover, when the most influential figures in the TUC threw their weight behind the policy of a Labour government, and these were the periods of the most effective administration of policy – the standstill of 1948–50, and the 'social contract' in 1976–8. It was seen as a remarkable step in principle when after the Joint Declaration of Intent that followed the return of Labour to office in 1964 the General Council of the TUC required affiliated unions to notify it of impending claims, and called before its own claims vetting committee any that seemed likely to overrun the guidelines.

Econometricians have attempted to measure the effect of phases of incomes policy on the rise of pay. To do this they develop equations which purport to show what course pay would have followed if there had been no incomes policy at the time. These equations are obtained by fitting the actual movement of pay in preceding years to a number of variables believed to be determinants of that movement. But it is possible to get a close fit from such a relation between time series over a number of years and lose it immediately afterwards: if we continue to calculate the course of the dependent variables, the projection now differs widely from the actual course. We therefore cannot be at all sure that we can tell how pay would have behaved in any period, solely from our knowledge of other variables, and this holds for the period of any incomes policy. We can only fall back on the report of many businessmen, administrators and trade unionists, that the constraints of the policy were a reality and often a hindrance and embarrassment to them.

But it is also a familiar observation that 'incomes policy has always failed'; no period of restraint has lasted long, and each has ended in an explosion. One reason for this is that the application of restraint has been uneven, and inequities have accumulated. The outburst has been mainly prompted by compressed differentials and distorted relativities. Governments, clear that they must set an example in their own house, have held back the public sector while much of the private sector has been under no such constraint. Large concerns and those in close contact with government are under more obligation to obey the rules than those whose proceedings are less exposed. Within the firm, those on time rates may be held back while those on piece rates continue to edge their earnings up – it was this disparity that broke up the standstill in 1950. The great defeats of governments in the 1970s were in struggles over relativities – the miners in 1972 and 1974; the public sector in 1978–9.

The distortions inflicted by incomes policy would be less hard to bear if there were more general understanding of its purpose. The lack of this is another cause of its breakdown. The very macroeconomic terms in which the case for an incomes policy is put are remote from the habits of thought and speech of many employees, and from their concern with the factors on which they are accustomed to base and uphold their own claims – the cost of living, some particular differential or relativity, and the expectation of an annual betterment. It may be true that if everybody's pay goes up, prices will go up too, but a rise in my own pay here and now is a clear rise in my purchasing power, and if my pay does not go up, prices will still go on rising and I shall be the loser. Even if all hold back together, breaking into the inflationary spiral will still mean that while prices go on rising for some time, real incomes are reduced. How sure must people be that they have much to gain from this in the end, for them to take the initial certainly painful step? The old issue of 'us' and 'them' affects attitudes here. The fall in real wages is a transfer to profits. It may be that those with higher incomes are subject to some reduction too, but that leaves them all the more noticeably higher – the manager director still has his Jaguar.

A further obstacle to the implementation of incomes policy has been the lack of control from the top downwards among the organizations of the labour market. The lack of discipline among the employers in this country we take, surprisingly enough, for granted. The TUC has always been only an association for the common purposes of its member unions, and its General Council can offer advice but not issue instructions: 'We are not an army', George Woodcock often said. Within the member unions, the authority of the national officers and executive has diminished with 'the shift of power to the shop floor'. Under full employment, just as the individual employee has aquired a new independence and assurance over against the foreman and manager, so he has within his union over against the district and national officer; and the shop steward whom he elects at the place of work has come to play an essential part in pay negotiation and administration. This has been matched, since the Donovan Commission recommended as much in 1968, by the widespread development of the negotiation of agreements firm by firm or plant by plant. But these agreements are not kept under the control of a national union in the way that 'plant contracts' may be in the United States. The decentralization of negotiation, and the underlying independence of individual attitudes, have thus come to preclude any form of central control such as is possible where both employers and employees are organized in large and disciplined bodies.

At the same time, the change in attitudes has made the problem of checking cost push more urgent. During the 1960s the size of claim generally regarded as normal was rising. In 1968–70 there came about in most OECD countries a sustained increase in the rate of rise of wages which it is not possible to trace to antecedent increases in monetary supply or current changes in business activity and the demand for labour, and which seems most probably to have come about through one of those waves of change in social outlook that roll through a number of countries simultaneously. At least we know that since this 'hinge', expectations of pay rises have ruled higher, and for some years at least the assurance of the employee has been shown in his readiness to press for very big rises in the presence of high and rising unemployment. In this setting the achievement of 'the social contract' in 1976–8 appears all the more remarkable. It shows the trust that could still be placed in an outstanding trade union leader, Jack Jones, and the simple plan proposed, while a Labour government was there to see fair play. But even so, two years were more than enough.

Against the heightened expectations and a steepening spiral, what we have seen in these latter days – if we put aside the theory of the remote control of the labour market by the money supply – is in practice a return to the economics of the trade cycle, and restraint by a steep rise of unemployment, as in 1921 and 1932. Depression used to exert a generally inhibiting effect on pay claims even where it did not impinge directly, and there are many signs of its doing that again today. But people have probably changed in their reaction to it, and in how they will reassert themselves when revival comes. It seems probable that the need for incomes policy remains and the country will have to see what lessons it can draw from experience.

In dealing with the lack of central control among the organizations of the labour market, we touched on the second main way in which the great settlement of our labour market procedure, as that emerged from the First World War, has been undermined in recent years: the principle that trade union activities should lie outside the purview of the law has been called in question by the greatly increased impact and frequency of unofficial strikes at the place of work. In the early 1960s these strikes had become a major source of anxiety to employers and government. Not only were they part of the process by which labour costs were continually being pushed up, out of the control of the multi-employer negotiations and even of plant management, but they also hampered production by harassing management and obstructing change. They were exploiting a gap in the established system. But they were also, in a sense, breaking an unwritten bargain, by which the trade unions used the powers conferred on them by their immunities only in certain channels – that was how 'the machinery' worked. In the early 1960s it was common ground that the unofficial strike must be brought under control. Before they went out of office, the Conservatives went no further than proposing to appoint a Royal Commission. Labour when it came back in 1964 did appoint one – the Donovan Commission – to examine industrial relations 'with particular reference to the Law.'

The Report of the Donovan Commission took the unofficial strike as its major problem. 'We have no hesitation . . .', its members declared, 'in saying that the prevalence of unofficial strikes, and their tendency (outside coal-mining) to increase, have such serious economic implications that measures to deal with them are urgently necessary.'[9] The measures they recommended were adapted to its cause, which they found in the lack of provision for negotiation within the firm or plant, to which much actual bargaining had shifted. 'Britain has two systems of industrial relations', they said. 'The one is the formal system embodied in the official institutions. The other is the informal system created by the actual behaviour of trade unions and employers' associations, of managers, shop stewards and workers.'[10] The remedy for present disorders was to recognize the reality of the informal system, and develop effective procedures for it to 'regulate actual pay, constitute a factory negotiating committee and grievance procedures which suit the circumstances, deal with such subjects as redundancy and discipline and cover the rights and obligations of shop stewards.'[11]

Though the Commission had been enjoined to have 'particular reference to the Law' its members did not see a new legal code as offering improvements: on the contrary, they set out fully their reasons for holding that any attempt at statutory regulation or compulsory procedure, on the analogy of some other countries, would be frustrated. They remained with voluntarism, and called for the formation of new institutions and procedures to fill the gap at the level of the firm. The initiative in this must be taken by management. But certain members of the Labour government were not prepared to be so inactive for their part. The White Paper *In Place of Strife*[12] contained proposals designed to help trade unionists in various ways, but it rode boldly up to their entrenchments with a statutory procedure for dealing with unofficial strikes. The Secretary of State for Employment was to be empowered to order the strikers back to normal working for a 'conciliation pause' of twenty-eight days. Any who did not comply could be proceeded against before a panel of the Industrial Court, and fined, though there would be no liability to imprisonment for non-payment. If agreement had not been reached by the end of the pause, the parties would be free to resume industrial action. This was a marginal use of legal sanctions, but it was sliding one foot over a passionately defended line. Could a worker really be fined for striking, in a free country? The intense opposition by the trade unions conveyed itself to the Labour Members of Parliament, and the proposal had to be dropped ignominiously within the Cabinet.

The Conservatives who came back to office the next year had long been thinking over the reform of trade union law, and were undeterred by the failure of *In Place of Strife*. They were convinced of the urgency of the issues, with reason, for in that year 1970 the number of unofficial strikes was twice what it had been when the Donovan Commission reported only two years before. Their Industrial Relations Act of 1971 therefore contained, amid much else, provisions that should have served to prevent or contain the unofficial strike. First, it provided that all written agreements should have the force of contracts unless they contained a statement to the contrary. Many unofficial strikes were also unconstitutional, that is, in breach of an agreed procedure for the processing of grievances or disputes: if this provision had been generally observed it would therefore have assimilated British agreements in this respect to American, which the parties were habitually agreed to treat as contracts. But in fact the unions always did insert the statement to the contrary, and the employers did not object. Second, the Act endeavoured to make clear the responsibility of unions that signed agreements for the actions of their shop stewards in carrying the agreements out; this it did by stipulations concerning the relevant rules of the unions. These stipulations were to be enforced by the Registrar of Trade Unions; but the great majority of unions simply refused to register under the Act. Third, the Act defined as 'unfair industrial practices' a number of actions which unofficial striking would involve. In particular, it was made an unfair industrial practice for any person to induce or threaten to induce someone else to break a contract – one might virtually say, for any person to bring others out on strike – unless that person was acting within the scope of his authority on behalf of a trade union. The remedy was in the hands of the employer, who could proceed against anyone accused of an unfair industrial practice in the Industrial Court set up by the Act. But in fact employers were loath to take any such actions against their own employees.

Thus the attempt to check the unofficial strike by law failed again, even before the Act itself was repealed as it was in 1974. But meanwhile a change had been going on in workplaces and board-rooms up and down the country, very much as the Donovan Commission had said it should. Largely on the initiative of management, industrial relations and wage negotiations within the firm were now receiving recognition and being provided with institutions and procedures. Formerly it had been held that industrial relations within the firm were confined to the application of a grievance procedure, with possibly the addition, out of benevolence, of joint consultation, a clear line being drawn between negotiation and consultation. It had also been held formerly that wage negotiation in the firm did not occur at all, rates being fixed in industry-wide negotiations or, so far as piece rates were necessarily fixed locally, being determined as an objective matter of measurement in accordance with standards negotiated for the industry. These views may have held true of much of the inter-war period, but the bargaining power that full employment placed on the shop floor made myths of them as they persisted in the 1950s. The Donovan Commission called for the gap at the firm to be filled. Since the Commission reported in 1968 much has been done to bring industrial relations and wage movements at the place of work under the control of agreed arrangements. The shop steward has been increasingly accepted, trained and accorded a constitutional position. Job evaluation has been used to work out acceptable wage structures. Procedures for negotiation have been established, leading to detailed agreements, firm by firm or plant by plant. The importance of multi-employer agreements has correspondingly declined. We are in the presence of a marked change in the structure of our methods of wage fixing in the private sector.

But while we have seen the endeavours of the Industrial Relations Act to contain the unofficial strike disposed of in this way, the larger issue raised by that Act remains open. In the light of the impact of trade union power in the contemporary economy, that Act called in question the principle of the great settlement, that the unions should be able to operate under the protection of legal immunities but without constraint and direction by positive law. In effect, the Act of 1971 went back to one of the choices open to the legislators of 1906. Between the extreme courses of restoring to the unions all the immunity they had enjoyed before the Taff Vale decision, and retaining all the liability to which they had been exposed by it, there had opened the middle course of distinguishing permissible from impermissible forms of 'industrial action', and restoring immunity only to the permissible. This in effect is what the Act of 1971 now did. The impermissible forms it characterized as 'unfair industrial practices', a term evidently adapted from the 'unfair labour practices' of the American Taft-Hartley Act of 1947. The practices of most concern were forms of the sympathetic strike and the secondary boycott. Where hitherto the courts had endeavoured to limit or repress these oppressive uses of the power of combination through the complexities of the law of tort, the Act made a fresh start with a new jurisdiction, meant to be of ready access, beginning with the Industrial Tribunals and going up to a new Industrial Court. For the rest, it contained provisions designed to protect the rights of the individual worker, and these were in the old tradition of the common law. It also envisaged the imposition of regulated structures: the Registrar was to enforce requirements concerning the constitution and rule books of trade unions, and the

Industrial Court could in the last resort, in a case of disputed jurisdiction, order the adoption of a recommended scheme of representation and negotiation. Here in all was a framework of positive law, specially designed to accommodate the workings of the labour market and guide them in orderly procedures; it was equipped with its own jurisdiction to repress aberrations.

If an old country could have made a fresh start these provisions would have been wholly reasonable. But the conception of them was completely foreign to the inherited notions of both employers and trade unionists. The employers were plagued by the unofficial strike, but they valued informality and flexibility, they preferred the devil they knew to the devil they did not know: as the Director-General of the CBI said when the Conservative proposals were put forward before the election, the employers did not want to hand over their industrial relations to 'a new profession of labour lawyers' or have to be 'constantly away from their business suing their workers and being sued by those workers in labour courts.'[13] The reaction of the trade union activists was no less instinctive but far more vehement, for the enactment of a legal code that made offences of many actions of their members, and the creation of a special court in which unions could be fined and their members subjected to injunctions enforceable by imprisonment, could in their eyes be nothing less that a return to the days when a criminal taint attached to trade unionism. So strong was the tradition that the law was inherently the enemy of unionism, so essential had they learned it to be that they should keep out of its clutches, that they can scarcely have paused to consider whether they would in fact be free to operate under the Act. When employers who would never proceed in court against their own workers did obtain injunctions against outsiders by whom they were being picketed, and the injunctions being ignored had to be enforced by imprisonment, the outcry, the rally in the trade union world forced two humiliating withdrawals on the Industrial Court, and destroyed its authority.

But the issue would not go away. It might be unthinkable that pickets should be subject to prosecution solely on the ground of a statutory distinction between primary and secondary picketing; but in 1979 the damage widely inflicted by secondary picketing in a haulage strike made its legitimacy an open and burning question among employers in the many industries affected. The closed shop – to take another subject of regulation in the 1971 Act – gained fresh significance in employers' eyes when, as was believed in the engineering strikes in the autumn of 1979, it enabled minorities of militants to bring out employees who did not want to strike. Militancy as it has grown in recent years has availed itself of a range of actions that extend the pressure exerted by action against the strikers' own employers – secondary picketing and the secondary boycott, blacking, the mass picket, the sympathetic strike. These have proved highly effective. But they are harassing to management and disruptive to the economy, and may be oppressive to individual employees. Though formidable weapons of aggression, they are not essential to the performance of their functions by the trade unions. We have seen that much has been done in the private sector to regularize practice by agreement in procedure; but over the wide field we are bound to return to the principle of distinguishing by law the permissible and impermissible uses of the power of combination. This is the principle that was considered but discarded in 1906, and applied too suddenly and extensively in 1971. It has been applied again, in a first step of caution and circumspection, by the Employment Act of 1980.

Will legislation of this kind be able, in the words of the Donovan Commission, 'to reverse the entire trend of our industrial history and to give to the law a function it has never had in the past'?[14] That depends first and foremost on the emergent attitudes of employers and trade unionists. There are signs that the employers have been goaded into willingness to accept the greater regulation of industrial relations by law, even where that means that they must go to law themselves. Among trade unionists the portents are mixed. Public opinion polls show a majority of trade union members in favour of trade union reform or of restraints on trade union action: but struggles in which particular unions have been involved have been supported, however ruthless or protracted they may have been, by the members generally. There is in any case the problem of representative leadership and the power of assertive minorities within trade unions as within other voluntary associations.

Beyond this there is another problem. Mr Callaghan gave his pledge to the Trades Union Congress in September 1980 that when returned to office Labour would repeal the Employment Act. Here appears one of the consequences most devastating to our industrial relations of the dramatization and enactment at the national level, across the floor of the House of Commons, of the war of 'us' and 'them'. In policy towards the labour market our electoral system and structure of politics work towards polarization instead of consensus; they generate demolition instead of construction. The development of labour market policy is bound up with political reform.

NOTES

1 I wish to record very gratefully my indebtedness for detailed and constructive commentaries to Dr Kenneth O. Morgan of Queen's College, Oxford, and Dr Barry Supple of Nuffield College, Oxford.
2 A. W. Phillips, 'The relation between unemployment and the rate of change of money wage rates in the United Kingdom, 1861–1957', *Economica*, 25, 100, November 1958, pp. 283–99.
3 This principle was embodied in the Corn Production Act, 1917, whose s.5(6) directed the Agricultural Wages Board in fixing minimum rates to secure wages which it considered 'adequate to promote efficiency and to enable a man in an ordinary case to maintain himself and his family in accordance with such standard of comfort as may be reasonable in relation to the nature of his occupation.' This directive was repeated verbatim for the county agricultural wages committees set up by the Labour government's Agricultural Wages (Regulation) Act, 1924.
4 At a gathering where, as William Robson told me, Keynes said to Beatrice, 'I owe it all to you'.
5 The Cotton Manufacturing Industry (Temporary Provisions) Act, 1934.
6 The Trade Disputes and Trade Union Act, 1927.
7 *The Economic Implications of Full Employment*, Cmd. 9725, 1956, para. 26.
8 Council on Prices, Productivity and Incomes, *First Report*, London: HMSO, 1958, para. 78.
9 *Royal Commission on Trade Unions and Employers' Associations 1965–1968 Report*, Cmnd. 3623, June 1968, para. 415.
10 op. cit. para. 46.
11 op. cit. para. 1020.
12 Cmnd. 3888, January 1969.
13 *Financial Times*, 11 April 1970.
14 *Royal Commission on Trade Unions and Employers' Associations*, para. 460.

Comments by
William Brown

There can be no industrialized country for which labour market problems have come to be more central to economic policy than is the case for Britain. There can be no democracy for which they have come to be a greater source of political hazard. The elegance with which Sir Henry has analysed the development of British labour market policy leaves me searching in vain for some shade of judgement with which to take issue. I am best employed in highlighting the key problems.

Any British government that seeks to influence employment relationships is confronted by an unusual pair of problems: our collective bargaining system is, by long tradition, both voluntary and decentralized.

To some extent the tradition of voluntarism can be traced to the decision of the Liberal government 75 years ago to grant trade unions certain legal immunities. But that decison was, to a large extent, a reflection of the prevailing wishes of employers. Besides having a distaste for government intervention they had, in those industries where trade unions were established, grown accustomed to collective bargaining at the workplace. That bargaining was – and still is – in many respects a legislative process. The agreements and understandings that emerge from the interplay of bargaining power acquire strong local legitimacy for those who work by them. When they are challenged by the laws of Parliament it has tended to be parliamentary laws that are shuffled aside. Thus, when employers have been offered laws which they could use against trade unions – after Taff Vale, after the General Strike, with the Industrial Relations Act, and probably now with the Employment Act – they have tended to ignore them. It is not that employers are opposed to labour laws in principle; it is just that they feel that it is *other* employers who need them and not themselves.

It is also to employers that we should look for an explanation of the second key feature of our labour relations system: its decentralization. British employers are remarkable by comparison with other Europeans for their lack of solidarity. For reasons that can be traced far back into the nineteenth century, including our early industrialization and our generally non-Marxist trade union movement, we have never developed strong, industry-wide employer coalitions to any substantial extent. In those industries where there have been multi-employer agreements, they have generally left much to be bargained over at the workplace.

In the scramble for scarce labour that came after the Second World War, these industry-wide agreements tended to fall apart;

employers have, in recent years, generally switched to single-employer factory or company agreements. But while this move has improved their control over the work and wages of their employees, it has not improved their co-ordination with other employers. The CBI has to contend with an ideology praising employer independence which would bemuse its continental counterparts.

These features have shaped our trade union movement. Voluntarism, and the practice of collective bargaining at the workplace, have provided it with incomparable control over both pay and the conduct of work. Decentralization, and the lack of the stimulus of a united employer organization, have inhibited the growth of an authoritative central trade union council.

In many ways the result is a remarkable democratic achievement. Spread throughout the length and breadth of Britain there are a third of a million shop stewards, subject to instant recall by their electorates, questioning and influencing employer decisions. No other country has anything remotely comparable. But its benefits to trade union members are mixed. Control over one's work has doubtful value when overseas competitors, unhindered by such civilized practices, can effectively close down one's factory. More urgently as the recession deepens, the over-dependence of the trade union movement upon decentralized bargaining is making it poorly equipped to beat a disciplined retreat.

But the greatest difficulty of our voluntaristic, decentralized bargaining system is undoubtedly its appalling power as an amplifier of inflation. Lacking either co-ordination or reassurance, conscientious trade union leaders have no option but to over-bid each other in an attempt to protect their members from falling real wages. Whatever the initial inflationary stimulus, this mechanism will tend to exacerbate it. By contrast, the damage caused by strikes, which are largely a by-product of the process, is relatively slight.

It has been during the last two decades of our seventy years that this profound institutional weakness has become most apparent. A confident workforce has had a higher level of world inflation against which to react. Governments have been obliged, always reluctantly, to intervene in bargaining processes from which they had previously stood gratefully aloof.

One form of intervention has been that of legislative attempts to control trade union power, either by seeking to inhibit the strike weapon, or by weakening the basis of union organization. So far these attempts have achieved more political trouble than practical success. Governments have shied from the risk of imprisoning trade unionists and employers have conspired to protect such valued institutions as the closed shop.

More effective have been attempts at incomes policies which have generally taken the form of unilateral actions by governements to control the bilateral process of collective bargaining. These have been unhappy experiences and it is perhaps inevitable that democracy as a whole suffers when government takes on the thankless task of regulating relative pay. More successful have been bilateral policies operated by governments and the TUC, although these have ultimately imposed intolerable strains on internal union government. Notably absent have been bilateral policies operated by the CBI and TUC, as in Sweden, or trilateral policies involving all three parties as in Australia. Once again, it has been the weakness of our employers' organizations that has prevented such developments.

Such direct attempts by the government to instill some degree of co-ordination into the pay bargaining process have, for the time being, been put aside. As at earlier stages in our seventy years, heavy unemployment is making direct intervention unnecessary. But this is a very short-term policy. When any sort of recovery comes, or when an imminent general election requires it to come, bargainers will bounce back, and they will do so with grievances based upon a more disordered pay structure than Britain has ever seen. The breathing space that is being offered to employers by the recession to regroup, forge larger coalitions, and raise the level of bargaining, is apparently being squandered. Both at industry level − as in engineering, printing, and shipping − and at the national level with the CBI, the signs are that employers are once more pursuing their individual, temporary advantages, apparently unaware of the opportunity that is being missed.

Perhaps one cause of the acute difficulty of policy implementation in this area is that economic problems tend to be seen as having economic origins. Or rather, that they are seen as being fundamentally the consequences of the price mechanisms that dominate economists' minds. When heavy unemployment cows employees into a passive acceptance of their pay, and when heavy competition between employers obliges them to pay a going rate, a market mechanism model is fairly appropriate. But when employees can combine without anxiety of job loss, and when employers have sufficient power within their product markets to pay for their employees' peace of mind, such models are wholly inappropriate. The driving force then becomes the desire of employees to protect their self-esteem, reflected in an obsession with relative pay; an essentially conservative motive which, when translated through uncoordinated bargaining, becomes deeply destructive.

Thus an understanding of our basic labour market problems requires a far more eclectic form of economic modelling than we have been accustomed to. It is hard to expect much to come from further attempts to alter the voluntaristic basis of our collective bargaining system. Even if it were desirable to do so, employer resistance would be implacable. But a great deal can be achieved by attempts to increase the coordination of decision making on pay. This does not mean a total centralization; experience in other countries suggests that much can be done with an authoritative 'umbrella' agreement under which separate bargaining units have some freedom to match their economic circumstances. Nor does it require the renovation of multi-employer industry-wide associations, most of which are, for these purposes, beyond recall. The government can help in the process by encouraging the CBI and TUC, instead of ignoring them, and possibly more positively by acting as midwife towards the voluntary coordination of the pay fixing process. It will be clear from the earlier analysis that I see the encouragement of the CBI and of employer unity as the single most important priority.

The picture we have of labour market policy from Sir Henry's highly eclectic perspective is one of success so long as government was able to abstain. Electorates have not allowed governments to abstain in more inflationary recent years. But the clear conclusion must be that it is only by helping to bring about the greater coordination of the collective bargaining process that governments can ever hope to abstain again.

Discussion

The discussion was opened by *Sir Arthur Knight* who found Professor William Brown's analysis almost entirely consistent with his own experience. There was a need for more activism on the part of the CBI, the TUC and possibly government as well. Greater centralization, however, had to rest on some acceptance of the general level that ought to prevail in wage settlements. The more centralized the bargain, the harder it was to fit it to individual circumstances, including in particular any productivity deal, plant by plant, that might be incorporated in it. This was his one reservation.

Looking at developments more widely, where in the end were improvements most likely to be made? It seemed to him that emphasis within the firm and within the plant on worker involvement was absolutely fundamental. It was only there that the worker could be educated to the realities of his situation. There has been a big advance in realism in the last year or two. Some of the most successful experiments had been in forming problem solving groups where workers developed a sense of personal involvement in making things happen. But very little progress had yet been made in what could be one of the most promising ways of reconciling policy making with an understanding on the part of the workers that their true interest lay in the prosperity of the firm employing them.

Although the *Chairman* emphasized, in the light of this contribution, that labour market organization might be at least as important in its effects on productivity as on money wages and inflation, the discussion tended to concentrate on incomes policy as underlying current dilemmas in economic management.

The prospects for such a policy, as *Sir Frank Figgures* saw them, were not very bright. In the last ten years the situation had become worse, not better. There had been an increase, not so much in union power, as in union sense of power. It was even more necessary to the stability and success of an incomes policy that it should have the acquiescence of the unions, and it had become much harder to get it.

It had to be accepted that the powers of government were limited: it was not possible to enforce an incomes policy of any kind by putting large numbers of people in prison. Not even in war had that been done. Reliance on the law could not be taken beyond a certain point. But to be durable an incomes policy had to be statutory. A voluntary incomes policy had to be very *simpliste,* as it was in the first year of the Heath experiment and in two successful years under the Callaghan government. But if the policy was *simpliste* it was incapable of lasting. An essential part of a durable policy was flexibility; but there could be no flexibility save on a statutory basis.

A statutory policy, however, was not likely to be enforceable against more than a very small part of the working population.

How could one get the trade unions to accept a statutory policy? Such an arrangement struck at one of their major functions. It was necessary, therefore, to be able to bargain about something of greater importance to them, such as the level of employment. The time might come when the trade unions might be moved by fear of inflation; but in the United Kingdom there was as yet no acute sense of danger from inflation. The moment inflation showed signs of subsiding it took second place in the minds of the population to other things.

If the trade unions were to be involved in a discussion of incomes policy a tripartite framework such as NEDC was necessary. This had allowed an exchange of views to take place and shown what would command at least the acquiescence of the unions. In his view, the experiment in the 1970s could have been prolonged by at least another year. There were, of course, hazards in these arrangements – hazards arising from the chances that Ministers might take wrong decisions. But Ministers were no more liable to that than the rest of us. Sir Richard Clarke, in a paper on incomes policies, had listed thirteen of them from Stafford Cripps onwards and all thirteen could be said to have failed in the end when governments slipped on a banana skin. One ought to beware, therefore, of devising policies exposing Ministers to this risk. But there was no chance at all of getting the trade unions to go along with an incomes policy if they would not do so with an operating framework on a tripartite basis.

Sir Frank also commented on the idea that it would be advantageous if more agreements were negotiated centrally. He would be very doubtful whether such negotiations would prove any less damaging from the point of view of inflation than negotiations at the plant level. It might be true that many of the productivity agreements at the plant level were bogus and inflationary but not all: many were valid. In most of the public sector, which formed one-third of the economy as a whole, negotiations were already centralized. The extension of centralized negotiations to the rest of the economy on that model did not seem likely to make much of a contribution to economic management.

Sir Austin Robinson raised the issue of indexation. What was new compared with pre-war days was that practically everybody was involved every year in a renegotiation of their wage or salary. This was because wage negotiations now dealt simultaneously with two sets of issues: there was a judgement relating to the movement in the cost of living and a judgement of the situation of a particular group as against other groups. If indexing wages on a much wider scale removed the need for the first of those judgements it would take away an important cause of the frequency of wage negotiations: cost of living adjustments. Now that the rentier could enjoy indexation through 'granny bonds', why not the wage earner too?

Mr Chris Allsopp suggested that something might be gained by finding a new name for incomes policy. The argument in favour of an incomes policy was that the alternatives were so awful. If demand management had been preempted by the need to control inflation or tied to the requirements of a fixed exchange rate, difficulties in the labour market appeared naturally enough as unemployment. That being so, incomes policy could be conceived of as a kind of employment policy and more progress might be made by calling it that. After all, there *was* an employment problem and it was easier to sell the idea that employment should be kept up than that wages should be kept down. It would be easy also to extend the idea of an employment policy so that it took in productivity as well.

Lord Roberthall said he had been one of the earliest advocates of an incomes policy. Economists would agree that the issue was crucial and almost all of them might also agree that they did not know what to do about it.

The discussions with the trade unions had all been in terms of making concessions so that they had come to think increasingly that in agreeing to an incomes policy they were giving away something. The last two Labour administrations, in what they called a Social Contract, had altered the legislative framework in favour of the unions. So at the start of each successive wage round the trade unions were more conscious of their power. The rise in wages accelerated from one round to the next; and as inflation mounted, groups who saw what others had achieved asked themselves whether they had not just as much muscle if they chose to use it. In a highly integrated economy it was more and more apparent how easy it was to bring things to a stop for so long as each group was backed up by the principle of solidarity: this gave strength even to the weaker groups and nobody was willing to drop behind for long. Inflexibilities built up in the system and would cause a mammoth explosion whenever the present government let up. There must, for example, be an acute sense of grievance in the private sector after unemployment had forced acceptance of lower rates of increase in pay than in the public sector. All this meant an abiding danger of serious social instability.

He agreed with Sir Frank Figgures that NEDC provided a forum in which there could be a tripartite discussion of the problem. But it had never been turned into a place for bargaining between the parties represented. It would have made all the difference if the Labour government had had the courage to repeal the legislation when the trade unions failed to control their members. This would have obliged the unions to face their members with the problems and organizational difficulties. However, the present government was unlikely to have any use for bargaining with the unions even though it might have offered to reverse its policies in exchange for a wage freeze.

Professor Giersch went back to the assignment problem discussed by Sir Bryan Hopkin. Demand management could serve two objectives if they were complementary: for example, if prices were falling in a world depression, an expansion in demand could move the economy nearer to full employment and to stable prices at the same time. But nearer to productive potential, the objectives would be in conflict and while monetary/fiscal policy could raise nominal demand, how that affected employment would be decided on the wage front. In the long run the assignment problem would be solved when incomes policy served the goal of full employment. The problem was seen in this light in an open economy like Switzerland where high wages reduced competitive power in international markets and hence the level of employment in the international sector. In the domestic sector it was more difficult to see this connection between wages and employment and for this reason the public did not see the assignment problem in these terms. It had been educated in the 1950s and 1960s to see the problem in terms of cost push with the level of prices rather than employment decided on the wage front. If economists did not agree that the problem should be posed as one of employment, at least in an open economy under competitive conditions, then this view of the matter would find no echo in public opinion. Unfortunately the unemployed were not represented at the bargaining table and in a decentralized system they would have even less influence. With centralized bargaining it was easier for the pressure of public opinion to be brought to bear and to represent to workers' organizations the need for them to show solidarity with the unemployed.

Professor Giersch said one should go further than take account of actual unemployment. There were also the young people coming on to the labour market in the future to be considered: there should be a kind of forward market in which expected future labour supplies would have an impact. These should reduce real interest rates sufficiently to ensure the creation of additional capacity by the time the larger inflow of workers began. But how far were trade unions in Britain aware of the effect they had on employment either in settling wage rates or in the institutional rules governing employment?

Everybody seemed to be agreed that this session had come to the heart of the economic problem but the economists who claimed no particular knowledge of the labour market like *Mr Maurice Scott* felt stumped. When they turned to those who did have such knowledge they were told all the problems, not what to do about them. Even those who were less negative were apt to insist on the length of the educational process that was necessary to bring about a change in attitudes. What then was the government to do in the meantime? Should it, for example, try to peg the value of GNP (i.e. MV)? If it did this, then the rate of growth of wages would determine the rate of growth of employment, and incomes policy would become in fact (and not just in name as Mr Allsopp had suggested) an employment policy. If, on the other hand, the government tried to peg the level of employment, as it had done in the post-war years, the result might be accelerating inflation, which is what had happened.

Professor Lundberg expressed some surprise at the claims made for more centralized bargaining. If one compared countries with centralized and decentralized bargaining procedures there was nothing much to choose between them in point of inflation. The rate of inflation was about the same in each group. On the other hand in a decentralized system like that of the United Kingdom was there not much more of a dispersion of wage relationships under the force of market pressure? In a centralized system two principles of wage policy were constantly in conflict: market forces pushed one way and equity considerations another. In Sweden, for example, this tug-of-war affected the industrial sector which was too small to keep the balance of payments healthy but paid wages that compared unfavourably with the public sector and could not, therefore, expand. The public sector unions were powerful and did not accept the contention that industrial work was harder and should be paid more. So the situation was one of disequilibrium and wage push. But the dilemma went deeper because if industry was to earn profits, wages would have to be lower, while at the same time if bright young men were to be attracted into industry wages would have to be higher.

Another example of the conflict between equity and market forces in the labour market was that while there was a chronic state of excess demand for skilled labour in Sweden, and this limited the rate of economic development, the differential in pay for skilled compared with unskilled workers was the lowest in the world. The majority of trade union members were unskilled and their bargaining strength was reflected in the wage structure. An increase in skilled workers' wages soon led to comparable demands from unskilled workers in an inflationary tug-of-war.

It was necessary, therefore, to take account of wage relationships as well as the need for wage restraint. Even where, as in Sweden, people were well aware of the conflict of principles and needed no education in it, the wage structure showed that the equity point of view was always stronger than the market point of view.

Looking back on the discussion on incomes policy, *Mr Christopher Dow* expressed some surprise that so much hope still reposed in it. He had advocated such a policy for many years but it seemed to have no chance either of acceptance, or of being effective, in present circumstances; and this was, moreover, likely to continue to be the case. It had to be admitted that, as Sir Frank Figgures had emphasized, it was against their nature for trade unions to behave in the way incomes policy required. To try to get them to do so seemed to him a basically hopeless endeavour. Even if an incomes policy was again possible, everybody was agreed that it would be a mistake to rely on it too heavily. If this was so, incomes policy was not a solution to the present-day problem of inflation: even if feasible for a brief while, it was too weak an instrument.

He was surprised also by Mr William Brown's advocacy for more centralized employer organization for purposes of wage bargaining. That kind of centralization, for example in the engineering industries, had shown a tendency to break down and give way to bargaining at the plant level. Was that not a good thing? In the United States where bargaining arrangements were more decentralized he had the impression that the problem of union power was much less acute.

Union power raised a wider question. It had increased partly in consequence of changes in the law and it might be necessary to reconsider those changes, and change the law back again if union power, so reinforced, contributed to inflation. Exactly what changes should be made was a highly complicated matter and there was always a question of what advantage employers would take of changes in the law. There was nevertheless something basically wrong about the present situation. Workers were using powers conferred on them by society to extort gains, not from their employers,but from the rest of the community. If employers were to do anything of that kind there would be an immediate outcry. The power of the unions to obstruct technical change raised very similar issues and might be limited if their other powers were more limited.

Some speakers had spoken of the urgency of making reforms to labour market institutions before the economy recovered and again was faced with inflationary demand. Mr Dow commented that we might be graced with quite a long period in which to make preparations before anything like that state was reached. He greatly feared that, whatever government was in office, it might well be at least five years.

Mr Nick Gardner asked what connection we were to believe exists between two kinds of labour market: the one in which pay bargaining took place and another that concerned itself with hiring and firing. In the textbooks these might be seen as one, but it was being suggested that in practice they showed a considerable degree of independence; so that there was often a wide margin between the actual movement in pay and what would be required to clear the market. Were we to believe that no self-correcting mechanism exists? There might be some natural selection process under which those firms survived that did reflect the state of the labour market in their wage structure and pay bargaining. But this would be slow and uncertain.

If there were no self-correcting mechanism, what prevented unemployment from rising without limit? A simple calculation showed that if productivity rose ½ per cent faster every year than output, unemployment could rise to 5m. by 1990. But if it were true that institutions were such as to produce such an ineluctable rise in unemployment they would not endure and changes would be made.

Lord Roll continued the discussion on incomes policy by pointing out that positive and negative attitudes to it had become aligned with the position taken up by Keynesian believers in fiscal-oriented, interventionist demand management on the one side and monetarist unbelievers on the other. This was a great hindrance to an understanding of the problem. Most economists would agree with the simple proposition that in an open industrialized economy adjustments *were* necessary in the level of incomes — sometimes quite significant adjustments — in response to endogenous developments in the domestic economy and more particularly to exogenous shocks like the big increases in oil prices. Even the present government recognized the need for some adjustment in incomes by its use of exhortation and tremendous pressure on the corporate sector in the expectation that it would be passed on in wage negotiations. The results of direct action on incomes had not in the past been brilliant but it had had some success. In the two years of the Social Contract it had helped to bring about the necessary adjustment although it was true that because of the re-entry problem its effectiveness had been very much eroded. The problem still remained: how to bring about general adjustments in incomes within a relatively short time without disrupting the economy through unemployment and trade depression. Institutional factors in other countries had enabled them to achieve necessary adjustments more quickly and smoothly than the United Kingdom. Examples he could point to were Germany, Sweden (until fairly recently) and above all Japan, which had survived the last oil shock largely by a substantial shift away from consumption. What could Britain in her totally different social environment substitute for what these countries did? There was no 'spring offensive', no lifelong employment guarantee, no Shinto religion encouraging non-adversary reactions.

Like Lord Roberthall he had been inclined to put his faith in NEDC but it had proved a broken reed. On the one occasion on which a major bargain had seemed possible in the NEDC the venue was immediately shifted to Chequers. The results were not particularly effective and the power and influence of NEDC were substantially weakened. It would be extremely difficult to recapture that influence. But apart from the need to give institutional substance to incomes policy there was nothing else he could suggest.

Sir Alec Cairncross found it baffling that those economists who were interested in demand management but disclaimed knowledge of the labour market were the strongest supporters of incomes policy while those who were familiar with the workings of the market but had no understanding of demand management tended to be sceptical. In 1961, when he was sent to see George Woodcock after the announcement of a wage pause, he was first reproved for asking how to make the policy work after and not before it had been decided upon. Woodcock then advised that if it was sought to continue the policy for more than six months it would break down from within. Experience had confirmed that anomalies did multiply and gradually undermine almost any form of incomes policy. If anybody set out to control prices of all kinds they would not find it very easy; and comprehensive control of wages, which were a kind of price, was almost as difficult, though not quite. He had therefore some sympathy with the labour market economists whose negative attitude had disturbed Mr Maurice Scott. Incomes policy was not simply a matter of clear thinking or of will or of power but also a matter of mechanics and the mechanics were bound to prove extremely difficult.

When it was proposed to embark on an incomes policy in 1961 he had warned his colleagues in the Treasury of the prevailing state of ignorance about how the labour market really worked and Sir Matthew Stevenson had said: 'We have to do something. Let us have a "pause" and then we will find out. All the economists who know about these things will come forward and tell us what we ought to do.' But twenty years later we still didn't know how to get an effective incomes policy.

The acceleration in inflation was not due simply to full employment. In 1945–50 when unemployment was as low as it ever was in peacetime the rate of increase in wages was no more than twice the rate of increase in 1933–9 with about 2m. workers unemployed. There had been a breakdown of attitudes over time – not just the attitudes of the trade unions but of the average worker on the shop floor. No doubt union power had increased and the unions had become more militant. But in addition there had been periodic shocks which were even more important. What nearly always brought on inflation in the United Kingdom was a rise in import prices. With it went, as a rule, a shift in the terms of trade and a loss of real income. This was certainly the sequence in the 1970s. Yet within a few years after 1974 inflation was going down, not up. It took time to adjust to such changes as a 25 per cent movement in the terms of trade, but the system had in fact adjusted a good deal of the way in a year or two. It was surely not surprising that it should be difficult to absorb a sudden 5 per cent reduction in real income or that workers should react to a very large increase in prices. One lesson of this experience was that one must allow time. In discussing education in economic realities, people tended to get impatient but one had to think in terms of years. If it were necessary to learn faster then things would have to be made very unpleasant at first. But attitudes wouldn't change any faster with 2½m. unemployed than with 'only' 2m.

Nobody had come forward with any proposal for getting rid of inflation other than incomes policy on one side and prolonged deflation on the other. Either way attitudes would take a very long time to change to the extent necessary for the resumption of a high level of employment.

Centralization of wage bargaining seemed unlikely to play a major role. But it was possible to have more centralization in the sense of instituting central machinery for bringing together the main participants in wage policy and more decentralization in the sense of leaving more of the details of wage structure to plant bargaining. Decentralized arrangements were more sensitive to demand pressures. Even without national wage agreements of any kind wages tended to creep up faster than productivity: the renegotiation of piece rates on the shop floor was enough to produce inflation without any intervention by the trade unions.

The fact was that full employment and free collective bargaining were not compatible with one another. The unions would have to make up their mind which they really wanted. The point must be rubbed in that if they wanted full employment they could not have free collective bargaining and would have to collaborate in working out bargaining arrangements that did make full employment possible. The government could not stand aside, as at present, from the bargaining system and leave everything to the employer. Government, employers and workers had to work out satisfactory arrangements together.

Sir Henry Phelps Brown, replying to the discussion, said he was grateful to Professor William Brown for his emphasis on the role of the employer. It was too readily assumed that the faults of the British system of industrial relations must be laid exclusively at the door of the trade unions. The 1906 Act, for example, conferred immunity on a trade union from a charge of civil conspiracy for action taken in furtherance of a trade dispute. But an employers' association was a trade union and, as such, was covered by the Act if its members locked out their employees in support of a member firm confronted with a strike. In the years before the First World War, employers in Germany and Sweden had done precisely that and by doing so had checked irregular activity. But in Britain, employers who had already reached a *modus vivendi* with the unions preferred not to make use of the Act in this way and accepted the unions as an integral part of society with which they were content to work informally, outside the law.

He had been surprised by Mr William Brown's advocacy of a movement back to more centralized wage negotiations and away from the works agreements or single employer negotiations to which he had himself called attention. Sir Arthur Knight had pointed to the benefits of those negotiations in worker involvement; and the Donovan Report had also wished to see single employer negotiations extended as a way of checking the unofficial strike and wage drift. Sir Henry's understanding was that they had been effective in both respects.

A number of speakers – Sir Frank Figgures, Lord Roberthall and Lord Roll – had discussed the potentialities of bargaining at the national level to arrive at an incomes policy. He himself remembered a two-day session of the NEDC under Mr Maudling at which the employers had gone so far as to accept price control. But the six members of the TUC General Council had rejected the proposed bargain. The reason was, as George Woodcock made clear later, that they could not hold to their side of the bargain – 'the lads weren't ready for it'. What the six members of the General Council might find acceptable could not be assumed to be equally acceptable to the 115 or so unions affiliated to the TUC. The General Council had no sanctions to apply to them then and had none now.

Indeed the situation was more difficult now. A wind of change had blown from Paris through the democracies of the Western world at the end of the 1960s. Power had shifted to the shop floor, and something like an 1848 change of outlook had taken place in the younger generation, which had not known the troubled inter-war years and was more willing to push ahead on its own initiative independently of its own trade union leaders and of central authority. With this change in attitude, there had been a 'hinge' in the rate of increase of money wages in nearly all the OECD countries except Germany and Japan which could not be associated with antecedent changes on the monetary side or in unemployment or the flow of demand.

Sir Henry saw much virtue in the suggestion made by Sir Austin Robinson that the two elements in wage increases should be separated and cited the example of Australia. The labour market there was currently in turmoil and methods of wage adjustment were under revision. But a procedure had been instituted in 1975 for a periodic National Wage Award, after an examination at the national level by a Commission of the scale on which a *general* rise in wages and salaries throughout the Commonwealth would be appropriate. Observations were submitted by the Commonwealth government, the trades union centre, the principal employers' organizations and the governments of the six states. Hearings were in public and an award was backed by a carefully reasoned statement. The award might not amount to full indexation but it was intended to compensate for increases in the cost of living since the last award. Workers were free to enter claims for an increase over and above the general rise if the circumstances of their own case warranted it. This procedure had succeeded in pulling back the rate of inflation in Australia very substantially since 1975. It merited study and proposals for reform in the United Kingdom which Sir Henry had in the press were based on it.

He then turned to Professor Lundberg's question on the effects of decentralized bargaining in the United Kingdom. Decentralized bargaining gave more conformity to local market conditions. Under conditions of high employment it had worked to accelerate inflation through a catching up process. Under current conditions of heavy unemployment it made for greater differentiation in wages.

Changes in the law, such as Mr Christopher Dow had suggested, were difficult to make ahead of public opinion. That very day there was a case before the court arising out of the limitation of secondary picketing under the Act of August 1980. This raised the difficulty of enforcing a prohibition of what had been widely accepted for very many years as a perfectly proper action in defence of workers' rights. But it was far more difficult to use the law to encourage positive behaviour and make people conduct their affairs in a particular way. The fact that the 1971 Act had to rely on a Code of Behaviour attached to it showed how hard it was to change the pattern of industrial relations by legal enactments.

He also doubted whether it would be helpful to adopt Professor

Giersch's suggestion of bringing up the level of employment at the bargaining table. The reaction of any group of workers would be to demand shorter hours (whatever the effect on unit costs) or more pay to increase purchasing power. They were unlikely to accept the textbook proposition that lower wages would mean more employment.

Finally he was cheered by Sir Alec Cairncross's belief that the impact of events since 1945 had brought about fundamental changes in the attitude of workers on the shop floor and that, as he had said, you had to give things time.

——— 4 ———

Industrial policy

SIR ARTHUR KNIGHT

This essay deals with some issues of industrial policy in the UK in the period 1911–81. Its themes are concepts of government responsibility for industry and changing fashions in weapons for intervention.

I have taken as my starting point an article three years or so ago of which Sir Alec Cairncross was one of the authors:

> Policy tends to take shape round some central idea (or slogan) such as nationalization, planning, investment, restructuring or industrial democracy, often without much regard to the ambiguities of the idea and with very exaggerated expectations of the likely impact on industrial efficiency. . . . A successful industrial policy pre-supposes a stable and encouraging economic environment. It is of the utmost importance to have steadily expanding markets, stable prices, satisfactory industrial relations on the basis of widely-shared objectives and a business atmosphere congenial to industrial innovation. No intervention by government can make up for the absence of these pre-conditions. On the other hand, if they are present much government intervention becomes unnecessary or counter-productive. . . . Governments have sometimes to bow to wrong-headed majorities.[1]

This quotation brings out the sense of the discomfort which is felt by economists (perhaps more in the UK and in the USA than anywhere else) at government actions which go beyond those seen as necessary to create the conditions in which markets can be relied upon to allocate resources.

What concepts or changing fashions have led governments into assuming in peacetime responsibilities in relation to industry much greater than most British economists would consider desirable? The period under review divides into two halves. I have taken the first as ending in 1939 and the second as the years since the Second

World War. I begin this half with a glance at the mood of 1945, reflecting so much the widespread dissatisfaction with the inter-war period as transmuted by the experiences of the 1939–45 war.

This is a period during which the UK was less governed than were most developed countries, with 73 public officials for every 10,000 inhabitants in 1911 compared with 113 in the USA, 126 in Germany and 176 in France.

Nevertheless there was more government activity than these figures might imply. In 1911, for example, the government bought control of the National Telephone Company. A purely nationalistic urge to prevent foreign control of essential supplies led the Admiralty (even before 1910) to support what became the Anglo Persian Oil Company in order to safeguard oil fuel supplies for the Navy. The same nationalism in 1926 led the government to encourage the formation of ICI, in part to ensure a UK source of supply for dyestuffs in a market otherwise dominated by the Germans.

In the 1930s government began to encourage experiments in industrial reconstruction. Here too the needs of defence appear initially to have been a primary consideration. But with growing unemployment the early experiments were broadened into a willingness to intervene more widely. Through much of the period, the key figure was Montagu Norman, the governor of the Bank of England. Ministers were informed about Norman's activities, and indeed at times he was responding to government pressures; but he was prepared to go well beyond normal banking practice to achieve his ends because he regarded the actual task of reorganization as too delicate and technical to be handled by government.

Norman's attitude to intervention appears to have developed as the most pressing economic problem shifted from post-war reconstruction to the growing pressures of unemployment and protection. Thus in 1926 he saw his dealings with Armstrong Whitworth and Vickers as 'a model for future experiments in rationalisation'. The problems of Armstrong resulted from the need to adjust to peacetime contraction, and from attempts to diversify which went wrong. Although the Admiralty had approached the Bank and the new arrangements were seen as essential to national defence, Baldwin refused to give any financial guarantee. The Bank did guarantee 'in view of the national importance . . . and the possibility of ultimate recovery'.

He took a contrasting attitude to the problems of the steel industry. In 1926 Baldwins & Beardmores had asked the government for financial help. Norman advised against. Many industrial firms needed new blood and economies; the government could not afford to help and would find it difficult to limit its amount; the industry was waiting for protection to avoid the need for drastic reorganization. By 1929 Norman was forced to help, as an alternative to government intervention.

There were other problem industries. It was agreed that J. H. Thomas, speaking for the government, should announce publicly the City's willingness to handle reorganization and re-equipment schemes; and the Bank set up arrangements with good management advice to assess schemes and to channel funds. It was emphasized that protection should not be given until there had been reorganization to reduce costs. Germany and the USA were seen as the sources of advice.

Where government is a major customer whose expenditures are declining it might be expected that the relatively few supplying firms would see a common interest in organizing themselves collectively to produce a sensible re-allocation of resources. But where few individuals are concerned with differing perceptions of each other's interest it can be difficult to reach agreement and within the time-scales which matter there may be no one party which can deploy sufficient pressures to force a solution. Governments can then feel an urge to intervene; and in the examples which have been quoted the preoccupation with avoiding protection and with international standards of efficiency indicates an approach informed by economic rationality.

The widening of the scope of Norman's activities and the new protective legislation suggest, however, that government came more to respond to rising unemployment and the consequent political pressures.[2]

The introduction of protectionism is a fascinating example of the pre-war attitude to industrial policy. An Import Duties Advisory Committee was established in 1932. Its underlying purpose was to keep the tariff out of politics. The Committee was given little guidance. It was to have regard to the national interest in restricting imports and to the interests generally of trade and industry; there was no reference to the interests of the ultimate consumer. The Committee decided to act first and enquire afterwards. The new tariff structure, imposing duties at varying rates on most manufacturers, was devised by the Committee's staff in five weeks with but limited outside consultation. Despite protests, Ministers made it clear that they were not going to interfere. Individual cases came up for consideration later.

The chief interest today of these events is that they reflect a belief at that time that, while intervention may be necessary, it is best handled without the influence of party politicians. In a period in which governments were dominated by men like Baldwin and Chamberlain who came from industrial backgrounds it was thought necessary to keep industrial problems out of the hands of politicians. They 'have never been fit to handle them':[3] so Eric Geddes, influenced by his experiences in government in the First World War, had been one of those in favour of positive government initiative, but came later to believe that government could do little in the existing climate. He became convinced that politicians had second-rate business minds and that political interests and red tape would sabotage effective action. In the pre-1914 years the social imperialists had entertained ideas about the state playing a positive role, but from 1918 to 1939 there were pressures to restore the traditional arm's-length relationship between industry and the state. This attitude had more in common with US concepts than with German ideas of organized capitalism with state support, much though the German model was admired by progressive businessmen. But, arm's-length or not, intervention took place and was influenced by the German model.

Cartels and combines were seen as promoting efficiency. At one stage Lord Melchett, then chairman of ICI, 'was satisfied that the industrial situation was serious enough to warrant sacrificing democracy for speed'.[4] He believed that coercion of minorities would be inescapable and that for single industries to go to Parliament would be time consuming and dangerous, giving politicians the opportunity to interfere with business and to make political capital out of technical economic issues.

These approaches to re-structuring and protectionism bear particularly upon the events of the post-1945 period which I discuss later. But throughout the whole seventy year period our industrial history has been dominated by far more important issues arising

117

from the growth of trade unions, the special legal framework within which they have operated and their political influence. This special legal position of trade unions has had considerable influence on industrial relations and performance, and has been the cause of continuing and still unresolved problems. To argue that the issue is one about the legal framework and not of industrial policy would be to emphasize the ambiguities which arise.

Sheer political opportunism appears to have accounted for the crucial 1906 Act which held that any action which is legal if done by an individual is legal if done in contemplation or furtherance of a trade dispute. This reversed the judgement of the House of Lords in the Taff Vale case of 1901 in which it was held that a union could not use its corporate resources to organize a strike and then claim to be only a number of individuals, not under contract, coincidentally withholding a commodity in their rightful possession. But the trade union representatives in Parliament had just been increased from two to thirty; it was convenient to please them.

The industrial relations issues are more important than any others and their handling has affected the management of all other aspects of industrial policy, especially in the post-1945 period. But they are the subject of a separate contribution to this book and in any case they did not impinge directly to any major degree upon the issues dealt with in this paper.

THE 1945 MOOD

There are two reasons why I want to pause briefly to look at the country's mood at the end of the war. First, it marks a turning point in attitudes in this country to the role of government. It is also the point at which I became an active participant, as it were, in industrial policy. I suppose my interest in the subject goes back to the 1920s. I have a vivid recollection of hunger in the 1926 strike (my father was a railway worker); of fear when the Jarrow marchers spent the night at the town hall next to the school I attended; and of my sense of resignation on leaving school at sixteen instead of aiming at university because an £18 annual grant made less contribution to the family budget than a £52 clerk's pay. It was these experiences which led me to switch from science into economics at the age of fifteen because it seemed important to know why unemployment was high and why the gold standard mattered. I went on to rigorous and exciting evenings at LSE under the influence of Robbins, Hayek and Arnold Plant − never quite satisfied that I was finding the answers to the questions which had led me there, but carried along on the belief (which had nothing to do with party politics) that we should be able through public policy to change society for the better. With my discovery in the early 1940s of Schumpeter's 'perennial gale of creative destruction' I felt I had at last found a more convincing approach to the real world than that offered by the policy prescriptions which my mentors derived from static equilibrium analysis.

The atmosphere was characterized by a new sense that government could and should have a wider role. This feeling developed during the war. The civilian sector had been efficiently organized by government; general health standards had been improved; a high degree of equality had been achieved. It was all so great a contrast with the tensions of the pre-war decade. At the end of the war a high proportion of the most able chose the civil service as careers, seeing government as the field in which the most interesting action would be.

As Dr Reader has expressed it:

> In the British war-time mentality the will to win was the leading motive force, but alongside it . . . there grew up an almost equally strong drive for radical reform of the country's society and economy. The very recent past came to be regarded with disgust and revulsion . . . and in the general atmosphere of the period it was not difficult to feel that the war was being fought as much to establish a new order in Great Britain as to overthrow one in Germany.[5]

Political sentiment swung well to the left and all the institutions of capitalism were suspect; though a general concern to preserve traditional political liberties characterized that part of the discussion which influenced policy making. Totalitarian solutions found little place in the attitudes which affected action. It was not just a party political matter − Harold Macmillan in *The Middle Way* had given voice to the collectivist strand in the conservative tradition which was to supply one element in the consensus (unusual in Britain) which came to be called 'Butskellism'. Neither was it just a matter of rejecting the past. Wartime administrative success in the civilian sector appeared to offer the prospect of effective action to improve performance. The public, the parties and pressure groups were for the most part in favour of planning, taken in the broad sense of state intervention with a view to coordinating the working of the economy and settling the broad lines of future development.

The difference between 1945 and 1918 could not have been greater. In 1918 and the early 1920s there was a general urge to return to normal with the pre-1914 situation as the model. Unresolved social tensions inspired some fear of revolutionary possibilities, heightened with the mass unemployment of the 1930s. The decision in 1925 to revalue sterling at an unrealistically high level was part of this search for the apparent security of the past, though it proved to be one of the factors which led to a worsening of Britain's competitive position and the unemployment of the 1930s. The timing of that decision depended upon a sufficient return to the more normal trading conditions after the disruption of the immediate post-war period; but there was never any consideration of choosing a rate of exchange for sterling different from the pre-war level.

So 1945 really was a turning point. A revolution was indeed beginning, but a peaceful one. Capitalist democracy may have shown intellectual and moral vitality in its period of crisis – Labour lost an election in 1935, and in 1939 looked almost set to lose another. But the mood of 1945, however wrong-headed, pointed clearly towards more activism in government.

I find it difficult to recall much discussion at the time of the point that what had been possible with the more limited and widely-accepted objectives of war, and with the draconian legal powers of government at war, might run up against more limitations in peacetime.

ACTIVITY IN THE POST-1945 PERIOD

Although the mood was one of activism, ideas about what government should do did not initially embrace much that could be called industry policy. The main interests of economic policy were in achieving full employment, an improved social framework, greater freedom in international trade, improved international monetary arrangements and the removal of wartime controls.

There were two exceptions. First, measures to create jobs in areas of high unemployment, initiated in the 1930s, were developed. There was a new emphasis on the deterrent effect of withholding building licences for projects in areas of high employment. The selectivity involved in operating the building licence system was an important exception to the general direction of policy.

The other major exception was nationalization. Ideas about nationalization often seemed to rest upon a belief that public ownership of itself would effect radical change; though workers' representatives appeared generally to see that change as consisting mainly in increasing the share of net output available for wages and related benefits. Herbert Morrison was unsuccessful in his efforts to set up some mechanism for monitoring efficiency. The setting of financial targets came much later in the 1960s.

It was fears of a continuing dollar shortage which provided the spur to further intervention in the late 1940s when, for example, Courtaulds were advised by Cripps, then Chancellor of the Exchequer, to find ways of reducing dependence on dollar sources of pulp, an important raw material. The advice was taken, a new and better source was established with heavy investment and proved a great success, giving Courtaulds a competitive edge. Would this have happened without the intervention? I doubt it. But although in this case intervention had happy results, the fear of dollar shortage inspired projects like the groundnut scheme which were costly failures.

REGIONAL POLICY

Throughout the post-1945 period, I worked for Courtaulds. The firm's experience can throw some light on the way policies worked. Take regional policy. In the early 1950s there were subsidies, to encourage investment in Northern Ireland. Courtaulds were considering a major plant, an investment of over £9m. (large at that time) and a 25 per cent grant could have been available. It was decided not to apply, for fear that acceptance of government cash would lay the company open to government pressure. A later change of policy about textiles brought a new attitude. In Northern Ireland, where the incentives were greatest, a number of projects were launched at various sites and the company's total employment for a while reached 10,000, more than at Harland and Wolff, till then the largest employer.

Other project decisions were influenced by the grants, especially in the North West and the North East. By 1972 out of a total employment in the UK of 122,000 some 80,000 jobs were in the assisted areas. Would the projects have gone ahead anyway? The parliamentary Trade and Industry Sub-Committee examined the question in the 1972–3 session. The general view of industrial firms who gave evidence was that investment grants had not been outstandingly effective. Courtaulds was the only company to assert unequivocally that their total investment programme had been influenced. In a six-year period in which investment in new assets had been £258m. grants had provided £62m. Because the firm's strategy was straining financial resources to the limit there could be no doubt that the grants had fostered investment.

Had they encouraged unwise decisions? It is difficult to know. The strategy was a risky one. The careful calculation of prospective returns project by project, the happy hunting ground of the specialists in decision analysis, is of secondary importance where each project, though large in the context of the firm's resources (typically £10m.–£15m. each), was justified primarily by reference to its place in the overall strategy.

Were investment incentives in the most suitable form? I find it hard to say. The details changed so frequently that a point was reached where it was assumed in financial planning that one way or another 15 per cent of expenditure in the UK would be provided by government. Since these observations relate to one quite large and relatively sophisticated company it is probable that for companies generally the incentives had less effect.

Courtaulds never suffered the sort of pressure which forced Ford to locate at Halewood. To what extend was Courtaulds a special case? A. J. Brown has reviewed the period to 1970 beginning with the immediate post-war rush to the Development Areas, when the search for suitable sites and for labour was more important than legislation or the system of industrial development certificates. He traces five short stages of policy between 1958 and 1970. The great success of the early 1960s lay in the diversion of major new developments in the motor car industry into Merseyside and Scotland, induced by the carrot of financial incentives and the stick of reluctance to grant industrial development certificates in non-development areas. He refers to the change in the rates of grants, free depreciation, the Regional Employment Premium, changes in the areas, the designation of special areas with additional benefits. He shows that from the late 1950s to the mid-1960s there was a massive diversion of moves to the peripheral areas which reached its maximum rate about 1963, and other evidence suggests that the process continued throughout the decade. But the regional employment premium introduced in 1967 does not appear to have had conspicuous effects on investment; which is not surprising since Courtaulds' experience showed how small an influence it would have on expected investment yields when compared with grants.

Brown shows that the capital-intensive industries became more concentrated in the development areas, no doubt encouraged by the form of incentives, and concludes that no obvious benefit to the assisted areas or to the economy as a whole stemmed from this.

Courtaulds' investments in the regions were certainly in capital-intensive parts of the textile industry and the textile and the motor car industries must have provided much of the impetus to the results which Brown had assessed. Far from being a special case Courtaulds was a part of the process.

INDICATIVE PLANNING

My experience in Courtaulds also has some bearing on my approach to that brief flirtation with indicative planning. Courtaulds was active in France with a reasonably big manufacturing business there, and for ten years I was director of the subsidiary company there. It was the period during which average GNP per head in France increased steadily from a level 20–25 per cent below that in the UK at a rate well ahead of the British. In the mid-1950s unease about British industrial performance compared with the French led me to ask Ennemond Bizot, later deputy chairman of Rhone Poulenc after the Gillet interests were acquired, what benefits there were in French planning. 'It enables me to know my competitor's expansion plans, and thus to go ahead in greater confidence with my own' was the reply. It seemed sensible enough and added point to joining the PEP group whose report was published in 1960. An FBI conference soon afterwards was persuaded and the FBI claimed much of the credit for the inauguration of the experiment by the Conservative government. NEDO was established with Robert Shone as its director-general, who had been chairman of the PEP group. It was the high point in consensus seeking in the whole period and in the closeness of industry-government co-operation.

It seems amazing now that we could all have been so naive.

Growth was inadequate, we all thought, because there had never been an objective to aim at, 'to enlist the enthusiasm of all sections of the community'. Even those of us who knew about the French techniques of persuasion, especially the role of Credit Nationale in allocating finance, were captivated. Christopher Dow expressed it in measured terms:

> . . . it would seem necessary for the government to give a general idea of the rates of expansion in both consumer and investment demand which – subject to capacity growing as planned – budgetary and monetary policy aimed to produce.[6]

The 1965 'plan' with which George Brown is identified was certainly clearer about objectives than anything which had preceded it, though not supported by anything likely to foster performance other than high aspirations. It was followed, however, by an interesting little modification to the restrictive practices legislation, removing from attack consultations between businessmen about their expansion plans (shades of the French!); and it was generally believed at the time that the oil companies took advantage of this dispensation.

The failure of attempts to realize hopes was followed by pressure for planning agreements with individual companies and by NEDO's sector working parties. It was difficult for an industrialist to see the point in either.

In the event only Chrysler signed a planning agreement – large government subventions were at stake. In 1976 one industrialist resisting pressure from two Labour Cabinet Ministers to delay plant closures was mystified at the intervention of the senior civil servant with the question, 'Why not enter into a planning agreement?' Some illumination came later from the left-wing ministerial adviser, who, when asked the point of a planning agreement, replied: 'We set your target, exports for example, and then use all of the weapons available to government to force you to meet it.'

The CBI's acceptance of sector working parties within the NEDO framework was seen as an escape from the pressure for individual company planning agreements. Sir Alec Cairncross and the co-authors of the article I quoted at the start of this paper find it difficult to say what practical effect the working parties have had. Those who have been involved, businessmen, trade unionists and civil servants, have seen them as educative, making people more aware of problems and possible solutions. This modest claim was endorsed by the Roll Committee on Finance for Industry.[7]

The flirtation with indicative planning is but one of the episodes which have reflected a sense of inadequacy on the part of the British. The example of other countries has frequently been a spur to thought and sometimes to action. In the 1880s Germany and the USA were seen as more competent at handling their industrial affairs; in the 1950s it was French planning; and from the 1960s onwards the Japanese in particular have been seen as examples, though the 'little Neddies' owe something to interpretations of German experience.

The British are not alone in seeking to build upon what are seen as the successful methods of others. The Japanese in their post-1945 thinking devised their own pattern of arrangements to meet their own situation, but in their product strategies bought in from others the know-how they needed; whilst the French have more recently been influenced in their national industrial strategy forming by the Japanese model.

RESTRUCTURING

In the UK two ideas have animated post-war approaches to restructuring: first the need to deal with situations where government is a major consumer; and second the urge to achieve the productivity of our overseas competitors. The motivations have thus been much the same as those which inspired the pre-1939 experiments.

As to the first, it is interesting to look at one aspect of the enlargement of GEC which the Industrial Reorganization Commission did something to foster. It relates to the supply of turbo-alternators required for the CEGB programme to expand electric power generating capacity. In the 1950s under the influence of F. H. S. (Stanley) Brown the generating authority had by stages, beginning at a time when only 60 MW sets were in use, developed its ideas about the use of 500 MW sets. This revolution was an economic and technical success. But it created difficulties for the manufacturers. By 1963 when the CEGB embarked on the 500 MW programme there were four in the UK capable of constructing turbo-alternators of the required size; whereas in the USA, needs of the much larger market were met with a sufficient degree of competition by only two suppliers. The four suppliers had not enough business and had been operating well below capacity. The authority had used its bargaining power to squeeze their margins. Since the early 1960s almost all orders were put to competitive tendering and the authority was able sometimes to take advantage of an attractive but uneconomic price offered to remain in business and avoid bankruptcy. But it was essential to the authority's philosophy that the manufacturers should shoulder the main cost of research and development in generation technology and it became obvious over a long period that the manufacturers did not have the financial and technical resources to meet the more demanding requirements of the new situation. By 1963 when the issue was debated it was said that prices in the UK were 20 per cent lower than those in Japan, and that net income in the electrical engineering industry was the lowest among the major industries, and not sufficient to pay for essential research.

It does look as though the firms in the industry took too narrow a view of their long-term interests. They should have seen earlier the need for some restructuring and acted to bring it about. The intervention of IRC can be seen as helpful in supporting changes which could have been made earlier without intervention of a government agency. Where there are four firms and few individuals taking key decisions there can be long delays. Market forces can be expected eventually to produce a situation in which something decisive has to be done, but the delays can be expensive. That is the justification for external pressures.

The second approach to restructuring, like the first, aims at improving productivity levels. But it does not depend upon the position of government as a major customer, and it might therefore be expected that normal commercial pressures would lead private sector managements to take the actions required to maximize their prospective profits.

The IRC's restructuring activities sometimes looked from outside like the pursuit of size for its own sake; and Grigor McClelland, a member of the Commission, was quite clear that the case for that institution must stand or fall on the proposition that in many sectors of British industry firms would not become large enough, soon enough, unless there were interventions. But the IRC's approach to restructuring introduced a new element – a willingness to use state funds to force people's hands, a feature so disagreeable to some that it continued to colour discussion of the role of the National Enterprise Board as recently as in 1979.

In all restructuring there is an element of picking winners, in the managerial sense. 'Kearton's method was to find the one most like himself in the industry concerned and give him the lot' wrote *The Economist*.

Although nobody could argue that the right decisions were always taken, the emphasis on people is far more important than any debates about the economies of scale or about more comprehensive strategic concepts. Good managers know where and how to use the techniques and concepts which are available; but good managers are rare and there is something to be said for action to help them to extend their influence. Who takes the action? The IRC was one attempt. In the post-1945 period private sector investors have occasionally asserted their power. Whether they could do more, and how, is a continuing debate.

COURTAULDS AND RESTRUCTURING IN TEXTILES

Relations with government were not seen as central to the formation and direction of Courtaulds' policy in the late 1940s and the 1950s. As a very junior member of the staff of a monopoly concern relying upon a protective tariff, I had a sense of being something of a renegade in occasional encounters with Arnold Plant at the Reform Club, or at the Thursday evening dinners which Hayek so much dominated. At the head office a small staff group dealt with Whitehall. One section dealt with trade negotiations and worked with the trade associations in lobbying for improved access to overseas markets or for continued protection of the domestic market. The other dealt with import licences, building permits and in the Korean War with plans to improve raw material supplies. One key product, rayon staple, was highly protected for historical reasons. Output was expanded and the domestic and overseas markets were developed. No competitor found it worth starting up and Courtaulds remained the sole supplier.

The UK textile industry was the firm's main customer. Its troubles were worried about, but no action was taken until the early 1960s. After 1958 new activities were sought to reduce dependence on textiles but it was soon apparent that these could not be on a sufficient scale to ensure survival. The alternative strategies then were either to integrate forward into the fibre-using industries or to accept a merger proposal from ICI. The latter was resisted.

In retrospect, Courtaulds' strategy can be made to look more coherent than it felt at that time. There were two strands. The first was to modernize the spinning and weaving 'Lancashire' industry, aiming at the EEC as the only accessible market large enough to offer any prospect of selling the volume of output necessary with new and up-to-date equipment to match US cost levels. The scale economies achieved by the Americans were a major influence in forming this part of the strategy. The second was to acquire existing fibre-using activities in the knitting and hosiery industries to get a captive market for enlarged production of newer fibres. Both strands of policy involved acquisitions and investment in new equipment. Acquisitions attracted public attention, but the sums required for new investment were much larger.

In the early 1960s government was worried about the Lancashire industry. The subsidies made under the 1959 Act had not achieved their purpose. For Courtaulds the rayon staple market was at risk and part of the prospective domestic market for their new acrylic fibre. Richard Powell, the senior civil servant concerned, made it clear that the industry would be allowed to go to the wall unless somebody acted. There could be no assurances in advance about improved protection. Courtaulds took the risk, made major acquisitions and embarked on big modernization plans, with the co-operation of the unions concerned. At the beginning of this process Richard Powell initiated a study in which employers, unions and civil servants took part. Courtaulds' staff played an active part in all this. The findings supported the argument that competitive cost levels could be achieved with modern equipment and volume production, but to secure the latter it would be necessary to improve protection. Improved protection was conceded, but haltingly and inadequately. It ran counter to the general thrust of UK trade policy towards freer world trade, and encountered strong resistance from those concerned with the less-developed. Later, when the EEC became the forum for negotiation, the arrangements were administered with less vigour than might have been expected.

Although these trade policy issues were handled by reference to the industry as a whole, Courtaulds was naturally active both within the representative bodies and in direct dialogue. The justification for the special support was improved performance and some attention was paid to the reduction in the number of firms in the industry. The productivity indices began to show a better record than those for UK industry in general.

But there was no detailed monitoring of the kind which might have been expected. Instead at the very time that Ministers were publicly supporting Courtaulds' activities there was a reference to the Monopolies Commission. This was limited to certain fibres, and did not refer to the acquisition policy or the general restructuring. (Yet the Commission's report and recommendations dealt with these matters, which had not been examined with care.) One can only assume that ambivalent attitudes prevailed. Some saw Courtaulds as a power for good in a depressed industry; others were worried at the scale of the merger activities and resulting increase in concentration. To investigate the whole would be costly and time-consuming. So why not compromise, investigate one part in depth, see what emerges and then go further? With the separation of functions between departments it seems a plausible hypothesis.

But this is all a far remove from the 'widely-shared objectives and a business atmosphere congenial to industrial innovation' seen by Sir Alec Cairncross and his colleagues as necessary to a stable and encouraging economic environment. The experience suggests that in this period government had too many incompatible objectives and too great a variety of instruments to permit any coherent, sustained policy in relation to one single industrial policy issue.

INNOVATION

Industrial innovation has long been seen as requiring government measures to encourage innovation and the patent system has been supplemented with bodies such as the NRDC and NEB and with subventions.

The economic case for generalized support, such as that which the patent system provides, rests upon divergence between the private and the public return on investment in innovation. Various attempts have been made to show how much bigger is the public interest than is any reward which accrues to the private investors. And this argument can be used also to justify general programmes such as, for example, those which aim to spread understanding of new developments in information technology.

But where government is a major buyer, as of defence products, it has to find ways of encouraging the necessary research and development activity and these require choices between products and so between firms.

The story of government encouragement of new high technology in the 1960s is disappointing. It seems that much of our massive programme of investment in defence-related high technology products was directed towards products which the Americans were bound to be able to manufacture more competitively, because the size of their potential market enabled them to reach cost levels we could never hope to attain with the more limited markets open to us. But these new activities were interesting and exciting and so they attracted a high proportion of our best young technologists; whereas in Germany the best young people were attracted into building up export-oriented more down-to-earth mechanical engineering activities.

These experiences have led to changes in two directions. First there was the 'Rothschild principle', aimed at simulating a buyer–seller relationship between research establishment and sponsoring department. More recently it has been the aim to place more of the expenditure in the control of supplying firms, in the hope that they will find ways to develop products which both meet the needs of the UK buying departments and in addition are designed to appeal to buyers in other markets.

THE NATIONAL ENTERPRISE BOARD

NEB is an example of an organization specifically intended to promote innovation. Set up in 1975 by a Labour government it had a number of roles. It was responsible for the management of Rolls Royce and British Leyland, two of the country's major troubled companies both (though for rather different reasons) requiring substantial government money. It seemed also at times to be active in promoting public ownership for its own sake. The situation with which I was concerned in my year as chairman between 1979 and 1980 was different.

The previous board had resigned because it was decided to place Rolls Royce under the direct control of the Minister and a new board had been hurriedly appointed. But the arguments which applied to Rolls Royce applied equally to Leyland and the new board pressed to be relieved of responsibility. Rolls Royce and Leyland had to report direct to the Minister not just because the cash sums they required were large. More to the point, strong political considerations attached to each major decision, whether about a new aeroengine project or about continued support of a vehicle which was improving productivity only slowly and with labour relations which appeared often to offer no prospect ever of success. In both cases, government had felt itself forced into taking responsibility because, although by all normal private sector standards the firms were bankrupt, the numbers employed and their importance as exporters made it politically difficult to let them go to the wall. Few governments escape completely from the need to respond to the democratic imperative.

Under a Conservative government there was new legislation which effectively limited new initiatives to investment in high technology and to the assisted areas (without restriction as to type of investment). Under this new legislation, and without Rolls Royce and British Leyland, NEB had some prospect of handling its affairs without getting involved in politically sensitive issues. True, its inherited portfolio included some holdings which had been the result of past troubles. But ICL, Fairey and Ferranti were producing results which made their shares attractive, using normal private sector financial criteria; whilst it was difficult to justify any more cash for Alfred Herbert and the sale of its parts provided continuing employment for 3400 of its 4000 employees.

Inmos, the integrated circuit chip project, presented a problem. £50m had been promised, the second £25m was needed but regional pressures delayed a decision until it was decided to build the first UK plant in South Wales and not at the preferred Bristol site.

After eliminating the saleable holdings, which I inherited when I took over at the NEB, the remaining portfolio had a value of some £100m. Its proper management was my first priority. I hoped to gain acceptance of the NEB as a worthwhile institution. There were suspicions, based upon memories of the past, and uncertainties created by those who appeared lukewarm about the body they were responsible for.

One of the new initiatives was biotechnology. It aimed in part at exploiting commercially the results of scientific work financed by government and the association with NEB was a factor in gaining the scientists' support. Private sector investors were willing to provide 56 per cent of the equity capital, taking a longer term view than is normal. The project was seen as a model – an initiative which would not occur without action by NEB but with private sector capital providing more than half the funds, thus responding to the political guidelines under which NEB acts and at the same time minimizing the likelihood of subsequent political intervention.

But my year's experience brought home to me the problems of getting effective initiatory action – the slow decision taking process of government, including the checking over the cases already well examined; the incursions and delays from other parts of the government machine; the diversions caused by the necessary monitoring of activities of the PAC; and the continuing effects of unresolved political battles.

CONCLUDING COMMENTS

Is it possible from this limited description of a few personal experiences and of a few experiences of others to draw conclusions about the large issues raised by Sir Alec Cairncross and his colleagues in the quotation with which I began? To draw conclusions would require an assessment of what the interventions achieved, compared with the reasons and hopes which inspired them and the resources devoted to them. To search properly for the reasons which explain these changing concepts of government responsibility for industry and changing fashions in weapons for intervention would be quite an undertaking. It would require, case by case, a study of the perceptions of the interest groups – industrial, union, bureaucratic or political – which led to pressure for government action, the intellectual validity of the arguments they deployed, and the processes by which decisions were reached. Depending on one's perspective, any or all of these could be said to explain acts of industrial policy. Many would argue that the game is not worth the candle. But let me try to pull together a few points.

In this country all governments have relied generally upon market forces to allocate resources and have pursued policies aimed at improving the working of the competitive process both in the UK and in international trade; but the examples which I have quoted suggest five ways in which governments have found that prescription inadequate.

First, the interest of national defence has always required governments to intervene and it explains some of what has happened in the period though not the full extent of the misdirected high technology projects of the 1960s!

The urge to survive politically is a second well-acknowledged

132

reason for action. Regional policies and the support of companies in trouble raise employment and thus votes, at least for a while; whilst the 1906 Act, to which I trace so much of our bad handling of trade unions, was presumably the result of some calculation about the parliamentary balance of power. When Sir Alec Cairncross and his colleagues refer to wrong-headed majorities, there is perhaps an implication that some of the pressures – the democratic imperative, as it has been called – might be modified with better education and wider understanding. But continuing conflicts of interest must surely also be a factor.

The limit of competition has been recognized in the traditional argument for the protection of infant industries. In seeking improved protection while carrying through their textile restructuring places, Courtaulds argued that they were engaged in something which amounted to the building of a new industry. The Japanese have carried this concept much further, using protection selectively to help industrialists first to capture the domestic market in order to establish the low cost levels needed to capture a large share of the world market.

A similar understanding of what is sometimes needed for competitive cost levels and growth can lead to accepting a one-firm monopoly. The Monopolies Commission report on the Courtaulds rayon staple case could perhaps be an example; though a better one might be the examination of Pilkingtons undertaken by the Monopolies Commission at much the same time. And a press report of a recent American case spells out the argument with some clarity. It was argued that Du Pont's strategy for titanium was unfair because it set prices high enough to finance its own expansion but low enough to discourage expansion by competitiors, and had expanded its production to capture all the expected growth in demand. It was held that the law should not impede aggressive competition, based on efficiency and growth opportunities, even if monopoly is a possible result. The case for nationalizing can sometimes be argued on similar lines, as with electric power generation. Nationalization is perhaps at one end of the intervention spectrum, and acquiescence in a private monopoly at the other.

A similar process of reasoning can justify intervention in restructuring where (for whatever reasons) capacity is too large in relation to any likely prospective market and there is doubt (a few dominant individuals impelled by pride rather than profit, for example) whether private sector firms will act quickly enough to minimize waste of resources. This argument had dimishing force as investing institutions develop their own ways of intervening.

In looking at innovation the patent system had been developed to bring the prospective return to the private investor more nearly to the social returns, and other kinds of support can be similarly justified, such as the programme for encouraging the use of micro processors or, more selectively, investment projects which the NEB tries to foster.

Since other governments are led by similar considerations into similar intervention, the scale and effectiveness of what they do can be a spur to action which might otherwise not take place. Until there are workable agreed codes of international behaviour, governments find themselves concerned with far more than their responses to individual and isolated instances of protectionism.

Finally, amongst the reasons for government intervention are philosphical attitudes which encourage collective action. Nationalization has been the outstanding example in the UK, where some have seen mere public ownership alone as bringing benefits.

The argument that government action was needed to obtain scale economies has been a pervasive feature of the discussion about industrial policy. It deserves some further comment.

Certainly in dealing with the case for UK entry into the EEC the government in its 1971 White Paper saw the major advantage for British industry in the ability to exploit economies of scale in the larger market; and in doing so was only stating in summary form the case argued at length by the CBI in its second industrial appraisal of January 1970, which included an estimate (how well founded?) that productivity was 3 per cent below potential due purely to the less-than-optimum size of plants.

Did we all become too interested in the economies of scale? A paper to the Manchester Statistical Society in 1972 examined the economists' measurements and concluded that these were not a sufficient measure of what we should be interested in. Because the firm is the mechanism through which the economies of scale can be achieved, the public interest in the efficient allocation of resources requires firms larger than those dictated by scale economies alone.

In retrospect it can be seen that the discussion of economies of scale did not emphasize sufficiently the dynamic features in the growth of a firm which create the conditions in which these economies can be achieved – the pricing policies which capture market share well before it is possible to realize the low costs which can justify the original decision; 'learning curve' effects; the use of relatively cheap borrowed funds and high gearing to improve the prospective return to the equity investors; and indeed the contribution from such financing towards making possible the low selling prices on which the success of the strategy depends. In the late 1950s and 1960s these ideas were well promulgated by some US consultants who specialized in helping firms with their strategy forming. But if they played any part in the UK discussion about the public policy or in the approach to planning of many UK industrial firms it was pretty well hidden. In particular in the debate about public policy the time it all takes was not generally understood. Mr Heath's anger at the industrialists was symptomatic. He had modified investment incentives to meet their expressed wishes and yet four months or so later there was no sign of increase in industrial investment. It was well into the 1970s before the CBI produced a pamphlet giving examples of the time it takes to bring a project to completion. Even then there was no reference to the dynamic factors and to the even more extended time-scales in which strategies are conceived and carried through.

If economies of scale or new investment programmes were the key to growth, then effective industrial policy would be much easier. But I find myself agreeing with those who identify technical progress as the prime determinant of growth. Picking winners is very difficult. The Japanese have managed it – look at the way they have planned and achieved an internationally competitive position in the supply of established products such as cars or television sets.

But it is often impossible to have any clear view of where a new technology might lead. Success comes to those who, step by step, make the judgements about where to go next in choosing product or process and about the scale of the resources to deploy. Some aspects of biotechnology development or of information technology appear to require this approach to strategy forming.

But those who point to the inadequacies of government policies based upon good macroeconomic policies alone must address themselves to two questions. They must ask whether there were valid reasons, including sound economic analysis, for each intervention, and they must decided why it is that past experiments in collective action have been erratic in initiation and implementation. The experiment with indicative planning, for example, was an attempt to transplant a technique which had been useful in France at a particular period. Its policy prescriptions for the UK were misguided because of full employment. We did not have the reserve of industrial manpower which had been available in France from the modernization of agriculture. Nor did we have the institutional arrangements, expecially the control of borrowing exercised through the Crédit Nationale, which had helped to give effect to central decisions about the investment plans of individual firms.

Reflection on this example suggests to me a definition of the difference between a concept and a fashion in weapons of intervention. A concept is capable of being made valid as a policy, in both political and economic terms, whilst a fashion is not – though individual mistakes of execution do not necessarily invalidate a policy. By this text the experiment with indicative planning was a mere fashion; it was not valid in the economic context in which it was introduced, neither did the institutional arrangements exist to operate it. The same might be said of planning agreements because there was no acceptance of the concept amongst industrialists and no way of enforcing it. Sector working parties by contrast are a valid, if limited, concept and in fact as educative as their supporters suggest. (This short essay is not concerned with assessing results in relation to effort expended.)

The other examples of intervention which I have quoted could be said, on the basis of the limited evidence I have presented, to reflect concepts – nationalization, regional policy, restructuring, promoting innovation – which are capable of being translated into political and economic policy. The issues for discussion relate more to the framing of precise measures, the resources deployed, the quality of executive action, and the possibility that more (and sometimes collective) private sector action might avoid or limit the need for government to be involved.

The story of industrial policy is a depressing tale of what happens when deep-seated ideological differences are allowed full expression in making policy about industry. In most of the post-1945 period, the results were exacerbated by exaggerated hopes of what could be achieved by government. Even if there had always been sound analysis and competent execution, these conditions made it inevitable that there would be a lack of persistence with any chosen mix of measures for any period of time long enough to improve industrial performance. Does the history of Montagu Norman's pre-1939 experiments offer a clue to that right analysis of the problem which will cure the disease whilst preserving freedom?

NOTES

1 A. Cairncross, J. A. Kay and A. Silberston, 'The Regeneration of Manufacturing Industry', *Midland Bank Review,* Autumn 1977, p.14.
2 Sir Henry Clay, *Lord Norman,* London, 1957.
3 Quoted in *Financial News,* 7 January 1929, p.7.
4 Quoted in unpublished paper by Professor Peter Mathias.
5 W. J. Reader, *A House in the City,* London: Batsford, 1979, p.161.
6 J. C. R. Dow, *The Management of the British Economy, 1954–1960,* Cambridge: Cambridge University Press, 1964, p.412.
7 'The tri-partite approach to industrial recovery', *National Economic Development Office,* January 1980.

Comments by
Andrew Likierman

In dealing with industrial policy we should remember that Britain had already lost world leadership at the beginning of this period and that the shift from manufacturing to commerce was already established. I would like to raise three question arising from Sir Arthur Knight's contribution. First, can intervention be justified? Second, has intervention been successful? And third, can intervention succeed?

The quotation at the very beginning of Sir Arthur Knight's paper suggests that intervention is likely to be either unnecessary or insufficient. If we accept this we need to ask whether intervention may nevertheless be desirable. Several possible justifications are given at the end of his paper, including the needs of defence, the protection of infant industries, political survival and purely philosophical reasons. Elsewhere in the paper he points to the need for intervention 'if market forces are too slow'. We need to discuss whether there are more reasons for doing so and I will suggest that these are likely to increase in the future.

The second question is whether intervention has been successful.

Sir Arthur Knight shows that there is conflicting evidence on some types of intervention. But I would suggest that the answer to the question should be in the negative, even though individual parts of the policy may have been effective. Although the period was marked by a greatly increased level of prosperity, there was continuing industrial decline relative to other countries. Further evidence of the apparent lack of success of industrial policy is indicated by the sheer variety of policies and the fact that they changed so often. Successive governments have tried permutations of competition policy, regional policy, investment incentives, public purchasing, planning, financing instruments of different kinds and so on. Nationalization has been followed by denationalization and a 'dash for growth' by a squeeze to improve efficiency. The list could go on and on. Many of these measures have been tied to macroeconomic objectives and it is not surprising that industry sees itself as the victim of changing economic fashions as Sir Arthur Knight's paper has suggested. The drive for more investment, planning agreements and a belief that practices in a variety of countries should be slavishly followed are just some of the ways in which a single solution has been sought.

We need to ask whether the sheer variety of measures has been a cause or a manifestation of lack of success.

Organizations have also been tried. Sir Arthur Knight's paper indicates more about the problems than whether they offer solutions. I would have welcomed more on whether the NEB might be a suitable vehicle and the discussion will, I hope, take this further.

The third question is whether intervention can succeed. I would like to deal with this in terms of expectations and attitudes, concentrating on those in industry and among government officials. From industry's point of view I wonder whether it is realistic for them to ask for consistency in economic policy and the separation of industrial from economic policy in general. I do not believe it is possible to take the politics out of policy. Industrialists surely also need to recognize that their attitudes to intervention are often inconsistent and that policy prescriptions carry much less weight when framed without regard to the constraints which surround any government.

The attitudes and expectations of officials also often appear unrealistic. Officials tend to discuss industry as if it were a single entity. Sir Arthur Knight invites us, rather, to look at people instead of organizations but I wonder whether this can fit into the normal framework within which officials work. Picking winners means making uncomfortable choices. A further expectation is that action should result quickly from political decisions. Those in industry know only too well that investment decision in particular cannot be taken as instant responses to policy changes.

Finally, I wonder whether too much of the thinking of officials is not dominated by the experience of a long period of relative economic decline and the fact that most of their contact with industry is with firms that are in trouble.

Three final questions. First, I would like to know what with the benefit of hindsight policy makers would have done differently and what economists would like to have seen done differently. Second, Sir Arthur Knight raises the question of whether Montagu Norman's pre-1939 experiments 'offer a clue to the right analysis of the problem which will cure the disease'. Is this right and how might it work in practice? Third, in writings a few years ago both Sir Arthur Knight and Sir Alec Cairncross referred to the need to establish mechanisms for closer liaison between government and industry. Would they still agree now? Do they think it is enough?

As we move into 'the next seventy years' to a world which may well have much lower growth rates, where there are high expectations of what government ought to do and where competitive government subsidization is becoming normal, the pressures for intervention will be very strong. We need to learn from the last seventy years how best we can cope.

Discussion

Professor Alec Nove opened the discussion by arguing that industrial policy immediately after the Second World War might have had considerable bearing on Britain's subsequent slow economic growth. There was no shortage of demand then, but the supply response of the economy was systematically obstructed. He recalled that when he had been in the Board of Trade in 1948–9 his job had effectively been to prevent people from investing. There was then a long queue of companies which wanted to modernize. Many of them were prevented from doing so by a government policy which put exports before anything else. Firms were only allowed to make new investment if they had a high proportion of exports – and not otherwise. The effect, he suspected, had been to make sure that while other countries were re-equipping their industries, Britain was not: except in those sectors which already had a high percentage of exports. Investment begun in the late 1940s would have come on stream in the mid 1950s – and so this policy might have had a significant effect on industrial capacity in the 1950s and 1960s. By contrast the French did not have a government under the Fourth Republic strong enough to prevent their firms from investing. The result was that they had four major devaluations – but did develop their industry.

Professor Sir Bryan Hopkin confessed that this was an area of economics where he had no particular expertise. But he thought that from an economist's point of view, Sir Arthur Knight's paper seemed distressingly empirical. There were an awful lot of cases in it where decisions had to be taken on their particular merits. An economist who started from first principles would hanker after some general economic rules which might be applied across the board.

He accepted that devising an industrial policy might be an expression of optimism: a lot of the difficulties which industry was in at the moment were the result of the fact that the whole economy was in deep trouble, and it might be optimistic to think that in the long run, the economy would do better on average than it was doing at present.

Like Sir Arthur Knight, Sir Bryan had began from a basic belief in the market as a way of dealing with economic problems. And like him, he agreed that there were cases where the market produced what most people would regard as a 'wrong' decision. An economist working from first principles would assume that industrial policy was necessary because of market failure and he thought this was of two main kinds. One was the problem of 'lame ducks', where governments supported firms in order to stop them going out of business. The other was the problem of expansion, where the government supported innovating firms or new technologies which the market was not prepared to back.

With lame ducks, the problem which governments faced was an industry or enterprise which was believed to have a healthy long-term future, but which was doing badly at the moment – perhaps because domestic demand was abnormally low, or because international competitiveness was abnormally weak. For this to be a genuine case of market failure, it was essential to argue that the capital market could not recognize accurately that the firm or the industry had reasonable long-term prospects. The right way to deal with this sort of situation, Sir Bryan argued, was for capital to be available on subsidized terms, with a long grace period, a low rate of interest, and eventually some sort of profit sharing. An economist operating from first principles might then ask who should be entitled to this sort of facility, and would probably believe that it should be rather widely available. If it were not, there would be awkward issues of where to draw the line: should the facility only be available to manufacturing industry, for example, or only to some kinds of manufacturing? An economist would, in short, want some more rigorous rule than the principle of helping companies simply because they were in trouble – the principle which Sir Bryan felt was currently being observed.

But from the point of view of dealing with the lame duck problem he thought that that feature of the present position that was most unhelpful was the high rate of interest. Much of the help the government was currently being forced to give to companies was simply an antidote to the effects of its own policies.

The problem of picking winners was a rather different sort of market failure, Sir Bryan argued. It was not just a failure of the capital market, but a shortage of entrepreneurial drive. That called not simply for a subsidized supply of capital, but for some kind of public sector entrepreneur: perhaps something like the National Enterprise Board.

He accepted that these were rather ambitious – even alarming – solutions to the problems. But he felt that it was essential not to confuse the two sorts of market failure he had identified. If lame ducks could be helped with subsidized capital, then the NEB should be left to pick winners. The two jobs should not be combined in the same institution.

Lord Croham took up Sir Bryan Hopkin's point about the need for more general principles in industrial policy. The real difficulty, he argued, was how to decide which winners to back and which lame ducks to save. Generalities were no help. There was a great gap between the generality and the specific case, and each application might be distorted by political considerations, by the mood of the moment or by the latest theoretical fad.

He gave an example of a solution which seemed plausible at the time, but which looked wrong in retrospect. A few years ago, when the steel industry was still in private hands, it had been popular to argue that the economy of the country depended almost entirely on the output of the metal using industries. The output of these industries was handicapped by a shortage of steel. It had been easy enough to demonstrate the theoretical proposition that a shortage of steel did vastly more damage than a surplus. So policy ought to be directed towards ensuring that there was never a shortage of steel.

It was, he said, easy to argue that the market had failed. It was much more difficult to be sure that if the government intervened, the results would be better than those which the market generated. It was very hard, looking back over the past seventy years, to find many occasions when the government intervened successfully. That might not prove much because policy had been so discontinuous. It might be that industrial policy could only work if it were consistent, and agreed between the political parties.

He drew attention to one highly damaging shift of policy in 1950–1, when it was decided to expand the defence programme far too rapidly than common sense suggested. The government took the extraordinary decision to replace the exports of capital goods which were diverted by the expansion of defence spending with exports of consumer goods. The gentlemen in Whitehall, he concluded, did not know best.

Professor Robin Matthews wondered whether governments, on coming into office, should set themselves in industrial policy the goal of simply not making things worse.

Professor Sir Austin Robinson said that his own aims in industrial policy when he had been in government had been to try to see where market forces were taking the economy, and how the resources of government could make the market operate more smoothly. He wondered whether more recent industrial policy had been aimed at deliberately frustrating market forces.

The only area of early industrial policy where the aim had been to frustrate the market had been regional policy. It was essential to remember that economics was ultimately about people, and this raised the question of what circumstances were most conducive to economic change and adaptation. He did not believe that the right policy was to deflate until entrepreneurs as well as workers were frightened into increasing competitiveness. He thought that change came about in a world of expansion. Every so often, the economy needed a good hot boom to pull people into the new activities which government wanted to see developed.

Sir Alec Cairncross recalled that in the period from 1945 to 1950, when he had been in Whitehall, there had been good reasons for the government to try to take a firm grip on industry and to try to create a different industrial structure. Exports had to be given priority, and imports had to be damped down. He felt that this period had been remarkably successful, partly because the government had a very clear purpose: that of rapidly expanding exports and reducing imports.

In the 1960s, when he had again been in Whitehall, there had again been a balance of payments problem. Much of the government intervention of that period had been a curious second-best for improving competitiveness by changing the exchange rate. He accepted that there had been some very odd decisions during the period – such as the decision to build two new aluminium smelters.

He argued that specific intervention was often not necessary, and that if one was aiming at a general improvement in industrial efficiency, that might be achieved by general policy. He pointed out that the aims of intervention had altered: early attempts had usually been aimed at dealing with a balance of payments problem, and it was relatively easy to judge success. More recently, industrial policy had been based on theories of how to affect the rate of growth. It had been based on quite different views of restructuring from the 1945–50 period: restructuring to achieve larger firms, for instance, or to break into or dominate a particular market. That inevitably involved government in taking decisions about specific industries and about specific companies. To do that implied that government thought it knew more than those who supplied capital to the industry, or those who ran the firms. He felt that there were times when this had been quite right, and when intervention had worked out to the advantage of industry. But this was largely random: there were inevitably some occasions when the government made things better and some when it made things worse.

Looking further back, he pointed out that there had been another kind of government intervention – when, for instance, the government intervened in the defence industry because it was a large buyer. In that case, the government had just the same justification as Marks and Spencers, the retail chain, had for intervening in the production policies of their suppliers. A buyer might reasonably became involved in making sure that the product was made as efficiently as possible. Where innovation was concerned, government intervention was a cumbersome tool. The more freedom individuals had, the more innovation was likely to occur.

His objection to the most recent kind of government intervention – intervention to promote faster growth – was that it was made either on no theoretical basis at all, or on the basis of theories on which economists had not really made up their minds. There were plenty of books which argued that only monopoly would encourage rapid growth in certain industries – and other books which urged the cause of free competition. A great deal of the argument was based on nothing more than producing examples of countries where a particular brand of industrial policy had worked – or had failed.

But he accepted that when there was only a limited number of big companies, there might be something to be said for them talking to the government departments which dealt with industry, to discuss what each planned to do. He thought it was curious that when the government was drawing up the economic forecast, it did not first talk to the fifty largest firms in the country to find out what view they took. That was one of the best ways of getting up-to-date information about the state of the economy.

Mr Christopher Dow felt that the distrust of government intervention which had been the theme underlying the discussion so far was a typically British attitude. In Japan, as he recalled from his years at the OECD, the government had in the past played an absolutely crucial role in accelerating the pace of industrial development. He thought that the government's role in both France and Germany since the war had also probably been helpful to industry. When large firms were themselves big bureaucracies, why should not even larger bureaucracies be successful entrepreneurs? It probably needed something which did not exist in Britain: a strongly entrenched, self-confident and powerful industrial bureaucracy in government which survived changes in government and pursued a consistent industrial policy. Even without this it ought to have been possible to do more in areas such as training and the treatment of engineers, where it had taken far too long to start making improvements the need for which ought to have been obvious long ago.

Professor Erik Lundberg missed the voice of the protectionist Cambridge Economic Policy Group from the conference. He felt that they represented a typically Keynesian retreat from an uncertain world. In Sweden, the Social Democrats were increasingly calling for protectionism: he felt this was very dangerous. One aspect of market failure which Sir Bryan Hopkin had not touched on in his his remarks was the increasingly risky nature of large investment programmes. The combination of the rise of the oil price, inflation, the emergence of the newly industrialized countries and uncertainty about raw material sources had all combined to make businessmen more aware of uncertainty than ever before. The least risky investment today was short-term financial speculation, which allowed you to make lots of money in a very short time, thanks to inflation and the tax system. That kind of investment was flourishing in many countries. It took a lot of brain-power away from productive long-term investment. That apart, the most certain investments were in computerization and the introduction of robot-controlled technology – because these reduced production costs. That was very different from long-term investment in the development of new markets. It created an incentive for companies to cooperate with government to spread the risk.

Another spur to industrial policy was the increasing proportion of industrial expansion which took place abroad. Sweden, said Professor Lundberg, had more multinational companies in relation to its industrial production than any other country – but all their expansion in the past decade had been abroad. This made very little contribution to domestic incomes, and induced trade unions to press for intervention to ensure that more expansion took place inside Sweden.

Another participant argued that the phrase 'industrial policy' inevitably implied selectivity. The main problem was 'picking winners': helping lame ducks did not raise quite the same sort of intellectual issues as that of picking winners. He felt that Whitehall now approached this issue in too humble a frame of mind. It should, he thought, be possible to bring together the influence which government exerted on industry through purchasing policy, competition policy, export assistance and sometimes through direct help in order to give selective encouragement to some parts of industry. That was, he said, something which some other countries appeared to do successfully. The British had not been very good at it – but the fact that other countries were clearly going to continue to intervene in this way was something which had to be taken into

account. He accepted that Whitehall had become tremendously inhibited about the idea of picking winners. The British tended to
guess: that was quite different from the Japanese getting together
with the banks and the large companies. The Japanese did not just
guess which industries would win – they decided which ones they
would make win. He admitted that if Britain had the Japanese rate
of growth of productivity, it would be much easier to make
industrial policy work.

A second reason for questioning the prevalent British humility
towards industrial policy was the one mentioned by Professor
Lundberg: the problem of persuading firms to take risks in a time of
acute uncertainty. It might be useful to re-examine the role of
government in sharing risk.

Thirdly, as Sir Arthur Knight had mentioned in his paper,
industry was tremendously ambivalent in its attitude towards
government intervention. Industrialists very often told officials that
they wanted more selective government help.

Mr Mića Panić raised three questions. First, he pointed out that
the pattern of industrial production in the UK was very similar to
that in more successful countries, such as Germany. So was the
trade pattern. So what was the reason for the difference between the
UK's industrial performance and that of other countries? The usual
explanation was in terms of factors such as the inadequacies of
British management, or the technical inferiority of British firms.
But, in fact, a relatively small number of companies in the UK
account for most of output, most of exports, and most of direct
investment overseas. Most of that investment had gone, in the past
fifteen years, into Western Europe and North America – highly
advanced countries, and the most competitive markets in the world.
That suggested that British management could not be as bad as most
people believe. In multinational corporations, he pointed out, it was
management at the centre which made the important decisions.

Why then did these firms appear to fail in the UK? One
explanation was that abroad they were working with superior plant
and techniques. But if that were so, why did the firms not import
this back into the UK?

Mr Panić also pointed out that almost a fifth of UK manufacturing production was accounted for by foreign multinationals. Yet
trade performance in the sectors in which these companies operated
was often worse, over the past decade, than the performance of UK

manufacturing industry as a whole. What was happening? Was the growth taking place elsewhere, leaving the more backward industrial capacity located in the UK? If so, could the country wait until 'the market mechanism' reverses the process? How long would that take?

Second, he argued that people often rejected industrial policy in the UK by arguing that it was much too complicated to administer. But corporate bureaucracies often had to make decisions which were far more complex than those which the Departments of Industry and Trade had to make in the UK. Coca Cola, he pointed out, operated in 148 countries. Somebody had to take decisions about that company's major investment projects.

Third, he questioned the impossibility of picking winners. In his time as chief economist at the National Economic Development Office he had spent months discussing precisely this question. There was little doubt, he thought, that, in their present form, NEDO and various government departments in the UK could not perform such a task. But this did not mean that, given the right organization and industrial expertise, the task was impossible – though it would still be very difficult. He had once asked a visiting Japanese professor, a former adviser to the Japanese Trade Ministry, to explain how the Japanese managed it. The professor had explained that in the late 1940s the Ministry had picked out a few sectors where they thought that the world income elasticity of demand would be greater than one – and had worked on them ever since.

One reason why the discussion had been rather inconclusive, thought *Professor Robin Matthews*, was the lack of a theory of government. If one asked what policies were appropriate to government, one had first to decide what were the distinctive attributes of of government. Government had central powers which the private sector did not have – but Coca Cola did not have to contend with by-elections, or with a complete change of power every five years. Economists really needed a theory of government to match their theories of markets in order to decide which was the better channel for policy.

Professor Herbert Giersch dismissed some of the glowing references to German industrial policy by saying firmly that industrial policy in his country was 'a complete mess'. Protectionism was no longer simply a matter of tariffs: there were now a lot of subsidies paid to coal and other industries. Regional policy had become a means by which industry got back some of the taxation levied on the more efficient firms: it might sometimes create new jobs, but it mainly provided an incentive for firms to choose more capital intensive methods of production. There were so many environmental controls that it had become difficult to set up a new plant. A huge ministry of research backed industrial research with enormous sums of money, but tended to pick particular projects with the advice of scientists who inevitably encouraged their own pet hobby horse regardless of cost. The supply of industrial subsidies tended to create its own demand, and large companies had bureaucracies of their own which, with the backing of the trade unions, applied for more government help.

The new trend in Germany, though, was to think in terms of what he called 'negative industrial policy': of dismantling controls and reducing the number of industrial subsidies.

Professor Giersch argued that countries needed information about which industries were likely to be most exposed to competitive pressures from abroad. But when the community was given such information, the results might be perverse. His own institute in Kiel had done some work on the subject, only to be faced with complaints from the industries which had been picked out because the banks had become less willing to lend to them.

Professor Giersch was also sceptical about the possibility of picking winners. It might be possible to pick them in a closed economy or in a backward country, where it was possible to look at trends in more developed economies. But in a country like Germany, it was easier to pick out which industries were likely to run into trouble than to spot future areas of growth.

Professor Arthur Brown pointed out that together with protectionism, the most venerable branch of industrial policy in Britain was regional policy. It dated from the early 1930s, and had perhaps been a British invention. There had been periods when it was relatively easy to make regional policy work successfully, such as the period just after the war when there was a widespread shortage of labour and firms did not need much incentive to persuade them to move to areas of higher unemployment. There had been periods at the end of the 1950s and in 1963 when the regional problem had re-emerged, in what would now be thought a very mild form. Professor Brown recalled that when he had reviewed the success of regional policy about ten years ago, it appeared to have been fairly effective.

There were quite clear links between policy and the diversion of growth from the centre of the country to the periphery. Given the urge of governments to reverse the policies of their predecessors, he felt that there had been a remarkable degree of continuity in regional policy. It had usually been the instruments which changed. Most other countries had eventually come to apply regional policies, too. He accepted that if one reviewed regional policy now, the conclusions might be different from the ones he reached ten years earlier: but he also pointed out that while there were some notorious examples of industries forced to relocated in the development areas in the 1960s running into trouble in the 1970s, there were also plenty of firms in the traditionally prosperous West Midlands which were in difficulties.

Lord Roberthall shared the view that people in government were less able to pick winners than industrialists themselves. One reason, he thought, was that business needed a very long time horizon to succeed, while governments tended to have a very short one. He gave two examples of industrial policy which had been successful. One was the abolition of retail price maintenance, which he felt had made a dramatic contribution to the efficiency of retail distribution. The other was agriculture, where he felt the industry's considerable technological efficiency had been greatly helped by operating in a very stable policy framework. This was the result of almost complete consensus between the political parties about the way that agriculture should be treated, with the result that the farm price reviews had been virtual formalities.

Dr Walter Salant argued that the problem of picking winners was not really one of shortage of competent civil servants. If a government really made up its mind to pick winners, it could always acquire the staff it needed. The problem was one of the time horizon of governments, and of the incentives built into the political system. It was inevitable, he felt, that government policy should express a political desire to slow down the process of adjustment.

Summing up, *Sir Arthur Knight* pointed out that he was the only 'amateur' contributing a paper to the conference. This was significant. He recalled how a recent visitor to Japan had inquired about the reasons for the success of Japan's post-war growth and had been told, 'At the end of the War, most of our good economists were Marxists. They could not be consulted about reconstruction. So we had to make do with commonsense and the advice of engineers and administrators'.

He took up the three questions posed at the start of the discussion by Mr Andrew Likierman: can intervention be justified, has it been successful, and can it succeed? The discussion had distinguished between 'negative' and 'positive' intervention. On the negative front, most governments had found it hard to resist the temptation to rescue lame ducks. He felt it was unavoidable, but wished that governments were more coherent. If they were, it would be more apparent how much more was devoted to this kind of intervention compared with the more positive kind.

The discussion, he pointed out, had not touched on reconstruction. The IRC had been modestly successful, and without it there was a gap which the private sector had not managed to fill.

The discussion of positive adjustment had developed two strands of thought. One was general policies of support: the other, selective policies of 'picking winners'. He had been fascinated to hear Professor Giersch challenge the popular British mythology that the Germans had been extremely good at policies of generalized support. He felt that Sir Bryan Hopkin's proposal for subsidized capital would be hard to justify and would create international problems. In the days when British industry was making profits, the tax system had arguably provided a form of capital subsidy.

Most of the discussion had focused on selectivity. Other countries − particularly the French and the Japanese − selected their winners on the basis of products with proven market acceptability elsewhere, especially in the USA. That suggested that the number of successful cases might be diminishing. But there was no sign of our competitors abandoning this policy. The Japanese and French had both published a list of industries which they intended to encourage. We had, therefore, to continue to think about selective encouragement, and he had been impressed by Mr Dow's point about the absence of an industrial bureaucracy in government. The most successful cases of selective intervention had been in Japan where industrialists had been self-confident in knowing what they wanted, and government had been prepared to help them, with protection, with support for research and development, with the removal of the pressure of competition policy for a limited period: all with the objective of increasing international competitiveness, but with the understanding that it might take ten to fifteen years to build up that competitiveness.

There had been a welcome change in attitude among the providers of finance for industry, he thought. There was now a greater willingness to take risks. But it was still not as great as it ought to be, given the changes which had to be made. He gave ICL as an example. Its future was undoubtedly important, if information technology was important. But the financial markets did not like it when companies ran into the sort of problems which ICL had hit. Ferranti six years earlier, had been pursuing policies too daring for its bankers to finance. It had to be rescued by the government – and its daring strategy had turned out to be rather far-sighted. It might be that the initiative for dialogue between government and industry should come from the financial institutions which owned a large share of British industry.

5

Evolution of the concept of international economic order 1914–80

JAN TUMLIR

INTRODUCTION

This essay will review the development of thought about foreign or international economic policy over the last seven decades. Put in more up-to-date terms, it is about the understanding, exhibited by governments at different stages of this period, of the nature of the international economic system, or order, in which the economies over which they preside are embedded and in which they seek to realize national economic interest.

It is an undertaking difficult to confine to any one of the standard historical specializations. It cannot be a straightforward history of economic policies for many acts of policy are hurried responses to unforeseen events, often insufficiently coordinated with other policies of the same government. It is therefore difficult to say how adequately the actual policy record reflects the general understanding which is our focus. The essay partakes more of the history of ideas, especially since it is impossible always to draw a clear distinction between ideas held inside a government and outside it. But since we are concerned with the evolution of ideas – that is, learning – some account of the events which imparted the lessons, some straightforward economic history, is also unavoidable. And I would be less than candid if I did not mention that a certain amount of polemic with some still widely held views underlies it all.

It may be helpful if I begin by summarizing the main problem of international economic order as I see it. The period chosen may be seen as containing two nearly complete cycles. The First World War destroyed what had been a relatively stable international economic order. The 1920s saw an extended effort to restore that order; the effort was unsuccessful and in the 1930s the ramshackle structure disintegrated almost completely. A much more successful effort at institutional reconstruction was made after the Second World War. The 1950s and 1960s were decades of stability and rapidly growing prosperity for the world at large. A new disintegrative tendency set in, however, in the second half of the 1960s, and has continued to gather strength. What remains of an international economic order at the beginning of the 1980s is a difficult question indeed.

My thesis is that beneath these two cycles – Juglars, one might call them – there is a trend, or perhaps a longer cycle – a Kondratieff as it were. The trend refers to the growth in influence, throughout the period covered, of what may be called 'the planning ideology' or, more simply, the politicization of the economy. It has not been a linear growth, of course, and the planning idea itself has undergone several qualitative transformations. Its main implication is that the involvement of the political authorities in the structure of the economy necessarily slows down the economic adjustments required for stable progress. Fundamentally the planning idea is but a reflection of a growing reluctance to adjust. It is in this respect that it poses an insoluble problem for maintaining international economic stability, or order. That order depends on two sets of closely corresponding arrangements, monetary and commercial, whose main – or, ultimately, sole – function is to induce a continuous and sufficiently prompt adjustment in all national economies to the changes generated in each, and diffused through their interaction in the global market. Since these are economies at very different stages of development but all subject to increasingly rapid technological change, large international flows of capital are a necessary condition of a dynamic equilibrium of the system as a whole. Without an institutional order compelling adjustment in the borrowing countries, there will be either a tendency for international loans to finance the postponement of adjustment, with the result that the loans eventually become uncollectable; or there will be a general insufficiency of investment outlets. At the same time, unless lenders are compelled to adjust, their loans will eventually also become uncollectable as borrowers will not be able to earn enough foreign exchange to service them.

THE CLIMATE OF ECONOMIC THOUGHT AT THE OUTSET

Much has been written on the change in social thought in the two or three decades preceding the First World War. All the main themes of this literature are already present in Dicey's preface to the second edition in 1914 of his *Law and Public Opinion in England.*

On the economic front, the more advanced forms of industrialization called for a better organized supply of skills. The growing complexity of the production process, which made it more vulnerable to disruption, led to increased concern about the contentment of the working class. On the intellectual front, the successes of science fed speculation about the powers of organized collective action. The influence of biology on philosophy, in particular, produced numerous 'organic', 'vitalistic' or 'holistic' concepts of society, all with more or less pronounced anthropomorphic features. In politics, finally, the extensions of the franchise, nationalism, and the fact that rapid urbanization was making poverty more visible even as it was being alleviated by economic growth, gave rise to the 'new conservatism' as well as 'new liberalism'. In both cases, the new elements consisted in different notions of state paternalism. From all these various impulses an ideology was crystallizing which opposed, and preferred, cooperation to competition. Cooperation represented the noble, competition the selfish and vulgar side of human nature. Through cooperation informed by science, society could deliberately determine its own development.

These trends in social thought were strengthened by the war in several respects. Governments governed with far less assurance than before 1914. In the aftermath of a war of those dimensions, as the nationalist fever subsided and people began to ask what it had all been for, all the belligerent European governments, whether winners or losers, felt weakened. There were two understandable political reactions.

Politicians and thinkers about public affairs were exerting themselves to salvage at least something from the carnage. The most obvious and promising issue was, again, 'the power of collective action'. E. M. H. Lloyd gave a clear expression to this effort:

> Just as (the) appalling evils (of the last war) exceeded in magnitude and horror those of all previous wars, so the self-sacrifice, courage, disinterested service – and even, one might add, the achievement of willing and effective co-operation, nationally and internationally, between vast masses of men, surpassed anything that would have been thought possible in time of

peace. . . . For the first time in history the world began to have a vision of what human association, raised to its highest degree, might accomplish. . . . People have come to realize that what is needed is not a mere transitory programme to enable life to resume its normal pre-war channel, but some larger and more permanent policy, conceived in the spirit the war has revealed. . . . Men who have breathed the larger air of common sacrifice are reluctant to return to the stuffy air of self-seeking.[1]

A similar reaction of John Dewey in the United States was described by A. M. Schlesinger – with an unintended but deadly irony – as follows:

What impressed Dewey most in 1918 was what he called 'the social possibilities of war' – the use of technology for the communal purpose, the subordination of production for profit to production for use, the organization of the means of public control.[2]

The experience of running a fully administered wartime economy flat out seemed to provide a firm basis for these dreams. Economics, presenting an infinitely intricate system the stability of which depends on infinitely fine adjustments, is easily bowled over by war. This is so for two reasons. Since war produces a unanimous society and is not expected to last long, costs do not matter much.[3] War also represents a suspension or a collapse of the international order; while it lasts, policy decisions are not encumbered by systemic considerations. It is exhilaratingly easy to administer a wartime economy.[4]

There was also a concern about 'the fruits of victory': about what tangible reward to offer to the people who had fought the war. Given the vast destruction that had just taken place, this amounted to a desire to obtain something for nothing.

Among the more concrete results of the war, the two most important for the following account were the large permanent increase of bureaucratic staffs in all governments, and the imbroglio of inter-Allied debt and reparations.

INTERNATIONAL ECONOMIC POLICY IN THE 1920s

In most European countries, the ultimate aim of international

155

economic policy was in conflict with the domestic political situation. The international objective was to re-establish the reliable order which the conjunction of gold standard with the system of non-discriminatory long-term commercial treaties had provided in the pre-war period. Domestically, however, political pressures demanded a much more active and detailed economic policy. The means for its conduct were at hand.

Even though most of the control and command mechanisms of the war economy were dismantled soon after armistice, governments' involvement in and influence on the economy remained great in all European countries, particularly so in the new states which had emerged from the peace settlement.[5] In Great Britain, the dismantling of direct market and foreign trade controls went farther than in other European countries. Nonetheless, as elsewhere in Europe, the share of government revenues and expenditures in GNP in the 1920s was, at 24 per cent, more than double the estimated proportion in the decade preceding the war. Furthermore, as in most European countries, the government's presence in the capital market was vastly increased.

Everywhere, the bureaucracies created to conduct the war economies remained much larger after 1918 than the bureaucracies administering pre-1914 society: so much so that Sir John Hicks, in his theory of economic history which spans millenia, could speak of an Administrative Revolution occurring in 1914–18. The simple availability of staff in peacetime made possible forms of control over domestic as well as foreign transactions which were unthinkable before 1914.

The inter-Allied debts and German reparations saddled economic diplomacy in the inter-war period with an unprecedented problem. What must first be emphasized is the sheer magnitude of these inter-state financial claims and liabilities in relation to the current flow of income. Just to underline the point: Germany, the ultimate debtor, was liable in the first reparations assessment for more than five, and in the last settlement for roughly three, times its annual pre-war GNP. If the original treaties could have been enforced, she would still be paying. The enormous debts not only had no foundation in productive assets. They had been incurred in paying for four years of large scale and intensive international destruction.

Securing these payments and receipts was a prime concern of

the governments of the time. They were also concerned with particular industries, mainly those established or significantly expanded during the war. Especially after the monetary consolidation, the production costs in many of these national industries could be seen to be clearly out of line with international levels. America's drastic restriction of immigration at this time created an urgent concern about employment opportunities, particularly in South-Eastern Europe. Unemployment was also being created by the segmentation of formerly internal trade in the Austro-Hungarian Empire brought about by the creation of new states – at the very time when the new governments most needed prosperity for consolidation. International payments considerations furnished another important motive for these governments to exercise active 'responsibility' for particular industries as foreign exchange earners or savers. The pressure of the restored gold standard on costs of production called into being the great industrial rationalization movement of the 1920s which in Europe assumed the form, not merely of amalgamations, but of concerted behaviour among independent firms aimed at limiting 'wasteful competition'. Governments either stood passively by or actively aided the effort with subsidies and enforcement of cartel contracts. (In the US, the Webb-Pomerene Act of 1918 was orginally intended, at least in part, to make possible the participation of American exporting firms in international cartels.)

Thus we have at least a sketch of the great expansion of influence which the democratic governments of Europe gained over the economies of their peoples. I now want to combine this picture with the understanding of the democratic political process developed in the theory of political economy of the more recent decades.

Democratic politics is very largely about economic change: about what we now call 'adjustment'. The losers, or prospective losers, in the market seek redress through the political process. To what extent they get it depends on the quality of that process and on the scope which the constitution provides for government intervention in the economy. When government's legal power to intervene in the economy increases, the nature of the political process changes, and it becomes even more intensely concerned with economic issues.[6] Even under the best conditions, such politicization of the economy necessarily implies the slowing down of adjustment.

These conditions explain the frustration of the League of

Nations' efforts to restore stability and security in conditions of trade. These attempts are recounted in a League of Nations' publication *Commercial Policy in the Interwar Period: International Proposals and National Policies* (Geneva, 1942). They can be said to have represented, over the 1920s, a declining spiral of ever more modest initiatives. The Genoa Conference (May 1922) recommended the removal of all adminstrative obstacles, the stabilization of tariffs and harmonization of their nomenclatures; the dismantling of export and import embargoes as well as of the most oppressive quantitative restrictions; and the generalization of Most-Favoured-Nation treatment. When progress along these general recommendations turned out to be slow, the Prohibitions Conference, attended by twenty-nine states, met in Geneva in October 1927 to negotiate abolition of exports and imports prohibitions, quantitative restrictions and administrative obstacles which had been generally used as discriminatory devices. The agreements of the conference were, however, ratified by only a small number of states and never became effective. Attempts were made afterwards to negotiate trade liberalization in particular product areas. Renunciations of embargoes and lowering of duties were achieved in the area of hides, skins and bones, signed by eighteen states in October 1929. Thereafter negotiating efforts concentrated mainly on bilateral agreements.

What accounts for the failure to restore a viable monetary framework for the world economy in the 1920s? That the gold standard was resumed by successive national decisions, rather than by coordinated simultaneous action, would not have mattered if it had thereafter operated as a system. Systematic forces would have aligned national price levels and thus made the originally chosen exchange rates realistic. The fact that countries denominated their monies in weight of gold, however, was not enough to restore a system. How United States monetary policy affected international monetary relations in the 1920s is described in detail by Friedman.[7] His conclusions can be summarized in three statistics and one sentence. From 1923 to 1929, US monetary gold stock was growing at an annual average rate of 5.5 per cent, high-powered money of 1.4 per cent, money stock at 2.8 per cent.

There can be little doubt that Britain's problems would have been vastly eased if the United States, and even more France, had permitted a greater degree of monetary expansion – enough in this country, for example, so that wholesale prices would have been stable from 1925 to 1929 instead of falling about 8 per cent.[8]

Similar or more severe criticism could be made of French monetary policy at the time, which was moreover buttressed by administrative restrictions on the flotation of foreign-capital issues in the Paris market, prohibitive taxes on income from foreign securities and successive increases in the French tariff. At the end of the 1920s France and the United States held between them some two-thirds of the world's monetary gold stock.

Before 1914, Britain's success in administering the gold standard from a very narrow reserve base owed much to the fact that trade, and thus national economic structures, responded fairly flexibly and promptly not merely to gold flows, but already to interest rate changes and accommodating capital flows. Our discussion of the trade relations in the 1920s shows that this condition no longer existed after 1918. The gold standard of the 1920s thus could be sustained, for a few years, only by a large volume of long- as well as short-term private American lending, much of it concentrated on Central Europe. International capital flows can be used to finance adjustments in the 'real' economy or, alternatively, the postponement of such adjustments, if only temporarily. Commercial policy in most countries was effective in delaying the necessary changes in the composition of production. As the volume of private debt grew, superimposed on official debt, and its international structure became more complex, the 'real' maladjustment (or the costs of the eventually necessary adjustments) continued to grow as well.

'Hot money' (destabilizing short-term capital movements) is generally considered to have been the new and central problem of economic policy in the 1920s. 'But these capital movements, and especially the American contribution thereto, were less dependable, more capricious, than the corresponding pre-war capital movements; and an undue proportion of them were short-term loans subject to sudden call.'[9] What was it that destabilized capital flows in this period? The answer is in two parts. There was, first, the increased presence of the government in the economy, the capital market in particular. It was a fundamental change from the pre-1914 business conditions, sufficient to make foreign capital jittery. Government actions in the market, not guided by any generally known theory, were unforeseeable. Governments' concern with their own capital transactions led them to various attempts to manipulate the private ones for political rather than economic ends.[10] Second, and more important than the increased government presence in the economy, was the fact that, in the absence of firm inter-governmental arrangements, there was no limit to government interference with private transactions. Without a believable commitment of the major countries to liberal trade, it is easy to understand that capital movements among them were unduly short-term and generally nervous.

It is thus possible to consider the 1920s a decade of laissez-faire in the traditional sense. It was, if anything, laissez-faire for governments which, for the most part, considered themselves wholly unconstrained in their interference with the private economy. After the Second World War, governments claimed an even larger proportion of national income but, having accepted certain rules limiting their intervention in private international transactions, they became more predictable in their behaviour. This is the main explanation of the difference in economic performance between the two periods.

THE WORLD DEPRESSION

Economists continue to argue whether the depression had one cause or many, and whether the main cause was real or monetary in character; but this is not an interesting debate. My interpretation follows the two leads provided by C. P. Kindleberger. First, no amount of 'distortions', 'disproportions' or 'maladjustments' in the structure of an economy, national or international, can of themselves cause a prolonged depression or stagnation. All such distortions need correction, and so represent opportunities for new investment. Their emergence may throw an economy into a recession. Indeed, it is the function of a recession to call attention to them and induce the corrective process which, within a proper policy framework, will eventually lift the economy into a new upswing. Second, on purely probabilistic expectations, a recession was due at the end of the 1920s anyhow. It is the failure to prevent it from degenerating into an international financial crisis and eventually into a monetary crisis that has to be explained.

An explanation of this failure must emphasize the interplay between trade and finance. The failures of trade and financial or monetary policy compounded each other. Net American lending to Europe had begun to decline sharply in 1928. Germany's industrial production peaked out at the same time as America's, and her imports show a small decline in value as early as 1929.[11] A cut in lending to Germany reduced the market for exports from East Europe which, burdened with high foreign debt service, reacted by increasing protection. Agricultural prices were falling steeply. In the early months of 1930, there was a brief upturn in the American economy. Imports stabilized, production increased; there was even a temporary revival of international lending with a peak in the second quarter.[12] In June 1930 the Smoot-Hawley Act was signed, after a Congressional passage of some eighteen months. Commercial retaliation by other countries was swift and widespread. International commodity prices resumed their downward trend. Primary exporting countries were hit particularly hard. The foreign debt service of the twelve most important among them was estimated by Kindleberger at $1.4 billion annually. In late autumn of that year, there occurred the first of the three successive waves of bank failures in the United States. It started with runs on rural banks in the agricultural exporting Southern and Midwestern states, before spreading to New York. The international financial collapse came in the following year: Kreditanstalt in May, Danat in July (causing the imposition of exchange control in Germany), London in September, followed in late autumn by a new wave of bank failures in the United States. Barriers to imports were by then rising at an accelerated pace in most countries.

Is there significance in the geographical and time path along which financial pressure moved from country to country? Much of the literature on the world depression treats the concepts of 'liquidity scrambles' and 'runs on banks' as ultimate facts, and is content with tracing their consequences. But bank failures cannot be explained from the liability side of the balance sheet. Why should depositors decide, all of a sudden, to liquidate their deposits? They must have suspicions about the quality of the banks' assets. These assets are debt, and their value declines with rising uncertainty about the collectability of that debt. Here is the nexus of finance and trade which it has been my purpose to elucidate. US farm debt became questionable as agricultural exports and prices resumed their decline in the second quarter of 1930. The collectability of US foreign loans became questionable with the passage of the Smoot-Hawley Act, which sharply reduced the ability of debtors to earn foreign exchange. The whole international credit structure collapsed when it became obvious in 1931 that the total value of international trade would continue to decline, making it impossible for debtors to service debts denominated in foreign currency.

There is little more to be said about the collapse. Only one point for future reference: at the several critical points when central bank cooperation might have made a difference, these institutions did not act as monetary authorities. They acted either as cautious private banks or, on the European continent, as servants of the 'jealous sovereignties', concerned with scoring political and strategic points even in the midst of a financial crisis.

EVOLVING CONCEPTS OF INTERNATIONAL ECONOMY

The failure of the effort to restore international order in the 1920s is ultimately traceable to the United States government's refusal to associate itself with that effort, and to a related error of commission on the part of the United States monetary authorities. Already a leading economy at the time and the world's principal lender, the United States was politically incapable of participating in the institutional reconstruction because of its split economic world view. It insisted on a world in which capital (increasingly American) could move freely and securely; yet in which any American industry which felt the need would be protected against imports. Despite French intransigence in the matter of German reparations, the United States was the actual pivot of the debt-reparations imbroglio. In the same way that Germany was the ultimate debtor, the United States was the ultimate creditor. That whole structure of inter-governmental debt, with no corresponding productive assets, was literally floating − on unyielding beliefs: in the sanctity of contract on the one side, in the victor's right to punish the victim unto the fourth generation on the other. Clearly, every debt is an expression of faith, belief; so much is implied in the word 'credit'. With all the understanding which we can summon today for the temper of that time, however, it is clear with hindsight that the United States' insistence on contractual obligations, and its consequences for intra-European relations, overloaded the bond normally expected to exist between the lender and the borrower – the bond on which the whole credit structure of a commercial civilization rests.

As the US government had largely withdrawn, Britain was the intellectual leader of the international reconstruction effort. Her initiatives were informed by two ideas which, together, can be taken to constitute sufficient conditions for international order. The first we may call the condition of 'effective multilaterality'. Essentially, the institutional framework of the world economy consists of arrangements between and among a relatively small number of the advanced or 'core' economies. If these arrangements are open to all others without discrimination, the necessary basis for an international order has been established. The second condition relates to the contents of these necessary arrangements. They consist of two sets of rules which jointly create *a multilateral system of trade and payments*. The central purpose of the rules governing payments is to ensure currency convertibility; that of trade rules, to ensure non-discrimination by limiting protection to tariffs which are stable, not subject to unforeseen increases. These two sets of rules have to be adjusted to each other in a precise way, given that the techniques of trade and exchange restrictions are largely interchangeable. When currency convertibility co-exists with price level stability in at least the few core countries, and when all foreign exporters have equal access to at least a number of the larger national markets, then an international market and price system exists and transmits precise information about incipient scarcities and surpluses in the world economy. Interpreted with skill and experience, this information permits conclusions about future trends in the world economy. It is thus indispensable for timely adjustments of the structures of national economies.

It may be noted in passing that the Covenant of the League of Nations provided only a very inadequate legal basis for that effort. The drafting difficulties are well known. 'Insofar as the Covenant of the League provided any basis for the later economic work of the League, it was largely due to British insistence and despite American indifference and even opposition.'[13] Britain provided initiatives for the most important of the League's actions in the field of international economic policy. British authorities were clearly aware of the inadequacy of the League's efforts with the United States absent and Germany not a member until 1926. The Genoa Conference in May 1922 was convened, on the initiative of Lloyd George, outside the framework of the League in order to ensure the participation of the United States, Germany and the USSR. The resolution of the Supreme Economic Council, which was the diplomatic basis of the conference, stated:

> *A united effort of the stronger powers is necessary* to remedy the paralysis of the European system. The effort must include the removal of all obstacles in the way of trade, the provision of substantial credits for the weaker countries and the co-operation of all nations in the restoration of normal prosperity. (emphasis added)[14]

I should also mention the beginnings of central bank cooperation in the 1920s. It was especially successful in the currency consolidations of the smaller Central and East European countries, in which the Bank of England showed greater ability than the Banque de France to keep economic and political considerations on separate tracks. The development of this cooperation in the 1920s was too slow, of course, to enable it to cope with the financial crisis at the decade's end. By way of criticism one could say that effective multilaterality was understood by the British governments as a desirable but not a necessary condition. It was not recognized early enough that the gold standard was no longer functioning as an automatic system and that without closer cooperation among the core countries it could not function at all.

It might also be said that full appreciation of the need for effective multilaterality was hampered by the very concept of the League which was a dominant influencing factor of British foreign policy at the time. International policy making by consensus among a large number of countries can lead to effective policies only when governments of the core countries possess a full theoretical understanding of the issues dealt with. The difficulty is that consensual international policy making already inhibits the process of policy formation in the governments of the core countries. It does so by providing arguments for groups and individuals opposing a particular policy, for they can argue that the policy in question, to be effective, would have to be adopted by all countries. And vice versa, domestic interest groups in the larger countries use failures in the smaller countries to keep the rules as an argument against compliance by their own governments. Arguments of this type, and arguments about the distortion of the relative competitive positions of national industries by exchange rate fluctuations, were used in the initiative for and passage of the Safeguarding of Industries Act of 1921 as well as in the 1923 election campaign which the Conservative Party fought on the issue of protection.

The British position, reflected in national policy as well as in the initiatives taken in the League, clearly acknowledged the inter-dependence of monetary and trade arrangements. This was in part imposed by the facts of the situation – no country was willing to make any significant concessions on trade before the monetary situation was stabilized internationally. Parliamentary discussion and the economic literature of the day, however, also reveal an understanding of the reverse relation: that a tolerable functioning of the monetary arrangements requires trade policy commitments to allow trade to respond to changes in monetary policy. This understanding was much less widely shared by other European countries. Certainly Britain was, by this time, no longer a free-trade country in the strict sense. The McKenna Tariff of 1916 and the Industries Safeguarding Act of 1921 provided protection for a significant range of industries, particularly for the technologically advanced ones. Nonetheless, in comparison with most European countries British tariffs were by and large moderate and stable; and with the single exception of synthetic dye-stuffs, for which an import licence was required, tariffs were the only means of pro-tection. Taken in conjunction with the freedom of monetary transactions, and with the course of monetary policy, it is correct to say that national economic policy in Britain on the whole forced rather than delayed industrial adjustment to changed international conditions.[15]

After 1931 British economic thought was evolving away from a concern with the international economy and the conditions of order in it. Nonetheless contemporary debate and literature on economic questions of the day reveal an understanding of the causes of the world depression far more complete than that prevailing in most other countries, especially in the United States. Even though the British initiatives for international action may have been imprac-tical, it cannot be doubted that British understanding was right on the two fundamental points. By 1932 it was abundantly clear to most British economists in and outside the government that the world depression was essentially a process of cumulative deflation which could be stopped by either a coordinated national or an agreed international provision of additional liquidity. Several proposals were made in this direction:

i Kindersley-Norman proposals for the Bank for International Settlements to borrow from governments; a similar proposal for an international fund of $1½–2 billion to make loans to central banks made by British Ambassador in Washington in early 1933;[16]

ii Henderson's monetary proposals for Lausanne (12 May 1932) which called for a special currency, International Certificates, to be issued by the BIS to the value of 50 per cent of a country's gold value exports in 1928; a similar proposal by Keynes in March–April 1933;

iii The Woytinsky–Keynes proposal for a coordinated – if not joint – extensive programme of public works in the main countries.

A detail is often the best illustration. For perhaps two decades after the Second World War it was generally thought that 'competitive devaluations' in the 1930s had been one of the main causes of the depth and duration of the depression. It was a major insight when several economists (Johnson, Mundell, Rolfe and others) pointed out in the 1960s that what had appeared as 'competitive devaluations' should not be viewed as a primary cause of anything but as a symptom of the system's need of liquidity, and as a roundabout way of increasing liquidity. In a memorandum to the Economic Advisory Council, dated 27 October 1931, Hubert Henderson presented a detailed analysis of the two alternatives of increasing the system's liquidity by (a) a joint devaluation of all the main currencies against gold and (b) a chain, or circle, of successive national devaluations.[17]

The second fundamental point acknowledged by British policy was that without the participation of the United States, no attempt at a joint action had a hope of succeeding. As for its refusal to co-operate, the United States could not be more explicit. 'Our international relations, though vastly important, are in point of time and necessity secondary to the establishment of a sound national economy. I favor as a practical policy the putting of first things first.'[18] 'The world will not be lulled by the specious fallacy of achieving a temporary and probably artificial stability in foreign

166

exchange on the part of a few large countries only.'[19] The frantic domestic experimentation of the first New Deal with gold, and with the corporatist programmes of National Industrial Recovery, was enough to undermine business confidence not only in the United States but also in the more trade-dependent European and other overseas countries. In this situation, to concentrate on second- or third-best solutions seemed the better part of wisdom.

FURTHER EVOLUTION OF THE PLANNING IDEA

The increasing concentration of British professional and political thought on the domestic economy after 1931 had several reasons, not the least of which was the beginning of recovery after sterling had been unpegged. This could be plausibly interpreted as a victory of national policy over international system, or of intelligence and will over blind forces of orthodoxy. An infinite perspective of future improvements and increasingly ingenious national policies seemed to open. Characteristic of this period of intellectual transition was the response of Keynes, Harrod and Meade to the message by which Roosevelt effectively torpedoed the London Economic Conference in 1933. He was judged 'magnificently right'. Further impetus to the idea of national planning was provided by the even more spectacular recovery of Germany, its influence on Keynes completing *The General Theory* in 1934 and the book's appearance in 1936.[20]

From the present viewpoint, the two salient aspects of *The General Theory* have turned out to be that it provided a theory of employment and money *in a closed economy,* and that its conclusion as to the government's ability to determine the aggregate level of investment without significantly influencing its allocation was an illusion. The UK government got involved in industrial investment allocation in several different ways, perhaps most importantly through the Import Duties Act of 1932 and the Import Duties Advisory Committee which it established. The heart of the economic problem of planning and investment allocation consists of two closely related questions: whether a sufficient amount of the knowledge and information dispersed through the economy can be centralized for government use, and what should be assumed about the motives and capacities of the politicians and civil servants to whom the planning tasks are entrusted. Both questions are

167

answered by an abundance of examples in Sir H. Hutchinson's *Tariff Making and Industrial Reconstruction,*[21] a work at once disarming and horrifying in its placid account of how the executive branch sought to promote 'cooperation' within industries and then to cooperate with, and accommodate, the articulated industry interests, to the point where the Committee 'was prepared to make use of its procedure in such a way as to aid a British industry in securing agreement with other members of a cartel on acceptable terms, or in maintaining or reviving a cartel that was failing' (p.79).

In the United States similar, though still less coherent, attempts at industrial planning were pursued through the National Industrial Recovery Act and the Reconstruction Finance Corporations.[22] They were gradually abandoned as a result of an increasingly explicit recognition of the knowledge and information problem on the part of the 'planners' themselves, and of their clash with Mr Hull over trade policy as well as because the Supreme Court invalidated the central statute of the programme.

With self-sufficiency impossible, some conceptions of the international context had to be grafted on the idea of an independent national economic policy. Basically, there were two. Together with the more rigorous idea of planning went a conception of the British economy minimally connected with the rest of the world by bilateral trade and payments agreements. The alternative conception it contemplated was an economy operating on an essentially liberal basis, though one circumscribed geographically by Imperial Preference. It must be added that, although the former conception seems to have held more sway than the latter over the influential minds of the late 1930s and during the war, it never became official policy. Even though correctly describing the arrangements in force during the war and early post-war years, it was even in this period officially considered a necessary but temporary expedient.

It is fascinating to observe in Harrod's biography and memoirs of other contemporary actors how the idea of bilateralism in trade, corresponding to the necessities of British war finance, were not far from Keynes's mind even when he was working on his Clearing Union proposal − how he could slip out from the Schachtian outlook and return to it when dealing with the pressing problems of current policy.[23] It is obvious now, however, that the idea of bilateral arrangements was never fully thought out. A nation's economic policy cannot be effective in the long run, unless it is governed by the Kantian universality postulate. When a single free rider is successful, others will imitate him; when all do all will lose, including the original one. Bilateral trade and payments arrangements cannot be generalized. Those between Germany and the small Central and East European countries were 'flexible' enough to be manageable: when Germany's suppliers could not obtain the stipulated locomotives or lathes, they could always take gramophones or harmonicas. Within the Commonwealth in wartime, flexibility was ensured by the tradition of friendship. But among large countries not necessarily friendly to each other, the product quotas of the bilateral trade agreements would have to be complied with exactly, and thus they would necessarily lead to detailed physical planning of production – which, in turn, would necessitate a simultaneous negotiation of the bilateral trade agreements in the framework of a world trade plan.

From the intensive wartime preoccupation of British economists with the post-war balance of payments of their country had emerged another development of the planning idea which came to exert a great influence on the economics of the last three decades. It was the instinctive, intellectually unexamined preference for slow over quick adjustment. In the circumstances of the time the preference was understandable, as was the belief that policy could control the rate of adjustment. But in strict planning theory, this preference must be translated into the notion of an optimal rate of adjustment. That raises the problem of the knowledge and information required for determining that optimum. From the international viewpoint, the notion of the optimal rate of adjustment is closely related to that of international reserves or liquidity, a complex of questions to which we shall return.

US ASSUMPTION OF LEADERSHIP – STEP ONE

The negotiations leading to the establishment of the post-war international economic order are recorded and interpreted in great detail, to which I have nothing to add. But being technical and chronological, these accounts miss, or at least pay insufficient attention to, an aspect which is still most remarkable. How did a logical and coherent conception of order emerge so rapidly out of the intellectual chaos prevailing in the Washington of the 1930s? There were two stages in the process. Already in the early 1940s, while the US was still neutral, the main ideas for economic reconstruction and a new international economic order of the post-war period were laid down in the bilateral negotiation of the Mutual Aid Agreement, Article vii of which paved the way to Bretton Woods and Havana. It was at this stage that British thought made its main contribution. The second stage can be described as the US 'taking charge' when the European reconstruction effort collapsed in 1947.

Even though our interest is primarily with formulation of policy, and thus with government, a focus so limited could not provide the explanation sought. If societies can be said to possess specific talent, that of the American society surely is for organization of resources on a large scale. In this case, there was a large-scale organization of the country's intellectual resources: H. B. Lary, A. Hansen, H. Simons, J. Viner, J. H. Williams outstanding among innumerable others. These academics shared the awareness that what had agitated the world economy in the past five or six decades was the entry of the US as an increasingly important actor into the world market. The stabilization of the US economy, and of the purchasing power of the dollar, was seen to be a key to stable, economic progress in the rest of the world. In its sure grasp of the vital issues this literature remains unsurpassed. There is nothing in economic literature of the last three decades to match, for example, Viner's 1943 article, 'German Reparations Once More',[24] in a clearsighted and humane analysis of an impending problem.

The first step consisted of the recognition by both the American government and public opinion of the need to learn from past mistakes. An important element of US foreign policy tradition was abandoned – the United States no longer insisted on 'avoiding entanglements', but was willing to get involved. Two other strong elements of that tradition were, on the contrary, reasserted: non-discrimination, and a precise specification of commitments.[25]

In the first and very rough conception the United States government imagined a largely self-executing system of self-denying ordinances and disciplining rules in the framework of which the main task of reconstruction and subsequent development could be carried out, more effectively than after the First World War, by private capital harnessing into the process the much expanded productive capacity of US industry. There is little doubt that this original conception focused mainly on arrangements for trade. These represented an extension of Mr Hull's reciprocal trade agreements, combined with the trade initiatives of the League of Nations. The British responded to the US initiative, rightly, by saying that a firm framework for liberal trade policy, together with freedom for capital movements, was not enough. They insisted on a need for formal arrangements in the monetary field to ensure that the traditional instability of the American economy would not be communicated abroad in repetition of the 1930s experience. The US policy makers had to acknowledge that without such an assurance, commitments to liberal trade were unobtainable. It may thus be said that the main British contribution consisted of restoring the necessary balance between monetary and trade considerations. In addition, there was the most valuable practical contribution of British economists in providing working drafts for the technical negotiations in both fields.

This is not to say that the British shared the American view on the necessary disciplining of the overall design. This came out most clearly in their view of the liquidity needs of the international monetary system. Keynes's concept of extensive automatic financing of the net balances outstanding in the Clearing Union can only be understood in the light of his concern with Britain's post-war balance of payments and the instinctive preference, mentioned earlier, for slow over speedy adjustment. There was a failure here of both economic and political reasoning: economic, because drawings on the abundant credit facilities he desired would still have to be repaid; political, because apparently generous credit facilities could not but influence the willingness of the component groups of society to adjust and thus, eventually, they affected the ability to service the debt. Thus we are again led to the notion, ignored at the time, of an optimal rate of adjustment.

At the end of the war, the IMF structure was completed, ratified, and formally in operation. The arrangements for trade were complete in conception if not in technical detail. Yet neither had any effect on the conduct of their foreign economic policies by the participating nations. A general assessment of these arrangements (the latter on the basis of the ITO Charter negotiated later) must begin by noting a fundamental contradiction inherent in both. Their main and avowed purpose was to make efficient operation of private markets possible. Yet both exhibited a high degree of distrust for the markets as such, and contained large number of escape clauses to allow measures of intervention in, and even the suspension of, market forces for the objectives of 'safeguarding full employment' and 'adequate development'. In this aspect the plans reflected an identical contradiction in Keynes's own mind, unresolved until the end.

US ASSUMPTION OF LEADERSHIP – STEP TWO

During the Second World War, the view gained almost universal acceptance that the inter-war economic disaster was due to laissez-faire, and in particular to the premature dismantling of government controls in the 1920s in the midst of economic dislocations so severe that private markets could not cope with them. This view was particularly influential in Britain but also in the underground movements of the occupied European countries, and strongly influenced their post-war governments.

Hence also the largely unquestioned assumption that reconstruction after the war would have to carried out under close government guidance and control. The assumption was initially unquestioned even by the US government which was at the time preoccupied with the reconversion of the US economy to peacetime production – or, rather, with a political fight about how it was best to be carried out. A series of statutes quickly enacted in 1945–6 decided against the planners and for reliance on the market. In less than two years, eleven million former soldiers and auxiliaries were absorbed into the civilian economy; the number of new jobs created was a multiple of the net increment to civilian labour force since several industries contracted output substantially (steel by one-third) while others expanded. Inflation rose to low two digits in 1946 but was back to zero in 1948. All in all, it was the most extensive, speediest, and most efficient economic adjustment in recorded history.

In Europe, attempts to restore prosperity proceeded on the basis of national reconstruction plans, under imperfectly suppressed inflation. They involved a degree of government allocation and control, including trade in strictly bilateral fashion, approaching a system of detailed physical planning. The only missing element was precisely the system, in the sense of consistency. Under bilateral trade agreements, governments not only set quotas for particular products but determined, through multiple bilateral negotiations, how much of each product should be imported from where. This could not work given that the control powers of democratic governments are limited by law, and that the governments of the time were not adequately organized to exercise such coordinated control as the law allowed them. Thus despite perhaps $10 billion of US aid granted in the first two post-war years,[26] when Undersecretary of State William Clayton visited Europe in the spring of 1947, all he saw and was told suggested an imminent economic collapse.

The basic insight into the European economic problem was provided by a team of State Department officials and experts. The last time Europe knew sustained prosperity, before 1914, it was a large continental economy. The 1945–7 reconstruction effort was not conducive to recreating that economy; on the contrary, it served to demonstrate the theoretically obvious difficulty of coordinating national economic planning in democratic societies so that benefits of international division of labour could be reaped. A basic policy reorientation towards recreating a continental economy had to be induced. The European governments agreed with the analysis but had fears of insuperable national balance of payments crises. Marshall Plan aid was offered to allay those fears.

One conclusion can be drawn from this episode. Britain was the leader of the reconstruction effort in the 1920s, offering the right ideas – but it had only ideas to offer. In times of crises, leadership requires material resources to back the right solution.

The UK's unsuccessful 'dash for convertibility' in 1947 suggests that the notion of effective multilaterality was temporarily forgotten on both sides of the Atlantic. It was a throwback to the 1920s, with its belief that a unilateral, uncoordinated resumption of convertibility, in an economic environment not so much planned as disorganized by attempts at planning, could advance the establishment of order.

One of the main arguments for a planned reconstruction of European economies was that of the dollar shortage. The term 'dollar shortage' was already used in the inter-war period in references to the difficulties of dollar indebted countries following the cessation of the US capital outflow after 1928 and the passage of the Smoot-Hawley Act in 1930. By 1933, with the US money supply barely two-thirds of what it had been in the first half of 1929, there was an acute dollar shortage everywhere, particularly in the American economy.

In the years after the Second World War, numerous attempts were undertaken to construct a theory which would explain the alleged dollar shortage as a long-term feature of economic history, resulting from the economic preponderance and/or more rapid productivity growth of the United States. In the early years, the discussion of the dollar shortage was, however, conducted virtually without reference to the price of the dollar, or exchange rates. When the idea of 'rationing by price' was finally raised, it was countered by studies purporting to show low price elasticity of demand for traded goods. Thus the dollar shortage thesis, reinforced by pessimism about elasticity, was the main argument justifying exchange and trade controls as well as the existence of a vast bureaucratic apparatus for their planning, bilateral negotiation and administration.

The dollar shortage theories obviously also lent themselves to arguments for more foreign aid. Their effect was to make the US see itself as causing serious trouble to others by its sheer size and productivity growth; perhaps it would try to alleviate that trouble by income transfers to the weaker economies suffering from its very presence. This might have seemed 'getting something for nothing', the aid serving to postpone or spread in time the economic adjustments that would otherwise be necessary. But it was a bad policy to use aid in this way – in ignorance of the full and long lasting costs of deliberately protracted adjustment, far exceeding the benefits even of aid given in the form of grants.

The reasons for the success of the post-war reconstruction of international economic order can be summarized briefly. There was, first of all, the willingness of the United States to be actively involved in the effort and to back it with its greatly enhanced productive capacity. Second in order of importance, in the author's view, was the low level of nationalist feeling. The Second World War, in contrast to the first, discredited European nationalism, at least for a generation. Finally, there was the spectacular failure of national planning in 1945–7 which made obvious the need to rely on private markets governed by stable, predictable and non-conflicting policies. The basis is on which policy was conducted involved adherence to an agreed system of rules.

DECLINE OF THE POST–1945 ORDER

From the failure of national planning and the success of liberal economy, the planning idea eventually re-emerged in a new form.

Scientific macroeconomics was said to have made the business cycle obsolete and steady growth paths possible. Seldom has an economic assertion been so eagerly accepted by politicians and governments, or so quickly acquired the status of conventional wisdom. Recessions were thereafter taken to signify not structural imbalances, but government incompetence, if not deliberate dereliction of duty. Once governments had promised steady economic growth, powerful social pressures were set up, simultaneously (a) demanding fulfilment of the promise and (b) making the fulfilment more and more difficult. Governments were thus forced into ever more intensive 'fine-tuning', designing their two macro-policies, monetary and fiscal, so that they would bear differentially on particular sectors of the economy: housing, industry, agriculture, etc. Together with an increased use of protection, mainly in the form of quantitative restrictions, this development represents a gradual return to physical planning.

The international implications of these domestic developments were first felt in the monetary field. The monetary order established in Bretton Woods was a dollar exchange standard with an increasing tendency to function as a pure dollar standard; this implied a deficit (on all of the possible definitions of deficit) in the US balance of payments. It could have functioned satisfactorily for an indefinite period if the US had avoided inflation.

The discussion of the system's 'confidence problem' in the 1960s was between a vast majority and miniscule minority of monetary economists. The majority view was of course differentiated, but based on the contention of Professor Triffin that the existing system was bound for self-destruction which would occur when the ratio of the (growing) official US liabilities abroad to the (diminishing) US stock of monetary gold reached some critical level. The main spokesman of the minority was Professor Kindleberger.

Triffin did not deny the usefulness of the dollar as an international transaction currency. His dominant concern was with the instability of the international system in which the dollar was the main reserve asset, given that the supply of monetary gold was not increasing rapidly enough. The dollar's other functions as an international currency were of secondary interest to him. Kindleberger started with an emphasis on the dollar's usefulness to private economic agents abroad. He noted the greater liquidity-preference of households in Europe than in the US. Given the less developed state of the European capital market (mainly due to its segmentation by national laws), this difference created a possibility for the United States to provide useful banking services to the rest of the world. Accepting deposits from those who wanted to stay liquid, it borrowed short; and it lent long by providing finance for industrial investment abroad. That these transactions, responding to and reconciling the different demands of households and firms, will leave a residue in the form of dollar holdings in the central banks abroad, Kindleberger rightly did not consider a fundamental defect of the system. Since the United States continued to have a large current account surplus, the accumulation of dollar balances by foreign central banks could not be interpreted as grants of credit on the basis of which the American economy could absorb more resources from the world than it earned through its current operations. The accrual of dollars in official reserves was, in part, the result of US direct foreign investment. There has been considerable international competition for that investment. If a government or a central bank considered continued accumulation of dollar reserves not to be in the interest of the national economy, it could always revalue its own currency or take equivalent domestic measures. From this analysis Kindleberger concluded the United States government should not worry about the country's balance of payments deficit. It was implicit in this position that the confidence problem was minimal. As long as the United States price level was stable, the dollar was as good as gold; there was no determinate 'critical level' of foreign official liabilities relative to gold reserves to trigger a confidence crisis. If, with its domestic price level stable, the United States were to take measures to end its payments deficit, it would trigger a new international 'dollar shortage' manifesting itself in a general rise of interest rates.

How did the liquidity and the confidence problems get confused? Between 1959 and 1964, the United States price level was absolutely stable. The deficit of the US balance of payments continued to fluctuate but within a narrowed range and the rate of growth of world reserves began to decline from 1963 on. It was at this time that worries about adequate growth of international liquidity began to be voiced in the IMF Board and Annual Meetings. The Annual Reports of the Fund, for all their cautious wording, communicated this fear effectively. One may question today its justification, especially since the concern continued even after 1965 when inflation started rising in the United States. There was a subtle shift in the argument over the decade. In the first half, with the US price level stable, the deficit in the US balance of payments was expected soon to disappear, limiting the growth of international reserves to the small annual accruals of newly mined gold. In the second half, the Reports seemed to be suggesting that adequate growth of world reserves might be impaired by an unwillingness of central banks to increase their holdings of inflating dollars. Throughout, the fear was that unless adequate growth of reserves could be ensured, obstacles to imports would start multiplying again. It was admitted, at the same time, that no precise quantitative criterion of reserve adequacy could be found.

It is impossible to overlook the basic similarity of the 1960s debate with the earlier ones recorded here: on international liquidity in the first confrontation of the Clearing Union and the Stabilization Fund concepts during the war; on the secular dollar shortage, from its beginnings before 1939 to the mid-1950s; and, intermittently since the early 1940s, on the desirable or politically feasible speed of economic adjustment.

The speed of adjustment is, essentially, a matter of social time preference (once the costs and gains of slower and faster adjustment have been properly estimated). It can be reliably ascertained only by the market in which preferences are expressed individually after a subjective calculation based on an assessment of the information on the economic costs of different adjustment alternatives. This information is dispersed through the market, each agent in it knowing its own adjustment possibilities and alternatives. Information of this kind cannot be easily centralized for government use. The politically expressed preference will always be for an adjustment slower than that which the market is tending to bring about, for the simple reason that politics is where people seek refuge from the economic rigours of the market. Once government declares its ability and competence to control the speed of adjustment, the nature of the democratic political process is subtly changed. The costs of a slower as against a speedier adjustment are to be reckoned in terms of the resources embodied in reserve holdings, increased uncertainty, and future income foregone. To get an objective assessment of these costs through a political process, by which different groups are trying to unload on others the costs they would have to bear themselves, is simply impossible. To pose the alternative of more international liquidity or more protectionism amounts to saying that the groups on which economic adjustment impinges are unwilling to adjust, and that governments stand ready to finance that unwillingness *without regard to social welfare cost.* They can do that either from reserves and international borrowing, or by income transfers from the society at large to the particular groups in question (which is what protection amounts to). If to this assumption about government behaviour a proposal is added for creating reserves by printing paper or making entries in international accounts, nobody should be surprised if the illusion spreads that the refusal to adjust can be financed costlessly: another version of the foredoomed effort to get something for nothing.

To say that increased liquidity is needed in order to avoid increased protection thus tells us what the additional liquidity will be used for. Neither of the alternatives represents a viable course for policy in the long run. It is even doubtful whether in the 1960s, with rapid economic growth facilitating all sorts of adjustments, governments of the core countries were actually willing to grant the degree of protection required. In any case, it would have been more productive to focus the debate on the true alternative: more liquidity or speedier adjustment. But it is easy to be wise after the event.

An element that helped to decide the debate was the growing belief in the existence of a trade-off between inflation and unemployment. It produced an acute dissatisfaction in the US government with the role of supplier of international currency. It was felt that the role condemned the American economy to an unfavourable point on the Phillips curve.

It remains an intriguing question, calling for some research effort, whether it was just an accident of timing that the deficit of US balance of payments, which in the preceding two decades fluctuated within the limits of $3½ billion to zero, exploded to $10 billion in 1970, the year at the opening of which the first distribution of $3.4 billion of SDRs took place. Somewhat smaller smounts of SDRs were distributed at the beginning of each of the two following years, in which the US balance of payments deficit amounted to $30 and $10 billion, respectively, before receding to lower figures. Between 1961 and 1969 annual increases in the dollar value of world reserves ranged from -0.5 to 5.5 per cent, with an average for the period of 2.8 per cent a year. In the next four years, the annual rates of increase were, respectively, 18.5, 40.8, 21.5 and 15.7 per cent.

At the very least, the episode shows that what governments manage to agree on need not always work in practice, and indeed may have the effect of locking them into activities which only make things worse and which, because of the agreement laboriously arrived at, they are unable to reverse in time. A useful initiative of academic economists was published in 1964 under the title *International Monetary Arrangements: The Problem of Choice*. The 1970–2 episode also seems to suggest that in matters of the institutional order regulating their economic interdependence, societies may have much less deliberate choice than social scientists are willing to believe.

CONTRAST BETWEEN THE TWO CYCLES AND THE RESIDUAL PROBLEM

The parallels between the disintegration of international order in the 1930s and the disintegrative tendencies at work now are so many, so obvious and so widely discussed that it seems more important to focus, in conclusion, on one difference between the two processes, and with its help to define the problem that remains.

The financial collapse of 1931 and all that followed may be attributed to insufficient cooperation among the economic, and mainly monetary, authorities of the four countries representing the cornerstones of the system. In our time, by contrast, disintegration continues amidst virtually uninterrupted negotiations, coordination meetings and professions of belief in close economic cooperation. Indeed one aspect of the trouble is that the words 'economic cooperation' have come to cover so many different things that they serve more as an incantation than to convey intelligible meaning. When, for example, governments meet at the highest level to agree how much oil individual countries are to consume or import, we must fear that the capacity of nations to cooperate is again being overloaded.

Sustained cooperation is possible only within a framework of rules derived from a cogent, compelling theory which, moreover, must be backed by abundant historical experience. It is ultimately destructive of the comity of nations when their governments arrogate to themselves, and then try to negotiate with other governments, decisions for which there is no theory to guide them and which only the free market, under the conditions of price level stability, can make in an optimal fashion. Under such conditions, the negotiations for joint decisions will, inevitably, be bruising; and when policies are agreed they will be impossible to implement. So the apparent difference between the two periods is only superficial. The underlying similarity is the lack of requisite theory or, perhaps, the governments' inability to act according to the right theory. After all, the best knowledge that contemporary economics can offer on the management of a floating exchange rate régime was already available in the 1920s; and the evolution of the IMF's practice went off on the tangent of a wrong theory when a more correct one was also available.

The residual problem is a variant of the old one: rules or discretion. In its old form, it has been answered. Rules are, by and large, safer than discretion. But we cannot imagine an automatic system relying solely on rules. The problem is how to recognize the necessary minimum of discretion, and how to make sure that only this minimum will be exercised.

NOTES

1 *Experiments in State Control,* Oxford: 1924, pp. 1–3.
2 *The Age of Roosevelt,* vol. 1, *The Crisis of the Old Order,* London: 1957, p. 42.
3 Churchill is reported to have said of the Armistice in 1918: 'A new set of conditions began to rule from eleven o'clock onwards. The money cost, which had never been considered by us to be a factor capable of limiting the supply of the armies, asserted a claim to priority from the moment the fighting stopped.' P. B. Johnson, *Land Fit for Heroes: the planning of British reconstruction 1916–19,* Chicago: University of Chicago Press, 1968, p. 299.
4 For this reason, J. K. Galbraith is to economics what J. P. Sartre was to moral philosophy: men who never got over a unique and brief moment in their youth, when economic and moral decision making seemed exhilaratingly easy.
5 Actually, the dismantling of quantitative restrictions and embargoes was almost complete by the end of 1919. A general trend towards their reintroduction started with the rising monetary instability in the early 1920s.
6 See D. C. North, 'Structure and Performance: The Task of Economic History', *Journal of Economic Literature,* September 1978.
7 M. Friedman and J. A. Schwartz, *A Monetary History of the United States 1867–1960,* Princeton: Princeton University Press, chapter 6, esp. pp. 279–87.
8 *ibid,* p.284.
9 J. Viner, *International Economics,* Glencoe, Ill.: The Free Press, 1951, p. 132.

10 See H. Feis, *The Diplomacy of the Dollar*, Baltimore, 1950, and the earlier remarks on French capital market controls.
11 In July 1929. The US industrial production series is seasonally adjusted, the German is not. It cannot be excluded that production declined earlier in Germany than in the US.
12 C. P. Kindleberger, *The World in Depression 1929–1939*, London: Allen Lane, 1973, p. 126.
13 Viner, op.cit., p. 285.
14 Quoted by J. S. Mills, *The Genoa Conference*, London, 1922, p. 12.
15 This process of industrial adjustment was more successful than general economic opinion may be willing to acknowledge. The development of the economy after the resumption of the gold standard is generally painted in unrelieved black. A revision of this view should begin with the acknowledgement that the average rate of GDP growth in 1924–9 was, at 2.3 per cent, more than double that recorded in 1899–1913 (1.1 per cent) and the difference in average growth of labour productivity between the two periods was much larger still.
16 Kindleberger, op.cit., pp. 210–11.
17 'Internal Credit Policy – and International', in Henderson, H. D., *The Interwar Years and Other Papers*, Oxford: 1955, pp. 81–90.
18 President Roosevelt's Inaugural Address, 4 March 1933.
19 His message to the London Economic Conference, 3 July 1933.
20 The history of economic thought of our century would be much enriched by a systematic account and interpretation of Keynes's almost life-long preoccupation with the Germany economy, from reparations to 'a somewhat comprehensive socialization of investment' (*The General Theory*, p. 378) getting under way in 1934, and finally to his fascination with Schachtian trade and payments policies.
21 London: Harrap, 1965.
22 Schlesinger, op.cit., vols. II and I.
23 In a letter to Dean Acheson, July 1941: 'My strong reaction against the word "discrimination" [from Acheson's context, the reaction actually was against the word "non-discrimination'] is the result of my feeling so passionately that our hands must be free . . . the word calls up, and must call up – for that is what it means strictly interpreted – all the old lumber, most-favoured-nation clause and all the rest which was a notorious failure and made such a hash of the old world. We know also that it won't work. It is the clutch of the dead, or at least the moribund, hand. If it was accepted it would be cover behind which all the unconstructive and truly reactionary people of both our countries would shelter.' Acheson, *Present at the Creation*, New York: Norton, 1969, p. 30.
24 Included in his *International Economics*.
25 In this respect, it is difficult to see the point of the insistent criticism of US planners by R. N. Gardner, in his otherwise valuable book *On Sterling-Dollar Diplomacy*, for 'excessive emphasis' on, or even 'obsession' with, economic issues at the cost of the political ones. The economic issues were, at that stage, the only ones that could be foreseen

with any degree of reliability. It is not so much that it was difficult to make equally detailed plans for the unforeseeable political conditions; in concentrating on the economic issues and deliberately separating and shielding them from the more volatile political ones, the State Department planners were implementing one of the most important lessons of the inter-war period.

26 Viner in November 1946: 'We have already made loans and undertaken commitments amounting, since the termination of Lend-Lease, to over $13 billions' (*International Economy*, p. 337).

Comments by
Mića Panić

A few years ago, in his Shell Lecture, Dr Tumlir observed that: 'It is not that nations never learn. They do. But then they forget again.'[1] It is this concern that the world has forgotten important lessons learned in the past and that, consequently, it may be heading towards economic disorders of the kind experienced during the inter-war period that provides the underlying theme of his paper presented to this conference.

The main aim of the paper is to 'review the development of thought about foreign or international economic policy over the last seven decades'. It is intended, therefore, to be an essay in 'the history of ideas', describing and analysing 'the understanding exhibited by governments at different stages of this period'.

As Dr Tumlir sees it, there has been a 'growth in influence, throughout the period' of what he calls 'the planning ideology', but what he believes to be more correctly described as 'the politicization of the economy'. This growth has not been 'linear'. Indeed, 'the planning idea' has undergone a number of 'qualitative transformations' over the period. What concerns the author is that 'the involvement of the political authorities in the structure of the economy necessarily slows down the economic adjustments required for stable progress. Fundamentally, the planning idea as such is but a reflection of a growing reluctance to adjust.' This, in turn, 'poses an insoluble problem for maintaining international economic stability, or order'.

The great similarity between the 1930s and the 1970s, in Dr Tumlir's view, is 'the lack of requisite theory or, perhaps, the governments' inability to act according to the right theory'. The problem confronting policy makers is an old one: 'rules or discretion'; or, perhaps more accurately, in my opinion, a continuous quest for the 'correct' blend of the two. Whatever this blend may be, Dr Tumlir obviously believes that discretion should be kept to 'the necessary minimum'.

The paper raises a number of issues of a general nature which are of considerable importance for economic policy at the moment and it is to some of these that I shall confine my comments. I should also add that the comments will be restricted to trade – or, more precisely, some of the factors which are likely to influence developments of the international order in that particular area – because financial aspects of the international system will be discussed in another session.

It is a great pity, for instance, that the 'planning idea', to which the paper attaches considerable importance, is not defined more precisely. Does this refer only to direct government involvement in resource allocation, income distribution and trade? Or does the concept extend more widely, to embrace government economic policies in general? The questions are relevant because the paper includes Keynesian macroeconomic demand management among the factors which have given 'impetus to the idea of national planning'. The reason for this is apparently that 'Keynesian' policies are not neutral in their effects on resource allocation. True, but the same can also be said of, for example, a tight monetary policy applied in conditions of flexible exchange rates and rigid real wages and prices, i.e. the conditions which prevail today. An 'accommodating' monetary policy will not be neutral in its microeconomic effects either. Should governments, therefore, also renounce any responsibility for monetary policy? If we are not prepared to go that far and if, at the same time, we believe that government policy tends to affect adversely the international adjustment process then a definition of the limits of government involvement is obviously a matter of considerable importance for economic policy. In other words, how much discretion, in which area and why? Or, if 'rules' are preferred, what sort of rules? Rules, like laws, make sense only so long as they are widely accepted or can be effectively enforced. As coercion rarely produces lasting solutions, any 'rules' formulated now have to be consistent with economic, social and political conditions at the end of the twentieth century. Rules based on hypothetical models of behaviour or utopian ideals are more likely to create chaos than to prevent it.

The acceptable 'mix' of the market vs. government involvement in the adjustment process is of crucial importance if one takes the view which is rather different from that put forward in the paper: namely, that it is not the government involvement which necessarily slows the adjustment process down but, instead, the slow adjustment process in the private sector which is likely to increase the size of government involvement. This proposition seems, in fact, to be consistent not only with experience over the past seventy years but with that over the last four centuries.

Economic policies are invariably influenced by social, political and other considerations because, as J. S. Mill pointed out:

for practical purposes, political economy is inseparably inter-twined with many other branches of social philosophy. Except on matters of mere details, there are perhaps no questions, even among those which approach nearest to the character of purely economic questions, which admit of being decided on economic premises alone.[2]

It is for these reasons that there is nothing new, of course, about 'the politicization of the economy'. It is always with us.

What may and does change is the extent to which governments become involved directly in the production and distribution of material wealth. There are many factors which influence this involvement – prominent among which is likely to be a country's relative position in the world economy. The leading countries are more likely to adopt 'liberal' domestic and foreign trade policies than the countries which are trying to attain such an advanced stage of economic development. Moreover, changes in countries' relative economic strength are also likely to lead to changes in their preference for 'liberal' policies. Given the difference in size of the required structural adjustments and income re-distribution that the two groups of countries have to undertake, this is hardly surprising. Inevitably, therefore, certain problems and policy responses appear to keep recurring in history, though never in exactly the same form.

Normally, these repetitions take a long time. What is remarkable about the period since 1950 is that – thanks to the unprecedented speed and scale of change – the world economy has moved from serious structural imbalances to a period during which most industrial countries were able to reconcile their internal and external economic objectives, and back to a position of even more serious

184

structural imbalances. And all this has taken place in less than thirty years! What is more, a number of important changes in the world economy over the period have left us without ready-made solutions.

The sheer increase in world industrial capacity since 1945, improvements in the standard of living, and the growth of population have combined to create extremely serious supply problems in the area of energy and certain other natural resources. The rate of growth of output which these resources will allow for some years – without a sharp acceleration in the rate of inflation – seems to be significantly below the rate of growth of productive potential of industrial countries in conditions in which there are no natural resource constraints, i.e. the rates that they were able to sustain until the mid-1970s. The unemployment problem is different therefore from what it was in the inter-war period, or in the 1950s. To solve it on a lasting basis nothing less seems to be required than either the discovery of cheap, non-polluting forms of energy, or a substantial restructuring of the world economy. Both take a long time to accomplish. In the meantime, many countries may be threatened by, or actually experience, social and political upheavals.

What makes these threats particularly serious is the concentration of economic power in large production and bargaining units, which has taken place over the past thirty years – each determined at least to maintain its share of total income. As the growth of the world economy and incomes slows down, the conflict of interests is bound to increase.

Moreover, it is this increase in the degree of concentration of economic power which was bound to disappoint, as it has done, the great hopes placed in the early 1970s in flexible exchange rates as the policy instrument which would enable deficit countries to reconcile external and internal equilibria. Instead, few structural problems were avoided, few jobs saved and the inflationary problems became even more serious.

It can be safely assumed that in the circumstances in which macroeconomic policies appear to have only a limited scope for correcting serious structural imbalances, governments will became obliged, whether they like it or not, to participate more actively in resource allocation and income distribution. The intention will be to facilitate the required changes or, if this is impossible, at least to prevent outbreaks of open conflicts within their borders. Normally, the extent to which they are likely to take into account international consequences of these actions will depend partly on the countries' size and, thus, the extent to which they have to specialize internationally; and, partly, on the existence of international financial arrangements which will enable them to adjust without increasing the possibility of internal conflicts. I will not say more about the latter for reasons that I gave earlier. There is little doubt, however, that the international monetary system is in a more precarious state now than it was, thanks to the United States, for the first twenty years after the Second World War.

Yet so far there has been no return to widespread protectionism of the 1930s type. There seem to me to be two reasons for this. First, the futility of such an exercise on a worldwide scale is still remembered. This is less true, of course, of large countries, but they have to take into account possible political repercussions in the rest of the world of such an action on their part – and risks to their own security that political upheavals abroad might create. Second, the authorities in industrial countries, in particular, realize that their economies are far more integrated now than ever before and not just in the sense that they are each others' best customers. A relatively small number of multinational corporations, banks and financial institutions have spread and diversified their activities globally to such an extent that it is not clear whether any industrial country can extricate itself from this highly complex net without great economic and social costs. In other words, a return to self-sufficiency is much more difficult now than it was fifty years ago. Consequently, greater international cooperation and coordination of economic policies than in the past seems inevitable. Past experience of such efforts in the absence of a dominant economic power may not be promising. But there is no realistic alternative. The important question is, therefore, what form should such coordination take to enable the international economic order to function properly – under the conditions likely to prevail over the next few decades?

Finally, when shall we economists begin to take much more seriously into account some of the great economic and social changes which have occurred over the past thirty years, anticipate their consequences and, thus, integrate them fully into our analytical models and policy advice? Judging by past experience, it usually requires a considerable shock to the system to bring about a significant change in perception of what the major problems are and how they might be tackled. The problem may have occurred in the past, but the world will have changed since then and the policies applicable at the time may be of little use, even counter-productive, now. The same is true also of institutions. Hence, the changes in perceptions will eventually bring about institutional changes needed to solve the problems.

NOTES

1   J. Tumlir, *National Interest and International Order,* London: Trade Policy Research Centre, 1978, p. 3.
2   A. W. Coats (ed), *The Classical Economists and Economic Policy,* London: Methuen, 1971, pp. 11–12.

Discussion

Sir Bryan Hopkin saw the international economic order as part of a wider conception of orderly economic conditions that would promote the wishes and welfare of the world's inhabitants. Did Dr Tumlir include in his understanding of the idea such things as full employment (or some approximation to it), stable prices, and progress towards greater economic equality (or the elimination of gross economic inequality) between nations? These were not, so to speak, legislated for in advance as essential components of the concept. Was it assumed that they would arise out of the working of economic forces in a free market?

Sir Bryan saw various factors disturbing the international economic order. First there were inflationary tendencies in the world economy. These encountered resistance which generated unemployment and slowed down growth. Second, there was the energy shortage: the gradual drying up of the cheapest and best available energy supplies and the exploitation of the shortage by the countries exporting oil. A third factor was the obstinate inequality between nations in capital supply, knowledge, and consequently productivity. These were the principal forces creating economic disorder in the world. It was not enough in face of them to have a free flow of goods and capital between countries in response to market forces. If any set of international economic arrangements was to be described as 'order', it should be such as to provide means and incentives, fostering rather than hindering a successful attack on the forces producing disorder.

Floating exchange rates did not strike him as a symptom of disorder: the strength of the forces making for inflation within different countries was so divergent that one could not hope to have a system of fixed exchange rates. On the other hand, he did regard it as an important symptom of economic disorder that there was a lack of any strong policy aiming at the collective rescue of third world countries from their extreme poverty by way of aid and through appropriate trade and financial arrangements. Another symptom of disorder was the lack of provision, either of a positive kind or through dispensation from rules of international behaviour, to help countries struggling with chronic industrial weakness or inflationary pressures. Such a lack arose from too *simpliste* a set of rules created to defend the system of free trade and capital flows.

Dr Tumlir saw at least three different levels of economic order. There was first the reality: stable money, orderly transactions, etc. Then there were the institutional arrangements enabling the situation to be orderly: law, rules. In addition there were ideal conceptions of order, or a theory of it, the general vision of how things hang together. His paper concentrated on the institutional arrangements which were certainly not perfect. In his conception, the international economic order consisted of arrangements for trade and monetary transactions among the 'core' countries of the world. These countries were relatively few in number: the United States, Canada, the EEC, Japan, Brazil and India, for example. If the commercial and financial relations between these countries were orderly, stable and non-discriminatory then the world had all it needed or could ever achieve, in the way of a working order: adjustment to changing global conditions of supply and demand would proceed promptly and the relatively poor countries would have the stability of trading conditions needed for accelerated development.

With his conception of order went a certain conception of sovereignty. In the 1920s, countries had entertained a very primitive view of sovereignty as absolute freedom and power. But sovereignty, Dr Tumlir argued, is highly vulnerable, both to lateral pressure from other countries and, most of all, to domestic pressures from various organized interest groups. These erode the effectiveness and eventually the legitimacy of government through the continuous grant of privileges to pressure groups. Sovereignty is in need of protection and this is one of the main functions of international rules. These may define the rights and obligations of sovereign powers to one another but thereby they also protect sovereignty (i.e. the power and authority to govern) from domestic pressure groups by calling in aid an international obligation.

Professor Meade went back to the conceptions of international order in debate at the end of the Second World War. Lord Keynes had been attracted by the idea of introducing Schachtian controls at the end of the war but 'gently persuaded' to espouse a more liberal view. Once he turned his mind to the building of a new international order in consultation with the United States he suggested a scheme of things which Professor Meade felt to be still valid. One liberal view of things might embrace a single international money, free trade and free capital movements but this was not Keynes's approach. He had reservations about free capital movements and he did not believe in an international currency. He insisted on the need for separate monetary authorities with power to alter their exchange rate, primarily because there were separate national labour markets. It was primarily for national governments to maintain price stability and full employment. But they should seek to maintain free, multilateral trade and the international economic order should be designed to secure this. It would be a misrepresentation of what Keynes tried to do (and killed himself doing) to lay stress on the special provisions that he wanted to add to deal with the post-war transition. The United Kingdom was in an extremely weak condition at the end of the war with heavy external debts and very low exports. There was also a need to guard against the possibility that the United States might return to the pre-war pattern of behaviour. Hence the scarce currency clause and the retention of exchange control and the right to impose import restrictions. These special provisions should not take from Keynes's contribution as an architect of a liberal international economic order.

Professor Meade went on to discuss GATT and the way in which it might be possible to go about restoring the international order. The system had worked well for a time after the Second World War. A multilateral payments system was developed, discrimination was reduced, trade became freer and exchange control and other restrictions were relaxed. All this was in the context of full employment and an expanding world economy, and it was arguable that the success of the system rested on Keynesian demand management policies, or at least on *expectation* that these policies would be pursued. The breakdown of the system was due to a variety of factors: excessive pressure of demand; wage-push; the oil crisis; and the wholehearted efforts of governments to control inflation through tight money policies. Nevertheless the system had not collapsed and the volume of trade, in contrast to the early 1930s, had held up remarkably well, and capital movements, as Dr Lamfalussy's paper pointed out (p. 203), were freer than at any time since the war.

What was now needed was an effort by national governments to restore full employment, combined with reasonable price stability. Professor Meade said he was still a believer in GATT and in a Keynesian international order. In reply to Mr Tumlir, he said he was in general in favour of maintaining freedom of capital movements.

Professor Erik Lundberg said that there were many fundamental similarities between the inter-war situation and the one we were now facing, in particular the under-utilization of capacity and the problem of unemployment, with inflation the main new feature. With excess capacity and heavy unemployment it was impossible to have a working international order and that was as true of the developing countries as of the developed world. Without an injection of additional demand, there would be an inevitable protectionist imbroglio with subsidies and import restrictions.

Professor Tom Wilson pointed to the difficulties introduced into economic management by large and sudden changes in the terms of trade. It was an old and familiar theme in economics that countries should try to expand together, but there were difficulties. In 1972–3 the major economies had moved up together, with disastrous effects on primary product prices. There could be too much synchronization as well as too little: perhaps what the world needed was 'an optimum degree of stagger'.

Lord Roberthall said that in the 1950s things had been relatively straightforward. There was an expanding world economy in which the United States had pursued a policy of benign neglect that made adjustment easier for her trading partners. Officials from different countries met frequently and since they talked the same language found it possible to reach a common understanding. But there was now more and more reluctance to adjust and although a period of unemployment offered a greater opportunity for adjustment it also increased resistance to it. The things we had to adjust to were getting worse and worse. One set of adjustments was being forced on us by OPEC but at least, taking the long view, these adjustments were desirable and necessary. Indeed, oil prices were not rising fast enough. The successful industrializing countries of the third world were also forcing adjustment on us while the others had adjustment problems of their own: reduced aid, trade restrictions and increasing population were strangling their development. On top of this, was the absence of any real international economic order and polarization between the two great powers.

Professor Giersch started by linking the discussion with the earlier session on demand management. Why was it that demand management had worked well in the 1950s and 1960s but not in the 1970s? The high rate of growth in output after the war had been helpful to price stability and the pattern of demand was clear to suppliers as everyone tried to regain the pre-war standard of living. The United States had pursued policies enabling other countries to enjoy export-led growth: it had been a kind of 'black hole' in the world economy. Output could expand along clear lines in the countries that were catching up on the basis of undervalued currencies: and with the expansion went rising productivity. This in turn facilitated demand management by making it possible to meet the expectations of labour in higher real wages. Trade ceased to be an engine of productivity growth, however, when the dollar shortage came to an end. Other factors sustained high productivity growth in Europe in the 1960s: the inflow of technology and capital from the United States and the continuing process of economic integration within the EEC. The role of the United States had not, however, been taken over by anybody else and indeed Europe seemed to be too inflexible to adjust to the expansion of the newly industrializing countries as the United States had done in the post-war period. These countries should be allowed to have undervalued currencies (in the sense of being able to offer lower prices on world markets for standardized commodities) like European countries after the war. On this basis they would then be able to displace such goods in the markets of the advanced countries while these countries adjusted their economies, by switching to new products. The countries catching up would need more capital goods and these could be supplied by the advanced countries which might well be in surplus.

Sir Alec Cairncross said that the discussion should be linked not only with the session on demand management but also with that on industrial policy. It could be argued that as trade became freer in the 1950s and 1960s governments had tried to feed some grit back into the system through industrial policies. So far as these were directed towards encouraging specific industries they were the modern equivalent of tariff protection. The experience of the post-war years also bore out the contention (which one could find in Treasury papers in 1944–5) that full employment was a far more important contributor to welfare than the removal of trade restrictions and could be a pre-requisite to their removal. The rapid growth in international trade after the war in spite of formidable restrictions of all kind was evidence of the importance of a high level of demand. Estimates of the economic gains from joining the EEC pointed to the same conclusion: an increase of the order of 1 per cent in GNP seemed to be all that could be hoped for by removing barriers to trade with the Community.

Dr Tumlir had spoken of an 'optimum rate of adjustment'. But it was natural to ask: 'adjustment to what?' Was it ever possible to know where we were really heading? In the 1950s there had been a recognizable order dominated by the United States and adjustments had been made to a general dollar shortage with American collaboration. Now what was called for was an adjustment to OPEC and an energy shortage. The world was facing enormous imbalances that made previous deficits look tiny and the resulting accumulation of debt would not, as in the 1950s and 1960s, be dissolved by international inflation. The outlook was complicated by the emergence on world markets of a number of countries that were in the process of industrialization. Although they had not yet become very substantial suppliers of industrial products they were likely to penetrate the domestic markets of other countries much more deeply in the next decade, and this would intensify the difficulties of adjustment. Some countries in the third world – particularly those in South-East Asia – would encounter other difficulties. For them the boom in the Middle East had served as a 'black hole' (to use Professor Giersch's phrase) in the late 1970s but after the second oil crisis they were unlikely to enjoy a further large increase in exports to OPEC countries or in workers' remittances from them. The whole problem of balance of payments adjustment was far more difficult than at any time since the 1930s.

Dr Tumlir, in summing up, commented first on the thinking of

British and American economists at the end of the Second World War. The Americans had concluded that the United States was too large to conduct its domestic economic policies without regard to their repercussions abroad, while the British thought that some degree of isolation from the United States was necessary for stable development.

The fundamental similarity between the 1920s and the 1970s lay in the fact that in neither period was international debt backed by productive assets. In the 1920s there was a continuous inflow of American capital into Europe that ceased in 1928–9 before the Wall Street crash. The Hawley-Smoot tariff a few years later aggravated the disequilibrium. In the 1970s OPEC capital was financing balance of payments deficits in a somewhat similar way – financing not new investments through which oil importing economies would adjust to the new situation but, in a large part, consumption, the postponement of adjustment.

It was no doubt possible to imagine an international order under which heavy investment in the third world by the developed countries assisted the adjustment process but this was hardly conceivable in a world suffering from two-digit inflation and rising protectionism. Under these conditions it was very difficult to elaborate bankable investment projects. It was all very well to insist on the importance of full employment but was the absence of inflation any less important? The rules of international behaviour are simple enough. They require the leading countries to maintain stable purchasing power of their currencies and, if they feel they have to protect national industries, to keep that protection low, stable and non-discriminatory. As long as these conditions were fulfilled, the world economy was expanding. But this was not the achievement of the rules as such. Since there is no enforcement mechanism behind them, they can only assist governments in maintaining the conditions of economic order.

6

Changing attitudes towards capital movements

ALEXANDRE LAMFALUSSY

This paper is in three parts. The first reviews the main changes that have occurred in government attitudes towards international capital movements since Bretton Woods. The second presents a few global figures on capital movements, especially since the first oil price explosion. The third discusses some current issues related to capital movements.[1]

OFFICIAL POLICIES AND ATTITUDES WITH RESPECT TO INTERNATIONAL CAPITAL MOVEMENTS

A basic principle of the Bretton Woods agreement was the obligation laid on member countries to avoid restrictions on their current external payments as soon as they were satisfied that their general balance of payments situation would permit them to do so. With respect to restrictions on international capital movements, however, the Fund agreement took a very different view. In Article VI of the agreement it is laid down that members may exercise such controls as are necessary to regulate international capital movements but that no member may exercise these controls in a manner which will restrict payments for current external transactions. Beyond this general principle, Article VI also says that a member may not use the Fund's resources to meet a large or sustained outflow of capital and that the Fund may request a member to exercise such controls to prevent such use of the Fund's resources.

Why did the Fund agreement treat capital controls so differently from restrictions on current external transactions, with the former regarded as a legitimate permanent instrument of economic policy and the latter only as transitional or temporary measures? Alec Cairncross himself has pointed out, in his paper on 'Control of long-term international capital movements' prepared for the

Brookings Institution in 1972 that it is 'very difficult to point to any official statement in which they (i.e. capital controls) are justified at any length'. Certainly no such justification is given in the Fund agreement, although Article VI could be taken as implying that the Fund's resources would be unduly taxed if they were used for the financing of large or sustained capital outflows from a member country.

Very briefly, I believe that the reasons for which the principle of capital controls was admitted can be grouped for analytical purposes under two headings. Firstly, there are external reasons. These have to do with the maintenance of balance of payments equilibrium and exchange rate stability. In the par value system established at Bretton Woods, capital controls can be seen as one instrument of exchange rate stabilization, in situations where capital movements are threatening stability. Secondly, there are internal reasons for which countries may wish to impose capital controls, either temporarily or on a more permanent basis. One of the reasons is in order to avoid long-term capital outflows that are seen as resulting in a loss of resources to the economy, or in misuse of those resources. As Alec Cairncross says in his Brookings paper, this argument for capital controls is usually associated with an emphasis on the importance of domestic investment in promoting economic growth at home. In that connection he remarks that 'it is undeniable that heavy foreign investment can reduce domestic investment and that this may have undesirable consequences'. Another domestic reason for imposing capital controls is that short-term movements of capital may interfere with a country's ability to control its own domestic monetary situation. This argument came to the fore in the last years of the Bretton Woods era, when the flight from the dollar caused very large inflows of funds to a number of countries in Europe, as well as to Japan.

Having summarized the Fund's philosophy with respect to capital controls and the main reasons why such controls are resorted to, I want to sketch the evolving attitudes and practices of governments in this field during the Bretton Woods era. In doing so I shall restrict myself to the policies of the main industrial countries, i.e. those of the Group of Ten. Before coming to them, however, I should say that the acceptability of capital controls, both in principle and in practice, does not mean that a large measure of freedom for international capital movements is not seen as being of benefit both to the individual countries concerned and to the world economy in general. I do not propose to state the general arguments for this view and shall simply take them for granted. I shall, however, in the last part of my paper try to set out the reasons why in present circumstances international capital movements have a vital part to play in the working of the monetary system.

Looking back at the evolution over the Bretton Woods era of the Group of Ten countries' official attitudes and practices with respect to capital movements, three main phases can be distinguished. The first phase covered the period after the Second World War, in which many wartime exchange control practices continued to be used. During the second phase, which extended roughly over the decade from the early 1950s until the early 1960s, there was a progressive, although by no means uniform, relaxation of capital controls. In the third phase, which began in 1963 and continued until the demise of the par value system a decade later, capital controls – particularly on international financial flows – were increasingly resorted to in an attempt to limit the very large balance of payments disequilibria which emerged in the United States and some other major industrial countries, and which were associated with very large disequilibrating capital movements, i.e. movements of money out of deficit and into surplus countries on a scale that presented great difficulties for the maintenance of exchange rate stability.

During the first years of the Bretton Woods era, in the post-war phase, virtually all countries, including those of the Group of Ten, made use of rather comprehensive controls on external transactions, both current and capital. At that time, only the United States and (with minor exceptions) Switzerland allowed freedom for capital movements, and in the Swiss case there was a separate exchange market for such transactions until 1949. As the foreign exchange shortages of the post-war period disappeared, the general movement towards greater freedom for current external transactions was accompanied by a relaxation of capital controls. The degree to which this happened varied from country to country, depending partly on the balance of payments situation and partly on countries' philosophies with respect to the desirability of allowing domestic savings to be used for foreign investment.

By the late 1950s, two groups of countries could be distinguished in Europe. On the one hand there were Germany, Switzerland and Belgium where complete freedom for capital movements existed, with such transactions being channelled in Belgium through a separate exchange market in which the price of foreign exchange differed very little from the 'official' exchange rate. On the other hand there were the remaining European countries, in which the process of liberalizing international capital movements had been concentrated mainly on outward direct investment, with other types of capital outflows still controlled more or less strictly, either on an administrative basis or through separate exchange markets in which residents could buy and sell foreign exchange, often at considerable discounts on official exchange rates.

A partial, and important, exception to the general trend towards more liberal practices in the 1950s was the tightening of restrictions on the international use of sterling by the UK banking system. This development, in combination with greater freedom for the UK and other European banks to engage in foreign currency business with non-residents and with interest rate ceilings on bank deposits in the United States, led to the emergence of the Euro-dollar market in the late 1950s, based in London and other European financial centres.

The extent to which the philosophy of greater freedom for capital movements had progressively taken hold may be seen from two events which occured in 1961. The first of these was the adoption by the Executive Board of the IMF in July 1961 of a decision in which it was said that the use of the Fund's resources for financing capital transfers was not precluded. This decision may be said to have been based on a recognition of the need, explicitly referred to a year later in the preamble to the General Arrangements to Borrow, 'to enable the International Monetary Fund to fulfil more effectively its rôle in the international monetary system in the new conditions of widespread convertibility, including greater freedom for short-term capital movements'.

Later in 1961, the Council of the OECD adopted a Code of Liberalization of Capital Movements. Article I of the Code laid down that members should progressively abolish between one another restrictions on movements of capital to the extent necessary for effective economic cooperation, with the rider added that they should endeavour to extend these measures of liberalization to all members of the International Monetary Fund. Although many OECD members entered reservations with respect to the liberalization of particular types of transactions, the Code amounted to a declaration of principle by the developed countries of the world in favour of a wide measure of freedom for capital movements.

In retrospect 1961 may be seen as the year in which the momentum of the post-war movement away from capital controls reached its first peak. In fact, even before the two events to which I have just referred, the first instance had occurred of new controls being applied in order to stem disequilibrating capital movements. This was in Germany, just before the March 1961 revaluation of the Deutschemark, when sales of domestic money-market paper to non-residents, as well as the payment of interest on non-residents' DM balances at German banks, were for a time prohibited.

But the real turn of the tide came in 1963 when the US authorities began to control exports of domestic capital in order to reduce the balance of payments deficit. The first such measure, taken in July 1963, was the imposition of an interest equalization tax (IET) on US residents' purchases of foreign bonds and equities. This was followed in 1965 by the extension of the IET to bank loans to non-residents with maturities of over one year, together with 'voluntary' measures to restrain short-term foreign lending by banks and other financial institutions, as well as outward direct investment by US corporations. Later, in 1968, mandatory guidelines for foreign direct investment were introduced.

While these various measures had some effect in restraining capital exports from the United States, by partially cutting off the US financial market from the rest of the world they also provided a strong impetus for the expansion of international capital movements through other channels. US non-bank corporations circumvented the limits on domestically-financed foreign direct investment by raising money for this purpose in the Euro-bond market, while US banks responded to the restrictions on foreign lending from their domestic offices by rapidly expanding their participation in the Euro-dollar market. Thus, the US capital controls were an important factor in the development of an international substitute for the US capital and banking markets, just as UK exchange controls in the mid-1950s had been a factor in the emergence of the Euro-dollar market in London.

Besides the United States, other Group of Ten countries that made extensive use of capital controls to limit outflows of funds in the latter part of the 1960s included the United Kingdom, France and Italy. In these countries, however, such controls had been a long-standing instrument of economic policy and their use at that time therefore represented, at most, no more that a broadening and/or tightening of well-established techniques.

Much more striking – indeed, no less striking than the conversion of the US authorities to controls on exports of resident capital – was the extent to which the retreat from liberal attitudes towards capital movements included the use by countries in balance of payments surplus of a variety of techniques – some market-oriented, some purely administrative – in order to control inflows of capital. The German authorities, following their first resort to such measures just before the March 1961 revaluation, used them on and off during the 1960s, and from 1968 onwards until well after the end of the Bretton Woods era they became a permanent feature of German policy. Similar controls were also employed in the final years of the par value system by Switzerland, Belgium and the Netherlands and, after the suspension of dollar convertibility in August 1971, by Japan and (for a time) even the United Kingdom.

The most important of these controls on capital inflows were those applied to the banking sector, through which a large part of the disruptive movements of funds were intermediated. Types of banking controls included: ceilings on overall net inflows through the banking system; reserve requirements on banks' deposit liabilities to non-residents; the prohibition of interest payments – or, in a few instances, the imposition of negative interest – on non-residents' bank deposits; and, as an extreme measure, an outright ban on any increase in the total of such deposits. A rather different sort of measure that may be mentioned under this heading is the conclusion of outward swaps of dollars from central banks to their commercial banks, in order to offset central bank purchases of dollars from the market.

Controls imposed on inflows to the non-bank sector can be grouped under two headings: those that restricted residents' borrowing abroad; and those aimed at inward portfolio or other non-bank investment by non-residents. Under the first heading come direct administrative controls on residents' foreign borrowing; the German 'Bardepot' arrangement, which was in essence a reserve requirement imposed on such borrowing; and controls on advance conversion of export receipts into domestic currency. Under the second heading come restrictions on purchases of domestic securities or real estate by non-residents.

Finally, some countries responded to disruptive inflows of capital by introducing separate exchange markets in which capital transactions took place at freely fluctuating exchange rates.

The role of destabilizing capital movements in the currency crises that led to the breakdown of the Bretton Woods par value system was the subject of a report to the Committee on Reform of the International Monetary System and Related Issues (usually known as the Committee of Twenty) established by the Board of Governors of the IMF in 1972. The Committee set up a technical group on destabilizing capital movements, with the following terms of reference: 'To define and analyse the sources of disequilibrating capital flows and the technical problems involved in the use of measures to influence them, whether applied nationally or to Euro-currency markets, and of measures to finance and offset them.' The views expressed in the technical group's report, submitted to the Committee of Twenty in May 1973, may be taken as representing the broad trend of official thinking on capital controls at the end of the Bretton Woods era.

The group recognized that the most important cause of disequilibrating capital movements in the late 1960s and the early 1970s had been the existence of major external imbalances and the inadequate working of the adjustment process. It therefore looked to improvements in these areas as the major prerequisite for reducing the scope of such movements. At the same time it took the view that even with a better working of the adjustment process disequilibrating capital flows could continue to occur from time to time, for a variety of reasons. These could include differences in national interest rate levels, inflation differentials, sudden shocks to market confidence and changes in the currency composition of international portfolios. Furthermore the group expressed the view that the potential for disequilibrating flows of funds had been increased by the secular growth of related magnitudes, such as international trade and domestic monetary aggregates, as well as by the tendency which became evident during the last years of the Bretton Woods era for the exchange market to typecast certain currencies as being prone to upward or downward secular movements in their exchange rates.

The group concluded that capital controls would have a role to play in influencing future disequilibrating movements of funds. However, it agreed that there should be no need for countries to maintain such measures on a permanent basis, that such controls had not in the past, and could not in the future, be expected to be fully effective in withstanding massive flows of funds between countries, and that beyond a certain point such controls could damage both international trade and beneficial international movements of capital.

As regards capital controls imposed unilaterally by individual countries, the working group took the view that these should be so designed and operated as to avoid creating problems for other countries. In addition, it suggested that the use of such controls might be governed by a code of conduct, such as that adopted by the OECD in 1961, and that such a code might be supplemented by consultations in the IMF and other international and regional organizations designed to produce over time a body of case law in this area. These suggestions were never taken any further.

The Committee of Twenty's technical group also considered the question, already discussed at length in 1971–2 by the central banks of the Group of Ten countries, of possible coordinated action to influence flows of funds through the Euro-currency market. As in the G-10 discussions, there were two views on this subject. A few countries, who believed that the Euro-currency market had added significantly to the volume of disequilibrating capital flows, favoured cooperative official regulatory action in the Euro-market – the main proposal being that reserve requirements be imposed on banks' Euro-currency liabilities. However, most members of the group, including the representatives of developing countries, questioned both the desirability and the likely effectiveness of such measures.

Thus, the end of the Bretton Woods par value system coincided with what may be considered to have been a reaffirmation by the membership of the Fund of the broad philosophy about capital controls embodied in Article vi of the Fund agreement.

During the period since the introduction of floating exchange rates in March 1973 two main developments have occurred in the Group of Ten countries with respect to capital controls. Firstly, a number of major countries have removed, or further liberalized, controls on capital movements. In the United States the Nixon administration removed in January 1974 the various controls over outflows of resident capital that had been built up from 1963 onwards. This decision enabled the domestic offices of US banks to play a major part in the financing of payments deficits during the rest of the 1970s, and between end-1973 and end-1980 the total external claims of US banks increased from $26.8 billion to $203.7 billion. In the United Kingdom existing exchange controls of all kinds were removed in October 1979. In both these instances, renunciation of the use of capital controls stemmed from the adoption of free-market economic philosophies. It may be added that the present British government's free-market approach has been applied also to controls on capital inflows,despite the very large size of inflows into sterling over the past two years and their unfavourable consequences, via the upward pressure they have exerted on the exchange rate, for the level of activity in the UK economy. A third major country which removed restrictions on capital movements was Japan where a thoroughgoing relaxation of exchange controls took place in late 1980. Finally, it may be mentioned that in 1980 the controls on inward and outward movements of capital between France and the rest of the world, both for direct investment and other purposes, were relaxed.

The second main feature of developments with regard to capital controls since March 1973 has been the continued use of this instrument by a number of G-10 countries in an effort to limit disequilibrating inflows of capital. In particular Germany, Japan and Switzerland, all of which countries experienced very strong upward pressures on their exchange rates from time to time after March 1973, with these pressures originating partly in portfolio shifts out of the dollar into their currencies, made use until fairly recently of the sorts of controls on inflows of capital that were employed in the late 1960s and the early 1970s to 'defend' existing par values. However, when the surpluses on these countries current account balances of payments disappeared in 1979, following the second round of major oil price increases, the authorities in all three countries responded by progressively removing controls on capital inflows.

Finally, I may mention the resumption in 1979–80 of the earlier central bank debate on the advantages and disadvantages of international banking capital movements and of the pros and cons of a coordinated approach to controlling the growth of international banking aggregates. In 1979–80 the G-10 central banks' discussion of this subject originated in a proposal by the US authorities that the monetary authorities of all G-10 countries should impose reserve requirements on their banks' Euro-currency liabilities including those of their banks' foreign branches and subsidiaries worldwide. To summarize even the main points of this debate, which covered all macroeconomic and prudential problems seen by different Group of Ten countries as arising out of the tremendous growth in the rôle of the international banking system during the 1970s, as well as a variety of possible ways of dealing with them, would take me beyond the bounds of this paper. I will simply remind you that the Governors did not agree that a case for co-ordinated control of international banking aggregates in general, or of Euro-currency aggregates in particular, had been made out. On the other hand, they did decide to strengthen their regular monitoring of international banking developments from the macro-economic point of view and to pursue further the efforts thay have been making since the mid-1970s to reinforce prudential supervision of international banking.

To sum up the present situation in the Group of Ten countries with regard to capital controls, I would say that there is now a greater freedom for capital movements than at any time since the end of the Second World War. How long this second 'peak' will last is, however, an open question. Many countries retain a pragmatic attitude towards the use of capital controls, particularly in situations where disequilibrating capital movements take place, and the arrangements for monitoring international banking developments which the central bank Governors of the Group of Ten countries set up in April 1980 do not exclude the possible use of capital controls, either by individual countries or even on an internationally co-ordinated basis, should circumstances arise which would make such action desirable.

CHANGES IN THE PATTERN OF INTERNATIONAL CAPITAL MOVEMENTS

In the second part of the paper I shall deal briefly with some of the most important features of international capital movements since the Second World War. In doing so, I shall devote most attention to what has happened since the 1973 oil price increases, so as to set the scene for a consideration of current issues relating to capital movements.

During the years following the war the main feature of international capital movements was the outflow of funds from the United States, shown in Table 1. During the three years 1946–8 total net outflows of US capital averaged $3.5 billion, most of which was on government account, and in addition there were average annual outflows in the form of US government transfers (excluding military grants) of $2.7 billion. Subsequently, during the years

Table 1 US capital movements 1946–61[1] (in billions of US dollars)

	1946–48					1949–55					1956–61				
	Total	Europe	Canada	Latin America	Other countries[2]	Total	Europe	Canada	Latin America	Other countries[2]	Total	Europe	Canada	Latin America	Other countries[2]
US capital (net)	-3.52	-2.53	-0.01	-0.38	-0.60	-1.30	-0.18	-0.42	-0.33	-0.38	-4.12	-0.70	-0.95	-0.99	-1.47
Private	-0.77	-0.14	-0.01	-0.32	-0.28	-1.04	-0.13	-0.41	-0.24	-0.26	-3.30	-0.79	-0.95	-0.69	-0.87
Government	-2.75	-2.38	—	-0.06	-0.32	-0.26	-0.05	—	-0.09	-0.12	-0.82	0.09	—	-0.30	-0.61
Foreign capital (net)															
Long-term[3]	-0.20	-0.16	—	—	-0.05	0.21	0.15	0.02	0.01	0.02	0.49	0.37	0.03	0.03	0.07
Short-term	-0.61	-0.23	-0.25	0.13	-0.25	0.99	0.57	0.09	0.14	0.20	1.62	0.83	0.27	0.07	0.45
Total capital flows (net)	-4.33	-2.92	-0.26	-0.25	-0.90	-0.10	0.54	-0.31	-0.18	-0.16	-2.01	0.50	-0.65	-0.89	-0.95
Memorandum item:															
US Government transfers (excluding military grants)	-2.67	-1.28	-0.01	-0.03	-1.35	-2.81	-1.96	—	-0.04	-0.80	-1.88	-0.40	-0.02	-0.13	-1.33

Source: US Department of Commerce, Balance of Payments Supplement 1961.

Note: Owing to rounding figures may not add to totals.
1 Annual averages.
2 Including international institutions.
3 Including foreign commercial credits.

1949–55, total US capital outflows fell off to an annual average of $1.3 billion, most of which were private capital outflows; but over the same period US government transfers to the rest of the world, which for this period included Marshall Aid transfers, continued at about the same level as before. In the second half of the 1950s the picture changed considerably. Total US capital outflows averaged over £4 billion during the years 1956–61, and 80 per cent of that figure represented private capital outflows, the annual average of which trebled between 1949–55 and 1956–61, to $3.3 billion. In response to the economic recovery in Europe, average annual net outflows to European countries rose between these two periods from $130m. to $790m.

In the immediate post-war period, the rest of the world was reducing its claims on the United States. But as the balance of payments and reserve positions of other countries began to improve, there were net movements of foreign capital into the United States. During the years 1949–55 these amounted on average to $1.2 billion, rising to over $2 billion a year during 1956–61. The largest part of these inflows were on short-term capital account and they included the rebuilding of monetary reserves in the rest of the world, to a large extent in Europe.

From the early 1960s onwards there was a large increase in the volume of G-10 countries' capital movements, accompanied by a widening of imbalances on these countries' capital accounts and by a change in the composition of capital flows, with the growing importance of the Euro-currency market.

As regards the growth in the volume of capital transactions, the sum of annual changes in US foreign assets and liabilites (excluding official reserve items) rose between 1960 and 1966 at a compound rate of 9½ per cent per annum, between 1966 and 1973 by 16½ per cent and during 1973–79 by 21 per cent. This was part of a general tendency for international financial transactions to expand faster than the turnover of international trade. In Germany, total monthly sales and purchases of foreign securities by German residents, and of German securities by non-residents, expanded more than ten times between 1960 and 1979, while the total of foreign loans received and extended by the German private non-bank sector expanded nearly fifteen times over this period. By contrast, the turnover of Germany's merchandise trade transactions grew sevenfold during the same twenty-year period.

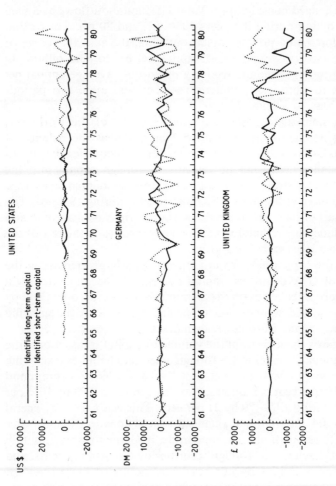

Figure 1   *Quarterly long and short-term capital movements (net) 1960–80 (in billions of national currencies)*

Source: BIS data bank

The widening of capital account imbalances which accompanied the increase in the volume of international capital transactions is illustrated for the United States, the United Kingdom and Germany, in Figure 1. The annual average of Germany's net balance on identified capital account went up from about $0.5 billion during 1960–6 to $3.8 billion during 1967–79, that of the United Kingdom from $0.6 billion to $2.8 billion and that of the United States from $5.3 billion to $13.6 billion. Moreover, with the exceptions of direct investment and long-term official capital, practically all other transactions, and in particular short-term capital movements, exhibited a growing volatility.

I may add that the US programme of capital controls was most effective in the banking sector. During the five years 1960–4 new gross lending to non-residents by US banks had averaged $1.4 billion; during the following five years this average came down to $100m. In the area of portfolio investment, US purchases of foreign securities came down from an annual average of about $1 billion in 1962–3 to one of about $0.8 billion in 1964–6. The controls had little effect on the level of US direct investment abroad, although they did shift part of its financing to foreign sources.

The change which began to occur from the early 1960s onwards in the composition of international capital flows, and in particular the growing importance of international banking flows, appears most clearly from the growth of the Euro-currency market. The earliest data collected by the BIS on the size of the market refer to March 1963, when the total external assets and liabilities in five foreign currencies[2] of commercial banks in eight European countries[3] amounted to some $9 billion each. By end-1966 these totals had reached $20 billion, by end-1969 almost $60 billion and by end-1973 nearly $190 billion.

I now come to the impact on international capital movements of the oil price induced shifts in the world balance of payments structure since 1973. Very briefly, this impact was threefold: firstly, the volume of net capital movements between capital-exporting and capital-importing areas increased dramatically in response to the size of post-1973 current external surpluses and deficits; secondly, the OPEC countries replaced the Group of Ten as the main net suppliers of capital to the rest of the world, i.e. the shortfall of national savings over domestic investment in the oil-importing world was met by the OPEC countries' oil price induced savings surplus; and thirdly the financing of post-1973 payments deficits took place to a large extent through the banking systems of the G-10 countries, with the result that flows of banking funds became the most important single element in international capital movements.

The figures shown in Table 2 illustrate the first two of these developments. As regards the size of net capital transfers, the annual average of net outflows from the capital-exporting areas of the world roughly quadrupled between 1967–73 and 1974–7, from under $10 billion to nearly $40 billion. As regards the pattern of capital movements, the Group of Ten countries virtually ceased to be net capital exporters in 1974–7, and their place as main source of net capital exports was taken by the OPEC countries. Net capital inflows to the non-oil developing countries more than trebled, in current dollar terms, between 1967–73 and 1974–7, and inflows to the smaller developed countries rose from little more than $1 billion a year to a magnitude not far short of that recorded by inflows to the non-oil developing countries.

Table 2   *The pattern of global capital flows 1967–80*[1]
(in billions of US dollars)

	1967–73[2]	1974–7[2]	1978	1979	1980
Group of Ten countries and Switzerland	−8¼	−¾	−22	22¼	50½
Smaller developed countries	1½	17¾	10½	13	23
Non-oil developing countries	6	21	22½	36	51
Oil-exporting countries	−1¼	−38	−4½	−68	−116

Source: IMF and OECD, various publications.

1   Total capital flows including monetary movements (i.e. current-account positions with the sign reversed); minus signs indicate capital export.
2   Annual averages.

In 1978, when the OPEC current external surplus was temporarily reduced to very small proportions, the Group of Ten re-emerged briefly as the main net exporters of capital; but then in 1979–80, OPEC became the sole source of net capital exports with, in 1980,

Table 3 Estimate of some regional capital flows between the main group of countries 1974–9
(in billions of US dollars)

	OPEC Inflows	OPEC Outflows	Group of Ten and Switzerland Inflows	Group of Ten and Switzerland Outflows	Smaller developed countries Inflows	Smaller developed countries Outflows	Non-oil developing countries Inflows	Non-oil developing countries Outflows
OPEC								
banks[1]	...	...	108	−53	...	...	...	...
other	...	...	108		...	...	15	...
Group of Ten and Switzerland								
banks[1]	53	−108			78	−36	119	−60
other	...	−108			63	...	105	...
Smaller developed countries								
banks[1]	...	...	36	−78			...	...
other	...	...	...	−63			...	...
Non-oil developing countries								
banks[1]	...	...	60	−119	...	...		
other	...	−15	...	−105	...	...		
I Total identified capital flows (net)	...	−178		−106	105	...	179	
II Total capital flows (= current account with sign reversed)	...	−224	105	−1	94	...	143	...
III Residual (II − I)	...	−46			...	−11	...	−36
Memorandum item								
IV Change in gross official foreign exchange reserves (− : increase)		(−54.8)		(−88.6)		(−9.6)		(−47.2)

Source: IMF, OECD various publications; BIS 50th Annual Report.
1 Includes branches of US banks in the principal offshore countries.

capital imports into the developed countries being significantly larger than flows to the non-oil developing countries.

The main features of post-1973 international capital movements, and in particular the channels through which the surplus funds of the OPEC countries were passed to finance the deficit countries, can be seen in Table 3. While the available statistics give only a rough idea of what happened, they nevertheless bring out two important points. Firstly, that the Group of Ten countries were both the recipients of nearly all the capital outflows from OPEC countries during 1974–9 and the suppliers of almost all the capital imports into the smaller developed countries and the non-oil developing countries. Secondly, almost half of the total OPEC outflows took the form of deposits with banks in the Group of Ten countries (including the branches of US banks in the principal offshore centres of the Caribbean and the Far East). These banks, in turn, supplied about 40 per cent of the identified net inflows of funds into the capital-importing areas. This financial intermediation involved a significant degree of maturity transformation, since OPEC deposits with Group of Ten banks were generally at short-term, while nearly 60 per cent of the banks' on-lending to the capital-importing areas carried maturities of over one year.

In passing, I may draw your attention to the extent of the increase in world exchange reserves that was associated with this pattern of capital movements. The memorandum item at the bottom of Table 3 shows the actual increases in the combined exchange reserves of the different groups of countries during 1974–9. For each of these groups except the Group of Ten, the increases in exchange reserves correspond fairly closely to the residuals in Item III of the table, which represent the differences between each group of countries' balance on identified capital account and its total balance on capital account, represented in the table by its current external balance with the sign reversed. For the Group of Ten countries, however, the $105 billion residual shown in Item III represents the accumulation of reserve liabilities to the rest of the world – an accumulation which, as the memorandum item shows, was accompanied by a considerable increase in Group of Ten countries' own combined exchange reserves.

The preponderant part played by banking flows in post-1973 capital movements can be seen from the enormous growth of the international banking aggregates. At the end of 1973 total gross external assets, in both domestic and foreign currencies, of the BIS reporting banks[4] amounted to about $300 billion. By September 1980 that figure had grown to about $1225 billion, an increase of over $900 billion. Net of double-counting arising out of the redepositing of balances between Euro-banks in the reporting area, the banks' total assets rose during the same period from $170 billion to $775 billion. These are compound annual growth rates in excess of 20 per cent.

Table 4 shows the main movements of funds through the BIS reporting banks since end-1973. OPEC countries supplied $88 billion net to the banks, their deposits rising by $142m. while their new borrowings from the banks totalled $54 billion; almost mirroring this inflow, non-oil developing countries took up a net amount of $83 billion from the banks during the same period, gross new borrowings of $146 billion being partly offset by a $63 billion increase in deposits. In addition developed countries outside the reporting area and Eastern European countries took up net amounts of $48 and $37 billion respectively from the banks, against which can be set an inflow of $80 billion to the banks from sources inside the reporting area.

CURRENT ISSUES RELATING TO CAPITAL MOVEMENTS

Let me now turn, in this third part of my paper, to some of the current issues relating to capital movements – and at the same time adopt a more normative, and hence more provocative, approach. What is the state of the debate concerning freedom for capital movements? Should capital flows be unrestricted or should they, on the contrary, be subject to controls?

An appropriate starting point is the recognition that at no time in the course of the last fifty years – except perhaps for a short period around 1961 – have Western industrial countries allowed a degree of freedom for capital movements comparable to that prevailing today. How should this state of affairs be viewed?

There are several possible ways of trying to answer this question. One would involve a detailed development of the very brief analysis presented in the concluding pages of the first section, with a view to exploring whether the liberalization of capital movements that has occurred in a number of countries since 1973, and which seems to have been motivated by reasons that varied from one country to another, has nevertheless been the product of the working of some

Table 4 Estimated external lending and deposit-taking of banks in G-10 countries and Switzerland and of the foreign branches of US banks in the Caribbean area and the Far East 1974 to September 1980[1]
(in billions of US dollars)

	Changes						First nine months 1980	Amounts outstanding September 1980
	1974	1975	1976	1977	1978	1979		
Use of funds for lending to:								
Developed countries outside the reporting area	8	9	14	16	16	15	11	116
Eastern Europe	4	8	7	4	11	7	2	53
Oil-exporting countries	2	4	10	11	18	8	1	65
Non-oil developing countries	16	15	18	11	24	35	27	182
Reporting area[2]	20	4	21	33	41	65	69	359
Total	50	40	70	75	110	130	110	775
Sources of funds:								
Developed countries outside the reporting area	2	1	2	6	15	10	5	69
Eastern Europe	1	–	1	–	2	4	–2	12
Oil-exporting countries	30	10	12	14	6	36	34	152
Non-oil exporting countries	7	–	13	12	16	12	3	92
Reporting area[2]	10	29	42	43	71	68	70	450
Total	50	40	70	75	110	130	110	775

1 Foreign branches of US banks in the Bahamas, Cayman Islands, Panama, Hong Kong and Singapore.
2 Net of double-counting due to redeposits between reporting banks.

strong, common historical forces. To raise, and *a fortiori* to answer, a question of this kind would go far beyond the scope of this paper. Another approach would entail discussing on a more theoretical level the traditional list of pros and cons concerning freedom of movement for capital. I propose to look at the problem in an intermediate and more pragmatic way, viz. in terms of whether there are any workable alternatives to the current policy stance. My answer to that question is that while freedom of movement for capital does not make the world an easy place to live in, in the present circumstances all other alternatives would be likely to create even greater problems.

The principal argument underlying this statement divides into two parts. The first is that the world is today living, and will in the foreseeable future continue to live, with current account payments imbalances of a nature and size that cannot be 'adjusted away' except at the cost of a worldwide depression – and even then the outcome would be uncertain. The second is that official financing can simply not be organized on a scale sufficient to finance these unavoidable current account imbalances – and it could even be argued that it would not be desirable for official financing to take on such a monumental task.

The most important and most visible kind of imbalance I have in mind is, of course, the OPEC surplus. In 1980 this surplus amounted to some $110–120 billion and it is expected to remain at around $80 billion in 1981, despite a sluggish world economy. I am fairly confident that in the long run the process of real adjustment to the higher price of oil will tend to erode this surplus, at any rate to a significant degree. The process of adjustment, in the form of both energy conservation and the substitution of other sources of energy for oil, has already begun, and is gathering momentum. But in a medium-term perspective, and excluding the assumption of a persistant worldwide depression, OPEC countries seem to possess sufficient monopolistic power to prevent the real price of oil from falling, and even to make it rise somewhat. It would therefore seem realistic to assume that the OPEC surplus will persist in the coming years, although it will fluctuate in line with the international business cycle.

The second source of global imbalance which is likely to persist is the current-account deficit of the non-oil developing countries. That these countries as a group will have to run a deficit if they wish to develop seems to be a fairly obvious proposition: how else could real resources be transferred to them? However, the growing burden of indebtedness they are assuming is in itself serving to raise the likely level of their deficit. A rapidly increasing part of their external debt has been contracted on the basis of floating interest rates, thus eliminating the benefits that borrowers have hitherto derived from inflation. It may be added to this that since the most likely scenario for the international world in the coming year is one of relatively sluggish economic development and the maintenance of a strong anti-inflationary stance, with heavy reliance on restrictive monetary policies, developing countries will not be able to count on a strong increase in exports (either in volume or price terms) or on a major decline of interest rates in the main financial markets to relieve their balance of payments situation.

Last but not least, we shall have to expect current-account imbalances among the industrial countries. With cyclical desynchronization, varying inflation rates, changing policy stances and differing attitudes towards external shocks, it is certain that the oil deficit will not be distributed evenly among the major industrial countries. The plausibility of this forecast is underlined by the dramatic shifts that have occurred over the last three years in the current accounts of the United States, Japan, West Germany, France and Italy. Even if these intra-OECD imbalances are not to be sticky – indeed, there is a good case for adjustment policies that would avoid their becoming so – they would add to the global financing problem. Implicit in this statement, of course, is the view of adjustment – a view inspired by my strong belief that undesirable 'overshooting' of rates has occurred during the last few years.

The contribution of official flows of funds to the financing of these current-account imbalances should be encouraged and is indeed likely to increase over time. The intra-OECD types of disequilibrium are an obvious candidate for official financing out of reserves, provided, as has been assumed, that these imbalances do not (or at any rate are not encouraged to) become sticky. But on the basis of recent experience it seems safe to predict current account swings of a size such that the authorities will be neither able promptly to implement successful adjustment policies nor willing to let their reserves take the full strain of current account movements. Private capital flows will have to play some role in the financing of such movements.

Reserve movements can, of course, do little to help to finance the global oil deficit and the transfer of real resources towards the non-oil developing countries. Official financing would in these instances have to take the form of bilateral or multilateral aids and loans, and loans by the World Bank and the IMF. There is no doubt in my mind that capital flows via all these channels ought to be increased. But two remarks are in order here. First, the scale of non-oil developing countries' payments deficits from both the sources that I mentioned above is such that official financings of these kinds, all combined, will certainly be inadequate to cover them. Secondly, even if it were possible to make the implausible assumption that the resources of the two Bretton Woods organizations could be extended so as to play a quantitatively decisive role in the financing of these deficits, it would seem legitimate to question the wisdom of any such extension. Given the unavoidable political influences that would come to dominate these institutions in such an event, it is more than doubtful that they could play an optimum role in promoting the real adjustment process that is needed to re-establish a better long-term balance in international payments. But this in any case seems such a remote possibility that the real problem in the near future is more likely to be the inadequacy of official financing, rather than any excess of it.

The conclusion is, therefore, that private capital should be left free to flow to finance these deficits. But will it flow in the right directions? If it does so, what kind of capital will it be? And will it be able to play a positive role in helping real adjustment? None of the answers I propose to these questions will be clear-cut − but they will together lead to the final conclusion that there are a few alternatives open to Western industrial countries.

To begin with the first of these questions, there were periods in the last seven years when some of the hard-currency countries had to cope with excessive capital inflows; and there were also periods when some of the deficit countries' reserves losses − or the depreciation of their exchange rates − were aggravated by capital outflows. But these negative experiences with disequilibrating capital movements, i.e. those which aggravate, instead of offsetting, current account imbalances, have to be set against the substantially positive role played by the international banking system in the process of recycling the OPEC surplus, as evidenced by the figures given in the second part of this paper. There seem to be no overwhelming reasons why banks should be expected to put an end to their intermediation between surplus and deficit countries – although there are good reasons for regarding banks' massive intervention in recycling as less than optimal.

One of these reasons is clearly that the non-conditional nature of the bulk of bank lending does not necessarily induce real domestic adjustment. On the one hand, banks may over-finance a current account deficit and thus in fact delay the adjustment process; on the other, when they refrain from lending, their caution will not necessarily push the country concerned towards the optimum kind of domestic investment policy that would be required for the purpose of long-term adjustment. Thus, it may be argued, they lend either too easily or, when they suddenly stop lending, they force debtor countries to embark on drastic domestic adjustment leading to the collapse of investment. But what is the alternative? Clearly, long-term direct investment, combined with wise conditional financing by official institutions, would be preferable. But direct investment is inhibited by a number of political factors, and is unlikely to be undertaken on a massive scale in the coming years. Therefore, the second-best solution is to arrive at a combination of bank lending and official financing – in the hope that an appropriate balance between the two will keep official financing wisely conditional and bank lending sufficiently prudent.

The word 'prudence' recalls another legitimate concern about the close involvement of banks in international capital flows. This involvement has produced a gradual, but over the years substantial, increase in the 'international' portion of the banks' balance sheet and, correspondingly, in the 'international' sources of their profits. In the uncertain, politically unstable and economically risky world in which banks operate, this may indeed be regarded as less than optimal from a prudential point of view, especially if account is taken of the gradual (and almost universal) decline of the banks' capital base. This is another reason for favouring an improved balance between official and banking financing flows, on the assumption that greater involvement of official institutions will lead to better adjustment and hence to greater stability in the world economy.

Let me conclude by emphasizing once again the pragmatic nature of these propositions. I have deliberately refrained from discussing the pros and cons for freedom of capital movements in a factual vacuum, and have come out, in present circumstances, in favour of this freedom. But circumstances may change: for the world economy as a whole, and even more likely, for individual countries. Keeping in line with my pragmatic approach, I could easily see situations in which capital controls would be warranted.

NOTES

1   I wish to thank Mr M. G. Dealtry and Dr G. Baer for their considerable help in the preparation of this paper.
2   US dollars, sterling, Deutsche Mark, Swiss francs and Netherlands guilders (to which French francs, Italian lire and Belgian francs were subsequently added).
3   Belgium-Luxembourg, France, Germany, Italy, the Netherlands, Sweden, Switzerland and the United Kingdom.
4   Commercial banks in the Group of Ten countries and Switzerland and the branches of US banks in the offshore centres in the Carribean area and the Far East.

Comments by
Chris Allsopp

Alexandre Lamfalussy presents us with a broad summary of the issues relating to capital movements and capital controls. In three parts, his paper surveys the changing attitudes to capital movements since Bretton Woods; outlines important examples of the practice of capital controls; indicates the way the underlying flows have changed in the disturbed 1970s, and takes a wise look at current issues. He ends up with a pragmatic conclusion. Having argued that capital movements are now freer than at any time since the war, he describes himself as 'in present circumstances, in favour of this freedom'. But, he notes 'circumstances may change; for the world economy as a whole, and even more likely for individual countries.' He can easily envisage situations in which capital controls would be warranted.'

I was struck, in reading this paper, that it covers not one issue, but many. To start with, even looking narrowly at capital controls there are many types of control which have been applied from time to time. Are we talking about long-term direct investment; about short-term speculative movements? From a practical point of view, the differences are great, and moreover the reasons, good or bad, that have been used to justify them vary also. This was well recognized by Sir Alec Cairncross when he gently chided academics as follows:

> But there are a great many types of control, and they vary in effectiveness. Such is the perversity of a world of control that the more they are needed, the less likely they are to work. For this reason, it is usually much more important to form a view about which controls will work and which will not than to consider the precise grounds on which it would be useful to have workable controls. But again, thanks to the perversity of these matters, most writers about economic controls dwell almost exclusively on questions of justification and high principle and leave in obscurity the more interesting question: how successful have controls been in accomplishing their declared purpose?

But what is their purpose? There is a standard list of purposes or objectives for capital controls. Broadly, however, it is possible to identify two rather different concerns — resource allocation reasons of one kind or another, and reasons which are fundamentally to do with national economic sovereignty. Although the concern over resource allocation is probably older, it is the second concern arising from the conflict between national objectives and the powerful international forces of integration which is the dominant one in the post-war period. Lamfalussy concentrates on this; which means that the subject of capital controls has to be seen in the widest possible context: in the context, that is, of the international monetary system, the exchange rate regime, and indeed the general economic performance of the world economy. It will be no surprise if discussion on Lamfalussy's paper focuses on the experience of floating exchange rates, and the problems of international recycling rather than on capital controls. Indeed, his own conclusion seems to be based on the not uncommon view that in present circumstances there is no alternative to some sort of managed floating, rather than on any attitude to capital controls as such.

Many will agree with Lamfalussy that there is no practical alternative to floating in the 1970s. Beyond this, however, it does seem to me that there is a serious question which has not received sufficient attention. Most of the discussion of capital controls in the literature is in the context of fixed exchange rates; and a standard view used to be that floating exchange rates would remove the need for controls. But controls have gone on into the period of floating. Do they have a place in a floating exchange rate world? What might that place be? Lamfalussy argues that, in practice, there is now greater freedom of capital movements than ever before. But it is possible to take issue with him on the significance of this change. Can it not simply be explained in terms of a reversal of roles after the second oil shock of 1979–80? Countries, such as Germany, with a traditional problem of inflows and a set of institutional arrangements appropriate for quelling them, now need to attract capital. The UK, with elaborate mechanisms for preventing outflows, suddenly found itself by an accident of geology with a positive need to encourage overseas investment. Thus it can be questioned whether these recent developments do really reflect any fundamental change in the attitude of national governments to capital controls. Certainly there is still an interesting practical issue as to what role capital controls might play in a floating exchange rate system. Before going into this I want to make a few observations in the experience of controls over the longer term.

Over the whole of the post-war period, Lamfalussy identifies various phases. The first, covering the immediate post-war years, saw a continuation of many of the wartime exchange controls on current account transactions. The second phase, until about 1963, was accompanied by a progressive relaxation of controls. After that, the progressive breakdown of the Bretton Wood system was marked by increasing experimentation and reliance on controls in a vain attempt by both inflow and outflow countries to shore up the system. Most of the evidence on the inadequacy and inefficiency of controls comes from this period. In the 1970s controls continued to be used, but recently there has been, as noted, a substantial relaxation.

There is little doubt in my mind that one of the reasons behind the retention of controls in the early post-war period was the fairly explicit pursuit of an international economic order which would be conducive to national economic autonomy (or sovereignty) in the reconstruction period. Capital controls were seen as one element in this. Far more important in practice, of course, were other elements: Bretton Woods itself, the temporary acceptance of continued trade restrictions etc. And, pre-eminently, it was the attitude of the

United States to problems elsewhere that allowed the international economy to get started on the extraordinary period of growth that continued into the 1960s.

Whilst the objective of national economic sovereignty was important in the first period, it was the experience of autonomy in national economic management that was the feature of the second. For reasons which are not very well understood – but which have been much discussed in this conference – developed countries managed in the 1950s and the first half of the 1960s to reconcile (to a surprising degree) internal and external objectives. This period saw the progressive dismantling of controls (both on trade and as Lamfalussy notes, on capital flows) as well as the development of a false optimism about economic management (reaching its peak in the mid-1960s in America). It has already been suggested at this conference that one of the surprising things about this period was that there was not greater conflict between high employment and price stability. Another surprise is that the Bretton Woods system worked far better than might have been expected, particularly as the practice was more rigid than the intention.

Clearly, the lack of uncontrollable inflation was itself one reason for the maintenance of the par value system; another was the de-synchronization of the international business cycle, and the attenuation of the transmission mechanism. I want to add a third-supply side flexibility in Europe and Japan. As many of these countries became 'undervalued' (or at least highly competitive in international trade) they were able to turn this advantage into rapid growth rather than awkward payments surpluses. Indeed the incipient surpluses were a powerful stimulus to expansion both directly, and through their effect on government policy. For a time, rapid growth in Europe and Japan was a substitute for external parity changes. In my view it is no accident that the German surplus became a problem when Germany slowed down for supply side reasons in the 1960s; nor that Japanese position only became problematical when she too slowed down.

As the Bretton Woods system came under strain the move back towards controls on capital movements was inevitable. Lamfalussy has described the bewildering variety of arrangements: a testament if any were needed, to the ingenuity of bankers and officials in the face of short-term problems. With hindsight, they were bound to fail; which means that the significance of that particular failure for the future of capital controls is not very great. The question remains: do capital controls have a place under floating exchange rates in the disturbed conditions of the 1970s and 1980s?

One thing is clear. The move to floating was not accompanied by a sudden increase in domestic economic sovereignty. The external constraint binds as never before, though it is more clear that its origin lies in domestic inflationary pressure, and in price and wage rigidities. Thus the sovereignty argument for controls may be as strong as ever. What is more, Lamfalussy expresses his 'strong belief' that undesirable 'over-shooting' of rates has occurred during the last few years and subscribes to the view that it is not desirable to let exchange rates bear the full brunt of adjustment. If this is accepted, there is a case for intervention, and capital controls are one way of intervening.

The question, it seems to me, comes back to Sir Alec's: would capital controls work, and would they work better with lower cost than alternatives? Lamfalussy can 'easily see situations in which capital controls would be warranted'. It would be nice to know more about what these circumstances are. But perhaps the choices can be illustrated by looking briefly at the situation of the United Kingdom.

The recent rise in the UK's exchange rate has been accompanied by a marked deterioration in external liquidity as well as by the familiar effects on competitiveness and on unemployment. The reasons for the rise are not well understood. There is certainly a possibility that it represents an example of overshooting. Suppose it were desired to lower the exchange rate − or to prevent its rise. Would inflow controls (such as the interest equalization tax proposed by Dornbusch)[1] be the appropriate policy? Would intervention on the exchanges be better? Or should the general stance of policy change? My preference would be for the latter − but let us suppose that were ruled out. The disadvantages of inflow controls are well known. The disadvantage of intervention is chiefly that it tends to interfere with domestic monetary policy. I just want to make two comments:

i the possibilities of sterilization may be greater than commonly supposed. Much historical evidence suffers from the same defect as evidence on capital controls; it is derived from the fixed exchange rate period when the market could indulge in one-way

bets. More research, theoretical and empirical, on the possibilities of sterilization under managed floating would appear to be required;
ii the major conflict appears to arise because an intermediate target (£M3) is made the centre piece of economic policy. With a concentration on the ultimate targets it would appear that intervention would have many advantages over controls of any kind.

Generally, it does seem to me that there are advantages in managing floating exchange rates by intervention rather than by capital controls (I take it for granted that countries will, in practice manage their exchange rates to some degree). That said, however, there is no reason why both techniques should not be used. In practice there are limits to intevention (obviously if the pressure on the exchange rate is downward, but also if inflows are very large) and intervention may need to be supplemented from time to time by capital controls. They are likely to be most useful where the pressure is expected to be temporary, or where time is needed to make other, more fundamental adjustments. If treated as temporary expedients in dealing with volatile capital movements then, as Lamfalussy says, it is easy to envisage circumstances in which they would be warranted.

Finally, let me return to the theme of Dr Tumlir's paper, the theme which underlies this one too: economic sovereignty. The scale and mobility of capital flows had clearly limited the scope of independent domestic action by nation states. Some have drawn the conclusion that the appropriate domain for policy action has moved to the international economy, and that the only hope (and a faint one at that) lies in international consensus, and international co-operative action. I believe this to be only partly true. The experience of the various summit meetings in the 1970s has illustrated the almost insuperable difficulties in agreeing joint strategies. But the immediate post-war years provide an example of cooperation of a different kind; cooperation in pursuit of an international order conducive to national sovereignty. As twenty years of rapid growth testify, it was enormously successful. The question is whether that kind of operation is possible under the conditions of the 1980s, and without the benign influence of a dominant country at the height of its power.

NOTES

1   See S. M. Dornbusch, Memoranda on Monetary Policy, Evidence to the Select Committee on the Treasury and Civil Service, House of Commons 1980.

Discussion

Dr Tumlir, opening the discussion, said that several speakers at the Conference had implied that the inter-war period demonstrated the failure of laissez-faire policies. Nothing could be further from the truth. The concept of laissez-faire was very difficult to define. It might be used to describe the economics of the nineteenth century but, as applied to the inter-war period, it was, to say the least, puzzling. Governments were prominent actors in capital markets. Many of them used exchange controls and, as for trade, they all practised a high degree of protectionism of an increasingly discriminating character. It was indeed a period of laissez-faire for *governments*: the intervention both in the domestic and in the international economy was virtually unlimited. In contrast to this, there were in the 1950s and 1960s internationally agreed rules which limited the discretion of governments and made their policies stable and predictable. It was this that enabled the private sector to develop strength and flexibility.

Lord Croham said that capital controls like other forms of control (for example, incomes policies) had to be applied in individual cases and it was here that the difficulty lay. Whatever the theory of the matter, the failures and distortion of the control came to light when the specific circumstances of individual cases had to be faced. One could find plenty of general justifications for control over capital outflows. Outflows would leave less capital for investment at home; they would help to build up the economies of competitors abroad; they were a form of tax avoidance by the rich; and so on. These justifications often amounted to an attack on the capitalist system. There had been controls also over capital inflows for which the justifications urged included the need to stop a foreign take-over of British industry or a rise in the exchange rate. Throughout the period when the controls were in force there had been a constant argument over their effectiveness. With exchange control there had been a variety of different kinds of sterling account. For security sterling and for investment currency there had been

223

separate markets with fluctuating rates. Nobody had known how effective the controls had been. But what was quite clear was that there was always a gap while new measures of control were under discussion before legislation could be prepared and passed into law. This gave time for capital to move in anticipation of such legislation so that when it came into force there might be little further movement to block. There could be large movements of capital within a short period that amounted to avoidance of the controls and that could not be prevented because of the interlocking of the monetary system with other systems. Of course, if what was sought was a particular statistical result, that could be achieved by manipulation of the figures. Fixing objectives in terms of statistics might merely distort the statistics; it was easier to control statistics than what went on in the real world and the links between the two were continuously changing.

Lord Croham said he was sceptical of the case for reintroducing capital controls. To do so would serve only to revive the idea of using controls as a means of securing the 'independence' of nation-states and would bring pressure for the introduction of other, domestic, controls in support of that 'independence'. Once controls were used at one end of the economy the pressure to use them at the other end could become irresistible. In the present state of the world to seek to move exchange rates up or down through capital controls was a very dangerous idea.

Professor Meade said he wanted to address himself to the question whether it was possible under a system of freely floating exchange rates to build up an international order that would allow free trade and free capital movements, and yet afford the nation-state sufficient freedom of action to stabilize economic activity. It was an illusion to think that floating exchange rates allowed a country freedom in its domestic monetary arrangements and since this was so, demand management had to be fiscal rather than monetary. Suppose, for example, that there was no great divergence in the rates of inflation expected in the US and in the UK; but that the US short-term interest rate was expected to be held at 20 per cent for the next three years and that the UK authorities were expected to hold their interest rate down to 10 per cent. If there was not to be a great outflow of sterling, the spot rate of exchange would have to settle at so low a rate that it was expected to appreciate at 10 per cent a year for three years. The effects of such extreme exchange rate changes, needed to look after the *capital* account of the balance of payments, could cause great disturbances to imports and exports on the *current* account. What his example demonstrated was that it was not possible indefinitely to maintain divergences of interest rates unless there were offsetting divergent rates (or expected rates) of inflation. The main conclusion to be drawn from this was that, if one wanted to avoid capital controls or if they did not work, it was necessary for the national authorities to rely on fiscal rather than monetary instruments of demand management.

Professor Tom Wilson, reverting to the consequences of the oil crisis, said that before the first big rise in oil prices currencies were already floating and capital controls had been relaxed. These were merciful developments in the light of after events. Not that changes in the exchange rates between oil suppliers and oil importers could do much to solve the problems then encountered, but changes in the relative rates of other countries did something to ease the maladjustments between them under the new circumstances. Capital controls would have enormously complicated the re-cycling problem.

The renewed oil crisis beginning in 1979 was far more serious than the first. The large OPEC surplus of the first crisis had been run down to a fairly small figure by the end of the 1970s. But the surplus rebuilt during the second crisis was likely to be kept high, even if variable, by successive steps to maintain the real price of oil. What this meant was that the task of recycling could become exceedingly onerous. He could see little prospect of this task being taken over by official international institutions; the banks were still doing the greater part of what had to be done. International bank lending was already far greater than the total lending power of the IMF. A situation of this kind was bound to be precarious. What was urgently needed was to ensure that there was an extremely efficient fire brigade that could be brought into action if there was an important default or some banks were badly caught out.

Sir Alec Cairncross said that there had been various capital controls before the war but that discussion could be confined to post-war experience. In the discussions leading up to the creation of the IMF, Keynes and others had been concerned to avoid the destabilizing effects of hot money and for this reason regarded controls over the capital account as legitimate in a way controls over the current account were not. The British government also saw capital controls as part of an armoury of controls carried over from wartime and adapted to the needs of a planned economy. But while other wartime controls were gradually removed, exchange control continued, largely because of the continuing weakness of the balance of payments. In a crisis the government almost invariably sought to tighten capital controls even although the effects on the balance of payments of such controls was not altogether clear. There had been reason to doubt their effectiveness ever since the convertibility crisis of 1947 and the devaluation crisis in 1949 when leads and lags on any scale first became apparent.

A case could be made for capital controls as contributing to economic stability. Changes in the exchange rate, whatever their origin, destabilized the domestic economy but might become unnecessary if the balance of payments could be strengthened, even if only temporarily, by capital controls. There was therefore something to be said for exchange controls in certain situations if they were genuinely effective. But were they? The record appeared to show that some forms of control were effective and some were not. An investment currency premium of up to 50 per cent showed that control over portfolio transfers could be effective. Control over direct investment where there was freedom to raise money abroad became largely otiose if the interest differential was such as to make foreign borrowing cheaper. But short-term capital movements (e.g. movements in commercial credit) were not easily controlled and the financial markets had vastly greater liquid resources to move to and fro than governments could muster. There did not seem much point, in the light of experience, in trying to use capital controls to steady the rate. Moreover, the task was far more difficult than in the past because the larger commercial and financial owners of funds were no longer prepared to abide by the government's view of what the rate should be. They had skilled staffs who reviewed the prospects for different currencies, formed their own view, and made their dispositions in ways that were out of reach of government control. Once this situation was reached it was not possible to get any real purchase on the exchange rate through capital controls; yet this had become almost the sole purpose of such controls, all the others having faded out of the picture one by one.

Sir Austin Robinson recalled that when demand management was under discussion, Sir Bryan Hopkin had emphasized that a single instrument had been required to secure four different objectives. Under those conditions, one should not lightly dispense with any instrument that was even partially effective. In the 1930s Keynes had been very worried because the interest rate appropriate to domestic conditions differed from the rate required to meet international conditions. That was a dilemma that capital controls might help to resolve; for all their imperfections they still had a role to play as one of the few instruments available.

Professor Tew pointed out that there were capital controls and capital controls. The issue depended on what capital it was intended to control and for what purposes. Portfolio movements had been controlled successfully. There was at least a chance of controlling direct investment case by case. But all the evidence suggested that control of short-term movements, on which the paper concentrated, was fantastically difficult. If this was the object, it had to be assumed that the controls would leak like a sieve.

A measure of the height of the dam holding back capital flows was provided by the difference between local interest rates and Euro-rates. One could, for example, look at the difference between short-term rates in New York and short-term dollar rates in London to measure the effectiveness of American regulations in force in the ten years to January 1974. Since the dam provided by the regulations would hold back *some* water there might be a difference of a few percentage points but never one as high as the 10 percentage points that Professor Meade had talked about. Similarly with the regulations instituted by the Germans over inward capital flows: one could compare the rate on Deutschemark deposits in Luxembourg with the rate on deposits in Frankfurt. The first would normally be the lower on account of the regulations but never by more than several percentage points. So if it were desired to maintain a 10 per cent interest differential, it would not be possible to do so through capital controls.

It was important to recognize that even if funds could not be transferred directly because of exchange control, it was always possible to dress up a shift of funds as a commercial transaction by giving extended credit or making quicker payment (depending on the direction in which capital was being moved). There was no difficulty about deferring payment, for example, since all that was needed was a letter from the customer to the effect that he could not pay within the period stipulated in the exchange control regulations. What could the Bank of England say in face of such a letter? Estimates showed that leads and lags of this kind accounted for enormous movements of short-term capital.

Professor Giersch said he would like to begin by saying something about overshooting. After the Bretton Woods system broke down it was not surprising that there should be difficulty in finding new equilibrium rates of exchange. There was always some overshooting after any major development before a new position of equilibrium was reached and one should not expect to avoid it. Moreover, it had been necessary to find a set of exchange rates that would foster structural adjustments in the relative position of the United States and other industrial countries. In Europe the international sector had become too large and in the United States it was too small: in the one case exports were overdeveloped and in the other underdeveloped in relation to imports. The change in dollar exchange rates had to be big enough to bring about the necessary adjustment; and the size of the change should not be put down to the volatility of markets. It was not a question of overshooting but of fundamental structural adjustment. Only a drastic change would have aroused people to make such an adjustment. It had meant the loss of a million jobs in Germany and the creation of several million jobs in the United States.

Under those conditions, control of capital movements would have got in the way of the necessary market signals and stifled responses that were highly desirable. It was always necessary to look beyond short-term adjustments and short-term capital flows and take account of the underlying forces at work. Real factors and capital movements had to be considered together.

Apart from this there was also a question, with full or approximately full convertibility of currencies, of competition between them, of their association in currency areas, and of the migration of currencies from one area to another. Such a migration had nothing to do with governments. There was a kind of oligopolistic competition amongst currencies which presented a major problem. There could be contractions in currency areas because of changes in the international demand for money and this could result in adjustments in exchange rates if the domestic money supply did not accommodate the shift. It was a weakness of monetarism that it did not take account of international shifts in the demand for money; and there was unfortunately little possibility of predicting how money would move from one country to another. The Swiss had found two years ago that a strong demand for their currency, for reasons unconnected with their domestic policies, was pushing up the exchange rate and creating an embarrassing dilemma: the export of banking services was squeezing out watchmaking. In such a situation the central bank had to decide how far it should accommodate this external demand by adding to the money supply (as the Swiss in fact did). It was one of the major tasks of the community of central banks to collect information about changes in the international demand for any currency and make it available to the IMF: action by central banks to change their holdings of other countries' currencies should certainly be reported. Such information would allow accommodating intervention to take place and help to make monetarism work better.

Professor Giersch said that he agreed with Professor Meade that the only additional freedom that a floating rate of exchange provided was the freedom to inflate at a different rate from other countries. The same discipline could remain if countries disliked a depreciation of their currency as much as they disliked a loss of reserves: the signals were different but the message for monetary policy was the same. The international currency market served to police the system and impose a discipline on national governments.

Dr Budd said that the problem posed by Professor Meade would look different to an extreme monetarist. He would say that if you had a more expansionary monetary policy in the United Kingdom than in the United States, it would be the rate of interest in the United Kingdom that was high and the rate of interest in the United States that was low because people would anticipate more rapid inflation in the United Kingdom and they would also expect an appreciation of the dollar. The problem would therefore disappear.

Replying to the discussion, *Mr Dealtry* said that he was surprised by the vehemence with which capital controls had been attacked, particularly as the main argument of Professor Lamfalussy's paper had been that there is a need for large private capital movements to finance payments imbalances. Controls had been dismissed as 'leaky', 'dangerous' and 'farcical'. But they were nevertheless from time to time still used. The attempt to use them at the end of the 1960s had been bound to fail but that did not prove that they would never work. At that time the hope that had been that by prolonging a state of disequilibrium for as long as possible with the help of capital controls it might eventually somehow go away. But the disequilibrium had been too fundamental for that.

What, then, were the circumstances in which their use was

warranted? In his view there might be a replay of situations in which capital controls had been used in the past. At the present time there was no longer a type-casting of certain currencies as 'strong' or 'weak': that had come to an end in 1980. There was a suspension of disbelief in the dollar and in the strength of the DM. At the same time movements had been strongly influenced by interest rate differentials. Inflation remained much higher in the United States than in Germany and Switzerland, and in 1980 short-term interest rate differentials between investments in dollars and those in DM and Swiss francs had at times exceeded even the 10 per cent mentioned by Professor Meade. These large differentials had had an undoubted influence on capital movements and exchange rates. But it was also possible to imagine a renewed run into DM or Swiss francs, should existing inflation differentials persist. If that happened the authorities concerned might well use the controls they had used before, even though they were well aware that the controls were 'leaky'. They might do this, as in the past, to keep down their exchange rate and combine controls with intervention by the central bank for this purpose. The Swiss had in the past gone so far as to require a negative interest rate of 10 per cent per quarter on foreign deposits with Swiss banks. When this, and other direct controls, didn't work, the Swiss National Bank had supplied $2 billion worth of francs to the market in three days in October 1978, thereby temporarily giving priority to exchange rate stability over control of the domestic money supply. The risks involved in an exchange rate of Swiss francs 1.50 to $1 had seemed greater than the risk of inflation.

Mr Dealtry then turned to Professor Wilson's suggestion of an efficient international fire brigade. After the Herstatt Bank failure in 1974, a statement had been issued from Basle by the central bankers expressing their confidence that if a fire brigade were needed to prevent a financial collapse ways and means already existed for providing it. It would be difficult for the central banks to do more in advance than say: 'it has not been forgotten that a fire engine may be needed but you must take our word for it that one will be brought into use if necessary'.

In a related area, there had been discussions in Basle over the previous decade about the possibility of exercising coordinated controls over Euro-currency markets. But, although that could not be altogether excluded, it was hard to see how an agreement could be reached between the Group of Ten countries either as to its desirability or on a method of carrying it out.

Mr Dealtry agreed with Professor Giersch that the devaluation of the dollar had had to be dramatic. The devaluation agreed at the Smithsonian Conference in December 1971 was notably un-dramatic. Whether that meant that the dollar had necessarily had to float down as it did rather then be devalued through a decisive change in the dollar parity was another matter. But a larger devaluation in 1971 would have met with opposition from other countries.

He concluded that, while there would continue to be a need for large private capital movements, capital controls, however imperfect they might be, would probably continue to be used from time to time by individual countries for their own individual purposes.

7

Are the British so different from everyone else?

GUIDO CARLI

The 'industrial revolution' had its origin in the United Kingdom in the seventeenth century. Afterwards it spread to the rest of the Western world. For a long time the other industrialized countries considered Britain as the country to look to for a model of capitalist development. Britain had the most dynamic productive system and the most sophisticated framework of financial intermediation in the world. American and European observers have been convinced for many years that, even in periods of acute crises and of weak performance, the British economy could never lose its fundamental stability since it was based on sound traditions and on the continuity of political and economic institutions.

Even the less informed observer realizes today that the position of the British economy with respect to the other industrial countries has changed. At this point in the century, all industrial economies are confronted with unprecedented problems. The continuity of our way of life will depend upon the way in which these problems are solved. Supply considerations have replaced demand as the bottleneck that prevents economic development accompanied by price stability. The scarcity of cheap energy sources contributes heavily to the co-existence of high inflation, high unemployment and low growth. Disequilibria in international payments create enormous financial problems, impose tensions on the international monetary system and help to widen the division among developed and less developed countries because the market, left to itself, does not allow an efficient and just redistribution of financial resources. They also threaten the stability of the relations among the industrialized countries, creating dangerous tendencies towards conflicting and competitive economic policies. More complicated economic relations, more sophisticated markets and the lack of selective intervention reduce the effectiveness of these policies, modifying or counteracting their results. The

232

political and social systems often lack the cohesion to make the necessary interventions work.

But amid the gloomy crises of the industrialized world the British economy shows peculiar weaknesses which push it even further from the leading position it had. The vulnerability of the British economy is increased by the legacy of several years of poor performance. The OECD economies grew more slowly in the period 1967–78 than in 1957–67, but in the same years the British rate of growth was slower still and reached only 60 per cent of the OECD average. The first oil shock affected Britain very strongly. The average growth rate of the UK from 1973 to 1978 was 1.1 per cent against 2.5 per cent for the OECD countries as a group. Per capita income growth was poor throughout the last two decades while inflation rates remained above the OECD average. They were higher only in Italy. Balance of payments deficits and unemployment often plagued the British economy and imposed restrictions on economic policy.

Britain's problems today are neither different nor more serious than the ones of other industrial countries. It has been said that every country has individual problems, especially in time of crises, since every country's experience is influenced by its tradition and its culture. I certainly believe that particular causes for the weakness of the British economic performance can be found, causes which take account of historical and sociological factors.

British industrial development started earlier than everywhere else and enjoyed both the benefits and the disadvantages of this privilege. The pioneering character of British economic development may itself have been a reason for the subsequent decline which left the country behind just as development was beginning in other nations. The early start led Britain to concentrate on sectors where the role of sophisticated technology was secondary. In any country the industrial structure is difficult and slow to change. Therefore countries starting the process of industrialization at a later stage were able to expand in sectors where technical progress was rapid and competition by British industry absent. The diffusion of production processes which was taking place in mechanized and automatized factories found Britain unprepared. Britain did not yet have a strong need to substitute specialized workers, and the problems of labour management and of production organization were not yet treated systematically.

Mechanization, automation and mass production gave the newer

233

industrial powers another advantage. They identified in the workers employed in industrial production the potential buyers for their output. For too many years the British continued to sell exclusive products to a restricted class of privileged consumers.

Furthermore, while everywhere else industrial development stemmed from a changing or, as in the USA, totally new social structure, in Britain capitalist production developed at a time when the feudal structure of society was still very solid. Capitalist wealth overlapped with aristocratic society. Wealth coming from economic activities and from class privileges was confused, and the first was often seen as a natural consequence of the latter. The consequent affluence was reflected in the habits of life of a leisured aristocracy. The entrepreneurial spirit weakened and insufficient energy was devoted to the enlargement or the defence of wealth which had already been won.

The British, having been the first to develop, then acquired an attitude of detachment and superiority towards the rest of the world. They started looking at the other nations with the coolness of those who have already achieved their political and economic superiority and do not take seriously the threat of competition from other rapidly growing countries.

All this helped to make the British economy vulnerable to the competition of the other western nations and more exposed to crises. Against this background more specific causes emerged, strictly economic in nature, for the poor performance of the British economy. I would like to concentrate on three of them, two of which are probably related to the date of birth of Britain as an industrial power. First, the early start of British development affected the position of the UK in international trade. Second, the importance acquired by London in world trade determined its role as the largest international financial market. Both circumstances imposed serious limitations on the continuity of the growth of the British economy. Third, socio-political factors caused the enlargement of the public sector and the erosion of the productive base. I shall try briefly to investigate these three aspects, the way they manifested themselves and the way they interfered with the expansion and the efficiency of the British economic system.

BRITAIN'S TRADING POSITION

The changes in the position of Britain in the flows of world trade played a fundamental role in determining the British economic performance after the booming expansion of the seventeenth century. Two possible reasons for a fall in any country's share of world trade can be identified:

    i the country's share in world trade of each group of commodities may remain unchanged, but the relative size of each group may decline, i.e. changes in the structure of world trade may affect the country's position;

    ii alternatively the country's share in each group of commodities, be it a declining or an expanding group, may fall, i.e. its competitiveness may be reduced.

Before 1850, Britain was the only industrial country and had a highly specialized pattern of production. More than twenty per cent of its labour force was employed in textiles. More than half the output of cotton, the main product in the textile sector, was exported. This allowed the industrialization of the production processes to proceed more rapidly than would have been the case if output had had to respond to internal demand only. At the beginning of the second half of the century, cotton was no longer the leading sector, as it was replaced by iron, and the market had to be increasingly shared with competitors. At the end of the century the new leading sectors were chemicals, mechanical and electrical products, and Britain found it increasingly difficult to defend its leading position.

In the first half of the twentieth century the British share in world trade declined sharply from 32.5 per cent in 1899 to 25 per cent in 1950, after having fallen to 22.4 per cent in 1937. The moderate recovery in the post-war period was probably due to the dramatic reduction of the German and Japanese shares. As a matter of fact if these two countries are not taken into account the UK position worsens by a further 4 per cent between 1937 and 1950.

The British share of world trade in manufactures declined between 1899 and 1950 by 14 per cent. Of this fall, 12.5 per cent has been attributed to the change in the competitive position of British exports in the sectors and the areas Britain was mostly dealing with, and 1.5 per cent to changes in the structure of trade. In the first half of this century Britain was affected by the same problem as other industrialized countries. Except for few countries like Italy, Switzerland and India, changes in competition were the dominant factors for changes in the world trade relative positions. The deterioration of competitiveness of British products was by far the largest.

These general trends were not reversed during the 1950s and the 1960s, not even after the institution of the EEC. The British share of world exports of manufactures declined from 20.6 per cent in 1954 to 11.2 per cent in 1969. The fall in UK exports to the EEC countries was larger than the fall of its exports to the world in the same period. In those years the Community showed no tendency to increase its share of world trade. Rather there was a redistribution among its members: strongly competitive countries like Italy improved their position. Although the 1960s were a period of favourable trends in the unit costs of British exports there was a further fall in their share in world trade probably because of the delayed effect of the increase of the costs in the 1950s. Different exchange rate policies might have helped, but they could not have permanently eliminated the consequences of differences in productivity trends.

There are several ways in which a weak international trade position and the growth rate of an open industrial economy affect each other. The relation between foreign trade expansion and growth rates is complex in nature and the direction of the causality is probably not unique. The consequences of an insufficient growth of the volume of exports and the effects of persistent current account deficits are certainly positively correlated in many ways to lower growth rates of the economy. The British economy followed this pattern because its openness had been one of the main causes of its industrial development, and when circumstances changed, the British were unwilling to abandon the principles of unrestricted trade.

The slow export growth has affected overall growth in several ways. Balance of payments troubles have caused pressures on the level of foreign reserves. This was certainly true in the 1920s when restrictive monetary policies were implemented, and also in the 1930s. In that decade the situation improved after sterling was cut free from gold. In the post-war period the protection of the level of reserves from the pressures originating in the balance of payments deficits led to stop-go policies. Until 1965 the economy operated almost at full employment. In the following period restrictive policies lowered the level of investment, reducing the potential growth of the economy. Thus, policies aiming at protecting the level of reserves affected the expansion of the economy.

Foreign trade also influences growth through its direct contribution to demand. The growth of exports induces higher investment which leads to a higher GNP and allows the virtuous circle of export-led growth to continue. Conversely, an increase in foreign competition may discourage investments by creating pessimistic expectations about the growth of demand, about profits and about possible restrictive policies. In the period after the Second World War, the effect of increased competition by foreign suppliers was offset by the boost in the world demand, which left more space for British exports to expand and hence for productive capacity in the UK to increase.

In conclusion it was the pattern of British exports and Britain's slowness in defending their competitiveness which deprived the UK of the benefits of the rapid expansion of trade among the industrialized countries and thus affected the continuity and the level of its growth rates.

THE IMPORTANCE OF LONDON AS A FINANCIAL CENTRE

I touched upon the way exchange rate policies in some periods failed to alleviate the consequences of changes in Britain's competitive position. This brings me to the second peculiarity of British economic development. I mentioned before the role of London as an international financial centre and the policies aimed at its preservation. As Britain was the first country with a modern industrial economy involved in worldwide trade, London developed as the first financial centre of international dimensions. The expansion of trade was promptly supported by a sophisticated system of banking and financial intermediation. The volume of such intermediation attracted funds worldwide and the role of the City expanded further.

London's growth as a financial centre contributed to the attractiveness of sterling. The demand for pounds increased continuously as sterling was the most widely used medium for international payments. The volume of transactions in which it was possible to use it, and the lowering of transaction costs caused by the sheer volume of sterling-denominated funds, made the pound the only currency demanded internationally for trade as well as for speculative purposes. International traders held most of their money balances in sterling funds, using it as a transaction currency. The pound was free from risks of exchange rate or purchasing power default.

237

In the periods when British exports flourished, when the external balance did not create problems, the activity of the City was welcome as a source of financial support. When British exports hit more difficult times, as we have seen, and when balance of trade problems started to recur, London's status as a worldwide market attracting funds from all over the world became a very important advantage. Before 1913, when the balance on current account was almost constantly in surplus, the capital account balance had only to be tailored to the needs of the current account balance. Later in the century appropriate exchange rate and interest rate policies aiming at preserving the attractiveness of the pound became an instrument for offsetting the consequences of the problems of current account balances.

It was against this background that Mr Churchill, then Chancellor of the Exchequer, decided to return to gold. In 1925 he re-established the gold standard with an exchange rate of $4.86 for the pound. It has often been said that the decision was taken with an insufficient understanding of the mechanism of adjustment that the consequent overvaluation of the pound, estimated at 10 per cent, would impose on the economy. The justifications for the decision were that it would insulate the country from foreign inflation and that it would allow the Bank of England to use more sophisticated instruments of control on the financial market. But there is no doubt that the argument of the role of the City of London was, more or less consciously, in the back of the mind of Mr Churchill's counsellors. The defence of the prestige of the empire, when the decline of the British economic strength appeared unquestionable, played an increasing role in determining the exchange rate and interest rate policies. The decision was affected by motives which were not strictly economic, as well as by misunderstanding and by a lack of effort to analyse its impact on the economy. These are probably the reasons for the title of the only systematic treatment of the subject: *The Economic Consequences of Mr Churchill.*

As a matter of fact the impact of such policies on the economy was strong. Factories and consumers were sacrificed to the banks. But these sacrifices were not necessarily rewarded by stability of economic growth and the improvement of the balance of payments. The cost of this policy demonstrated that the defence of the role of the City was no longer justified by the underlying strength of the British economy and put a heavy burden on the productive system.

This cost, which we might call the cost of the City, can be identified in recurrent exchange rate crises, and fluctuations in short-term capital flows which repeatedly led to general deflationary policies to defend the pound.

After 1931 dangerous crises of the pound occurred periodically, and resumed during the Labour government's period after 1964. The origin of these crises was in the over-valuation of the pound. The attractiveness of the currency was no longer based on the general belief of the soundness of the economy behind it, but on particular inducements to hold it. As soon as doubts arose about the strength of sterling, runs on the pound started promptly. The fact that the effects of these crises were somehow limited is amazing if one considers that the total amount of readily mobilizable sterling assets in the hands of foreigners was certainly larger than those owned by the government. From time to time these crises forced the government to ask for official foreign loans, which made it necessary to impose on the economy the policies needed to secure the trust of creditors.

All the instruments used to induce foreigners to hold funds in sterling, that is, high interest rates, the over-valuation of the currency, and deflationary policies reduced the growth rate of the economy. The consequent stop-go probably hampered growth even further. The uncertainty itself discouraged investment. The unsteadiness of British growth may not have been worse than in any other country. But even a small variation has more harmful effects on a slowly growing economy than on a fast growing one.

While the slow growth in productivity started to affect the competitiveness of British exports, and while changes in the structure of foreign trade further reduced their importance, the over-valuation of the pound, imposed by the defence of the role of London as a financial centre, was a further burden imposed by the City on the economy with serious consequences for the current account balance and, via its effect on exports, for the growth rate.

The general consequences of sterling policies can thus be seen as the results of an unjustified pretence. As Leland Yeager puts it in his book *International Monetary Relations,* 'Just as a man's insistence on too high a salary keeps him unemployed and in turn lessens his value to employers, so Britain's insistence on too high an exchange rate for sterling probably worsened the country's economic "fundamentals".'

Changing Perceptions of Economic Policy

Let me now turn to the third feature of the British economy which in my view has affected the soundness of its development and its response to current crises: the expansion of the public sector and its consequences.

The attitude of the British government towards the economic activity fluctuated in past centuries between opposite extremes. During the years preceding the industrial revolution the dominant idea was that the government had to do something about it. After the mid-nineteenth century the prevailing position was that the government had to create the conditions for the business sector to operate as smoothly as possible. This attitude remained until the outset of the 1931 crisis.

During the heyday of laissez-faire in the 1860s, there were strenuous efforts to reduce the most evident forms of government intervention, like mercantilism; traditional forms of social assistance, like the Poor Law; and the protection of the interests of social groups opposing wider industrial development, like the landed classes. In that period the British government totally surrendered responsibility for economic activity. Thus the government steadfastly refused tariff protection to industry, and was the only one in Europe which neither financed nor participated in any way in the construction of the railways. In those years the main ways in which government manifested its presence in the economy were through taxation and currency control. The first aimed at the greatest possible reduction of the public indebtedness. The second one followed the lines I have already described to ensure the pound remained as stable as possible.

The turning point for laissez-faire came around 1870. As other countries' industrialization advanced, international trade could no longer be the major engine for the growth of the economy. Low taxes and stable currency were not enough any more. New economic powers, like Germany, Japan and USA, were growing rapidly. The threat to world peace and then the First World War led to an increase in military spending. An unrestricted industrial system could no longer be assisted by a modest public administration.

Nevertheless the growing feeling against laissez-faire policies never became 'socialist', until the Labour Party, in 1918, began to preach socialism more widely. The original justification for greater public intervention was the defence of efficiency and the need to improve the working of the economic system. After 1919 the growing influence of socialism led to government activity on a larger scale and to the spread of nationalization. Important service sectors became state-owned or partially nationalized: railways, electricity supply, the steel industry and the coal cartel. Meanwhile the collapse of some industries had legitimized the principle of state subsidies to industries.

In the 1930s laissez-faire was just a memory. Keynes's *General Theory* and its impact on government attitudes after the Great Depression started an era of changes in basic ideas from which Britain, of course, did not remain immune. Meanwhile there was growing admiration for the experience of the Soviet Union and, with the enlargement of the basis for socialism, economic planning became fashionable.

The Second World War interrupted any discussion on the theoretical issues, but *de facto* made Britain the non-socialist economy with the largest state sector. A mixture of the new Keynesian economics and of socialist pressure for the government to achieve social equity led to massive recruitment in the civil service and in the universities. 'A high level of employment' and advanced welfare legislation became explicit objectives of government policies. It was hard to go back from these positions. After the war, policy statements in support of private enterprise and the free market tended to be abstract.

A high share of public activity and a large number of public employees became, from now on, a constant characteristic of the British economy. The Labour government of 1945–51 continued the policy of nationalization. To achieve this, it set up 'public corporations', operating autonomously and theoretically making profits. In 1946 the National Insurance System was introduced and in 1948 the National Health Service. The variety of services supplied by the government increased to unprecedented levels, not equalled by any other country in Europe. In the 1960s total public spending was not much higher than in other European economies. But the public had acquired high expectations for government intervention. Thus the number of British civil servants multiplied, as did the variety of services citizens could expect from them.

The economic consequences of this have often been described as another burden put on the productive system, weakening the economy and its ability to overcome recurrent crises and the recent external shocks. Whatever one's theoretical approach to the problem, it is hardly questionable that a large share of resources, employed by the public sector to produce non-tradeable service, takes labour and capital away from the production of manufactures and or marketable services.

One of the obstacles preventing Britain from keeping up with newer industrial powers like the USA, Germany and France was the failure to see in the workers the potential buyers of its output. Public employees soon gained enough purchasing power to compete with private sector workers. The result was more social unrest, as the industrial workers refused to accept the reduction in their living standards caused by the expanding number of civil servants. Once again, the outcome was damage to stability, investment, growth and ultimately, the rise of inflation.

THE COMPARISON WITH ITALY

In describing other countries' problems one can forget the maladies of one's own country. As I said at the beginning, our economies are affected by unprecedented evils. These cannot be defeated except by a common effort of solidarity and cooperation. So no country can look only at its own problems, forgetting about the rest of the world. To share problems, to establish where trends run parallel, is of fundamental importance. I intend to conclude by trying to point out some elements of similarity between the British economy and the Italian one.

Italy shares with Britain a large involvement of the government in the economy. The public sector participates in economic activity in a number of ways: a large number of services are supplied by the State, several forms of social assistance are granted by state agencies, there are enterprises partially or entirely owned by the government in several sectors of the economy. In Italy, the increased activities of the government grew out of the desire of the parties supporting the government during the 1960s and 1970s for more socialist economic policies. Social security, health insurance, larger pensions were the most important achievements of this new political wave. Moreover, almost all political parties wanted more government involvement in employment protection, unemployment subsidies and incentives to investments in less developed regions.

Soon the economic system was deeply affected by these changes. The resulting massive public sector deficit had its counterpart in an increasing flow of public expenditure to subsidize unemployment or unproductive work. Inefficient industries were kept alive artificially. Welfare and social assistance programmes created expectations of a guaranteed revenue without regard for the need to produce the corresponding income. Public expenditure became a burden on the 'productive' part of the economy. It created incentives for both workers and entrepreneurs to take refuge in the public protection which the state did not deny to anybody. In Italy as well the public sector has been drawing real resources away from the 'productive economy'. Moreover, the need to finance record levels of deficit has attracted increasingly large amounts of credit which would have otherwise gone to the private sector – thus further discouraging initiative.

The last point brings me to another element of similarity between Italy and Britain which is somehow consequent to the first one: that is, the large amount of intermediation taking place in the Italian financial system. The gap between the personal sector, which generates savings, and government and company sectors which invest savings, became wider with the enlargement of the public sector deficit and the worsening of the financial conditions of firms. The differences between the preferences of suppliers of savings and users of savings became larger. The savings producers looked for forms of investment of their balances which were profitable and protected against inflation. The savings users' need for cheap finance and for longer term funds meant that they faced increasing difficulties in finding adequate financial flows. The authorities had to intervene in the mechanism of intermediation. This introduced rigidities and distortions which, after apparently easing the access to finance of government, local authorities, public agencies and firms in crisis, actually imposed burdens on the rest of the economy and on the financial system itself.

The discontinuity and the low level of the growth rates are another element of similarity between the British and the Italian system. Similar problems, like recurring balance of payments crises, high inflation, and exchange rate troubles required similar political responses, such as stop-go policies and frequent deflations. Similar uncertainties and similar discontinuities discouraged investment by lowering expectations. Structural problems, like the public sector deficit and the effective indexation of wages made the problems recurrent.

As in Britain, frequent balance of payment crises have often plagued the Italian economy. We have seen to what extent the weak performance of British exports affected the economy. This was true also in periods when the volume of imports was declining. The Italian response to the first oil shock has revealed a surprising capacity to react, using the country's ability to concentrate on sectors whose competitiveness in the export markets is high. The weakness of the Italian external balance is mostly due to Italy's heavy dependence on foreign imports of primary products, and particularly of energy of course, where Britain has a great advantage. This condition introduces a rigidity in the system which makes Italy, even more than Britain, extremely vulnerable to external shocks.

Large similarities between the current situations of our economies exist. Nevertheless our similar problems stem from very different historical experiences. Most of the Italian difficulties can be traced to the outburst of the unprecedented economic boom of the late 1950s and the early 1960s. They can be traced to some peculiarities of that boom, to the pattern of pay settlements it originated and to the consequent lack of social and political cohesion. The need for defending a clouded prestige and a declining international role affected the British response to the peculiar weaknesses of its economic performance. From time to time this led to contradictory actions. Perhaps even the current trends of British economic policy can be interpreted in the light of conflicting tendencies towards the defence of the role of Britain in the world and the need for the expansion of the British productive system and of employment. If this is the case it might be that the misunderstanding or the underestimation of the consequences of the current monetary and exchange rate policies will bring about, a few years from now, investigation into the 'economic consequences of Mrs Thatcher'. If this happens it will demonstrate that the current British policy is facing the same contradiction of the first half of the century, between the interest of the City and the interest of manufacturing industry.

Comments by
Andrea Boltho

Dr Carli's paper presents a very interesting and stimulating survey of the main reasons for Britain's longer-run economic decline. At the risk of oversimplification, there would seem to be two main strands to his argument:

i The legacy of empire and, in particular, of the international role of sterling, which meant that periodically 'factories and consumers were sacrificed to the banks'. In other words, restrictive policies were followed at frequent intervals from the 1920s onwards in a futile attempt to defend a position that 'was no longer justified by the underlying strength of the economy'.

ii The rapid expansion of the public sector and of the welfare state, particularly after the Second World War, which lead to a significant weakening of the economy's tradeable sector and compounded the debilitating effects of stop-go policies.

In these brief comments I would like to stress the first point, but place the second one in a wider context.

It will probably be generally accepted that the pre-eminence of financial over industrial capital over the past sixty years lies at the root of many of the United Kingdom's problems. As a further confirmation, one can point to the example of France, the country which perhaps most closely resembles Britain in terms of some of the historical characteristics Dr Carli describes – early industrialization and empire. In the inter-war period, between the 1926 Poincaré stabilization and the 1936 Popular Front experiment, the country followed orthodox policies designed to safeguard the value of the franc, policies which attracted to Paris 'most of the safety-seeking capital whose movements so damaged the world economy between 1929 and 1931'[1]. Over the decade, output rose by 3½ per cent in all – the lowest rate in Europe (and according to some estimates it actually fell). Partly because of this legacy of stagnation, France entered the post-war period in a position almost certainly less favourable than that of the United Kingdom. It had, *de facto,* lost the war (but it had not been given the 'advantage' of Germany or Japan in terms of large scale destruction of its industrial base), it had lost trade shares to an almost equal extent as Britain,[2] it faced stagnant labour force growth until the late 1950s and, more importantly perhaps, it clung to its empire much more doggedly, going as far as fighting two protracted and expensive colonial wars. But unlike Britain (and unlike its earlier experience), it evaded the pressures of a balance of payments constraint and the

245

onus of being a strong currency country by direct controls first and 'aggressive' devaluations later. No doubt, a good deal of the French post-war success story is to be found in the fact that the authorities had learnt the lessons of the 1920s and 1930s and did not worship the shibboleth of a fixed (and high) value for their currency.

But there must be other dimensions to British decline and French resurgence. Dr Carli selects the growth of the public sector. Yet neither in the 1950s nor later was this particularly rapid by European standards. Welfare expenditure, including or excluding transfers, rose by relatively similar percentages of GDP in France, Germany or the United Kingdom. But something else may have been at work in the early post-war period of a perhaps subtler nature. The pioneering of the welfare state in the late 1940s may have signified a break in the outlook and attitudes of the country *vis-à-vis* the earlier model of industrial capitalism. The creation of a national health service, the institution of family allowances, the adoption of a more progressive taxation system designed to reduce income disparities, the preference for leisure, illustrated by a relatively short working week, the strengthening of ecological concern shown by the rapid growth of 'new towns' – even the more or less conscious rejection of empire – may all have been expressions of a search for 'quality of life' which came earlier than elsewhere. Continental Europe expressed the same preferences, and in a much more articulate form, in the late 1960s and early 1970s, but by then it had achieved a large productivity advantage over Britain. In other words, it is not rising government expenditure *per se* which is a reason for Britain's troubles, but the premature choice of a new model of society which France, Germany or Japan were not yet ready to make their own. Moreover, this popular preference for greater personal leisure and welfare coincided with the Establishment's preference for a continuing world role, be this in terms of an overseas military presence or the City's prestige. The contradiction was obvious and the results perhaps inevitable.

In conclusion, I would like to raise a third peculiarity of the English which is probably less important in macroeconomic terms but closer to the economic policy theme of this conference. Looking at Britain in a comparative context, one is often struck by the rather extreme nature of the policy choices that are taken. Fine tuning, for instance, was strongly believed in and carried to great lengths. Monetarism is at present being followed with almost total dedication.

246

Other countries have fine tuned their economies or have moved towards more monetarish positions – none seems to have pursued either doctrine as wholeheartedly as Britain. No European country would have indulged in the saga of nationalization and denationalization, none has tried as many varieties of incomes policy, none would probably have introduced fairly major and radical reforms almost solely on the basis of economic theorizing, as in the case of Selective Employment Tax or *Competition and Credit Control*. And even in the brief flirtation with indicative planning, Britain seems to have taken the idea more seriously than France, the originating country, was (wisely) doing at the time.

For a country which has traditionally prided itself on a pragmatic and common-sense approach to policy making, this strong belief in the power of economic theory seems surprising. Clutching at straws in the face of a mediocre economic performance may be one reason. The high esteem in which economists have traditionally been held in Britain relative to the Continent (where they were, until recently, largely relegated to the role of company accountants, with prestige going to lawyers) may be another. But perhaps and more importantly, the absense of a real ideological divided of the sort which monopolized attention in countries such as France or Italy may have encouraged the emergence of a surrogate ideological debate fought not in terms of freedom versus equality, or communism versus democracy, but rather in terms of the need for stabilization policies versus the natural rate of unemployment.

NOTES

1 W. Arthur Lewis, *Economic Survey, 1919–1939,* London, 1949, p. 98.
2 Maizel's figures show that where the United Kingdom's share of world manufactured exports fell from 32½ per cent in 1899 to 25 per cent in 1950, that of France fell from 14 to 9½ per cent over the same period – a smaller absolute but a larger proportionate decline. A. Maizels, *Industrial Growth and World Trade,* Cambridge: NEISR, 1963, p. 189.

Discussion

The theme of an early start was taken up at the beginning of the discussion. *Professor Arthur Brown* said that he had expected to be surprised by what a distinguished foreign observer would say about the United Kingdom but it was what he said about Italy that had surprised him. What the paper said about the United Kingdom was very much in keeping with what had been said in this country for many years — and so frequently repeated that one began to wonder if it was true. It was so long since we had grown faster than other countries — over a century — that nobody remembered it. Italy, on the other hand, had shown a surprisingly fast rate of growth since the war: per capita incomes had increased twice as fast as in the United Kingdom. The biggest difference between the two countries lay in the initial difference in economic structure. As in other continental countries, but more dramatically, population had streamed into the towns in Italy: the rate of urbanization had been twice as fast as in the period of fastest urban growth in England in the mid-nineteenth century. The structural change that this involved had already been accomplished in the United Kingdom and was an important factor in the difference in economic performance. Similarities between the two countries were harder to find. As the paper showed, the expansion in the size of the public sector was not peculiar to either country but what did set them apart from other countries was that they both experienced pure wage push inflation.

The *Chairman* asked what one should make of the early start that the United Kingdom had enjoyed. The country had experienced slower growth than other countries for a hundred years but because of the earlier start average income per head remained relatively high until the 1960s. Thus it had taken longer to get to much the same point and the whole process of economic change had been more gradual. The rate of change in the industrial revolution had been very moderate by comparison with that undergone by more recently industrializing countries. There had been a capacity to resist change which was founded in the absence of any great revolutionary change in economic structure or, for that matter, in political arrangements. Some of the barnacles adhering to the ship of state had thus been able to stick more firmly than in other countries where change was more rapid.

While the paper focused on the last fifty years, *Dr Tumlir* went back to the 1920s. This was a decade seen in a very different light by economic theorists and economic historians. For the theorists it had been a total disaster: monetary instability, high unemployment, deflation, tariffs. On the other hand, the historians could point to an acceleration in the growth of GNP from 1.1 per cent per annum in the years 1899 to 1913 to 2.3 per cent per annum in the 1920s (and a somewhat higher rate in the second half of the decade). The growth in productivity was several times as fast in the 1920s. Unemployment was concentrated in the old and declining industries: textiles, coal mining and shipbuilding. These accounted for nearly half the total. What can one conclude from the coincidence of a high level of unemployment with high rates of output and productivity growth? The British economy in that decade was almost the only one in Europe in which structural adjustment was really taking place: the newer industries were expanding while the others contracted. It would also appear from available price indices that by 1928 purchasing power parity had been restored. But for the world slump, it was more than likely that the British economy would have followed a much more dynamic path in the 1930s. In that decade rising barriers to trade brought the contraction in the older industries to a stop. True, the UK economy performed much better in the 1930s than most other industrial economies. This was not due to more planning, however, which merely made growth more chaotic. The main explanation was to be sought in the tremendous improvement in the terms of trade consequent on the collapse in import prices for primary products.

Dr Tumlir then turned to the argument in the paper that the interests of industry and the working people had been sacrificed to the interests of the City. The City provided services to the rest of the world and its interests were international, like those of other export industries. In the controversy over the return to gold in 1925, the interests of the City's clients appeared to be left out of account. A lower parity would have reduced the value of their deposits in London.

The loss of confidence on which Sir Arthur Knight had commented had nothing to do with the end of empire or collapse of demand management but had its origins in 1931. It was then that the predominant concern with domestic welfare came to the fore, forcing national policy to draw on external resources or seek postponement or external claims. The 1920s, he believed, was the last decade in which the United Kingdom had a role in the world economy of which it could be proud.

From economic history *Mr Andrew Likierman* turned the discussion to the kind of diagnosis that begins with the phrase: 'the trouble with this country is . . .'. It was all too easy to put forward explanations in terms of some single factor that could not possibly do justice to the complexity of the facts. Not enough attention was paid to the link between economic and social factors. One must look outside the purely economic differences to social factors, where there seemed to him to be a real difference, and take account of social history which could never be quite the same in any two countries. What worried him was the lack of agreement in the United Kingdom on social parameters which might help to improve economic performance.

While agreeing with the Chairman's emphasis on Britain's very long experience of gradual industrialization, *Mr John Wright* thought that one should guard against attributing too much to the more remote past. It was the case that the problems of the steel industry, for example, had deep historical roots. They went back to the third quarter of the nineteenth century when the rest of the world was industrializing and the steel industry invested heavily to meet the demands made on it from abroad. The industry had then to adjust, over a prolonged period, to the building up of competitive supplies in the industrializing countries. But, by the late 1930s, there had been a long period of adjustment.

Meanwhile, inter-war experience showed that Britain was quite a good place for copying American techniques, thanks in particular to her inheritance of skilled labour, in engineering and other industries. The Second World War expanded the industries needed in the post-war period so that by 1950 Britain was in a good position to take advantage of the growth in world markets. Why had full advantage not been taken of the opportunities of the next two decades? What had been the snags? Perhaps the economy was over-committed: nearly 40 per cent of the labour force was already in manufacturing. There was no reluctance to supply labour such as Mr Boltho had suggested: the male overtime rate was high and the female participation rate was amongst the highest in the world. What had been damaging was the commitment to rearmament at the beginning of the 1950s which diverted resources at a critical period when, as it happened, the government was also freeing consumer demand from rationing and other controls. The coincidence of these two factors had taken the pressure off manufacturers to develop export markets.

The scope of the discussion was widened by an important contribution by *Sir Henry Phelps Brown*. International comparisons allowed one to eliminate many of the alleged causes of inferior economic performance: the burden of taxation and the disincentive effects of high marginal rates of tax; the 'bloodymindedness of labour' and its proneness to strike; the class structure of the British economy. A comparison in terms of the tax 'take' in relation to GNP, whether social security contributions were included or not, showed Britain in the middle of the league table, below Scandanavia for example. International comparisons of the incidence of strikes had to be handled with care; but again the British record compared quite favourably with many other democratic countries such as the United States, Canada, Australia and Denmark, although the frequency of unofficial strikes was a black mark against the United Kingdom. As to class structure, it was an illusion, widespread among foreigners, that British managers were drawn from a different social level and educated in a different kind of school from the shop stewards. An instance to the contrary was that of the British Leyland plant at Longbridge where the general manager and the convenor of shop stewards ('Red Robbo') had begun side by side as apprentices in the toolroom. This was not an untypical case. British managers were not old Etonians but came predominantly from the grammar schools. The City was a different matter but then the City was a successful exporter. Studies of social mobility also indicated that upward intergenerational mobility (measured by comparing the occupations of fathers and sons) was very much the same in a number of Western countries, and did not seem to be lower in Great Britain than in the land of opportunity, the United States.

Although one could dispose of those alleged causes of poor performance, there was plenty of evidence of inhibiting factors somewhere in the social structure or in customary attitudes. C. F. Pratten's well-known study[1] of 100 manufacturing companies making similar products by similar processes in the United Kingdom, North America, Germany and France brought out the large differences in output per employee-hour in the different countries. British levels of output were exceeded by 56 per cent in North America, 35 per cent in Germany and 28 per cent in France. Some of these differences could be attributed to economic factors: for example, the length of production run and the degree of utilization of capacity. When these were taken out, the residual 'behaviour' differences, associated with the attitude and performance of employees, accounted for 12–13 percentage points in the North American comparison, 19 percentage points in the German and 10 percentage points in the French. These differences reflected differences in the contribution made by workers *and* management and should not be attributed to workers alone. 'Those of us', said Sir Henry, 'who have had the experience that many of my generation have had of serving in an army of high morale have no patience with those who see the British worker as bloody-minded.' There could be no question of his response to leadership in willing work, steady endurance and loyalty. Pratten's 'behavioural differences' should therefore be attributed to the interaction between management and labour and not uniquely to the qualities of the labour force.

These differences arose out of the traditions of society and led back to the thought that by some accident of history an industrial revolution had taken place in a society which it did little to modernize. The attitudes and values of that society had remained those of a society ruled by country gentlemen. Perhaps the Cabinet of 1905 had been the first in which the majority of the members were not landed proprietors. Business men in the nineteenth century had not made much money and when they did, went out and bought land with it. The great fortunes were those of landowners and bankers.

The fundamental problems of the way forward were the problems of changing attitudes in a society that was profoundly conservative, comfortable, steady and slow-moving. In the 1830s we had embarked on what the historians now called an 'age of reform'. Threatened with an outbreak of cholera, we had achieved marvels in the development of public health. Now we must set out upon a new age of reform. Sir Henry said that he had been daring enought to set out a programme of reform under four headings.

i We should get back to a forum for industry far wider than NEDC. Lloyd George had made a brief attempt of this kind in 1919. There might be a gathering including the CBI and the TUC but more widely based. Reform of the second Chamber was an associated possibility.

ii There was a need to get away from the cowboys and indians style of political confrontation, by adopting proportional representation. The harm done by the alternation of policy was illustrated by the enactment and repeal of legislation on industrial relations.

iii There should also be development of the constitution of the firm:

252

some form of workers' representation, and development of the Works Council.

iv Finally, a change was needed in trade union institutions.

The result of the Pratten analysis, which Sir Henry quoted, was supplemented by figures given by *Mr Maurice Scott*. He claimed that a simple regression equation could explain 93 per cent of the variance in growth rates between the ten countries covered by Denison's study for the period 1955–62.[2] Not only that, but the United Kingdom, the United States and Japan were right on the regression line. The explanatory variables in the equation were:

i the level of output per head in relation to that of the United States (countries grew faster the further they were behind the United States);

ii the share of investment in GNP;

iii the rate of growth of the 'quality adjusted labour force' (allowing for education and for transfers from agriculture to the rest of the economy).

The last factor was of particular importance. It would seem that a 1 per cent faster growth in the labour force led to a more than 1 per cent faster growth in output (in keeping with the Verdoorn Law). This was not very surprising since one would expect, with imperfect competition, that the marginal product of labour was higher than the wage. So far as the United Kingdom was concerned, the fact that it had much the lowest rate of growth in the labour force of any country helps to explain why the growth in productivity was so disappointing. The relatively low investment effort of the United Kingdom operated in the same direction and matched the reluctance to change things on which other people had commented. Investment implied a wish to change the economy and if it was low this was a symptom of a disinclination to change it very rapidly.

Mr Christopher Dow brought the discussion back to Dr Carli's paper. The paper suggested that the management of the economy had been dominated by concern for the strength of sterling or City interests and this was a common enough journalistic view. But what did it mean and how could one test it? It could mean that extremely cautious demand management policies had been followed so as to boost the exchange rate and induce more foreigners to come to London and use the financial services of the City. But could the policies be said to have erred on the side of caution? Any error, surely, had been the other way. Or was the implication that we had been reluctant to devalue and clung too long to fixed exchange rates? There were many other possible explanations of that without bringing in excessive attachment to financial symbols.

If Britain was different, so was Italy. There seemed to be an absence of effective government there. Yet the economy was able to thrive without effective control by the authorities. Decisions, if taken at all, were apt to be taken late; to represent weak compromises and to be implemented weakly and with long delay. Decisions about government expenditure often took years to begin to be implemented. Taxation was widely evaded. The black market was everywhere. All controls were subject to a margin of bribery. So if the economy was relatively stable it must be self-stabilizing. The question raised by a comparison with Italy was: does government matter? Or was it, as Dr Carli might think, the central bank that mattered?

Finally, he made the suggestion that the success of an economy might be related to its possession of a confident middle class – confident both of its ability to manage affairs and of its right to be well paid for its services. The British middle class was not confident in this sense. Was the reason why it had submitted to a long drawn out diminishment of its position that it suffered an over-developed sense of guilt – a luxury that developed with affluence, an inbuilt destructive device such as people had in mind when they talked of 'clogs to clogs in three generations'?

Lord Roll subscribed to nearly all that Sir Henry Phelps Brown had said. It had been salutary to be taken through the process of elimination of popular explanations of poor performance of the economy. At the end of it we were left with a residual difference that lay in areas that were not exclusively economic and perhaps not economic at all. He would like to take up two points from Mr Andrea Boltho's commentary: the loss of the pragmatic attitude that had once been thought a British characteristic; and the role of the economist.

The path by which 'the burden of the past' is made manifest seemed to him very obscure. For example, it was much too facile to speak of the sacrifice of industry to the interests of the City. The City was not a uniform entity: there were different and conflicting interests. Moreover, those who operated in the City could misjudge their own interests like anybody else. Yet if one drew up a list of major errors of policy after the war there was something to suggest a common origin. Such a list might include the settlement of the sterling balances, premature convertibility in 1947 (admittedly under American pressure) and the defence programme of 1951–2. Of the latter, Sir Richard Clarke had said 'The greatest mistake that Gaitskell made was to be in favour of the defence programme. The Chancellor has no business to be in favour of *any* spending programme!' Another major error had been the failure to understand the strength of the movement for European integration whatever attitude the United Kingdom had to take in the end. The famous three ring theory, with the United Kingdom regarding itself as in the middle of the ring made up of the United States, the Commonwealth and Europe, was a symptom of the same failure to appreciate the changes occurring in the post-war world. All the specific policy mistakes of the period had their origin in failure to understand the changes in power relationships, economic and political, in the world and our role in it. The loss of pragmatism seemed to him to be traceable to our failure to react quickly enough to the change in our situation in the world. The Italians were in a good position to judge these matters because they were now perhaps the most pragmatic people of all: although one important French statesman had claimed recently: 'We are the pragmatists now. You are the theorists and Cartesians.'

As for the role of the economists, it was extraordinary that the Permanent Secretary of the Treasury should only once have been a trained economist (Lord Croham). It was paradoxical that in what passed for a 'business' government there was only one trained economist (Mr Nigel Lawson) and yet there was probably a greater reliance than ever on economic theorists and particularly on matters of theory that are highly sophisticated, obscure and controversial. This must be a debilitating factor, whether it led to indecision or affected decisions of the utmost importance.

Lord Roll ended by quoting the replies he had been given in Austria and China to questions about economists. He had asked the Austrian Minister of Finance how it was possible for Austria to be such an oasis of prosperity in a Europe in depression. 'It's perfectly simple,' said the Minister, 'all the Austrian economists are in America advising the government there.' In China a prominent member of the Academy of Social Sciences had astonished him by saying: 'Of course, you know what we need in this country. We need another million economists.' It turned out that what he was really asking for was not economists at all but cost accountants, clerks of works, foremen, and so on.

Professor Erik Lundberg was glad to find from Mr Maurice Scott that British economists still thought that the investment ratio mattered. Following the Salter type of analysis, he thought that the low British ratio must mean that there was a long tail of obsolete plants in most branches of industry, and too little Schumpeterian 'creative destruction'. This would account for the slower growth in productivity. In Sweden it was often suggested that the age distribution of managers in Britain was like the age distribution of equipment, and he seemed to remember figures confirming the higher average age of British managers. The vitality of business growth depended on not keeping managers too long. Governments changed and managers, too, needed to circulate. So, for that matter, did economists.

Mr Geoffrey Penrice entered a caveat about the strike statistics to which Sir Henry Phelps Brown had referred. Unofficial and short destructive strikes had an enormous effect on certain industries, notably motor manufacturing. The effect on output might be ten times as great as the number of days lost. It was also important that employers held back from making changes because they felt they wouldn't win. He recalled a report from the Labour Attaché in France in which he said that he could recall no major long-lasting strike that the employer didn't 'win'. This was far from true in the United Kingdom. If the employer didn't actually lose the strike he often seemed to lose the settlement. This necessarily had its effect on the self-confidence of the management.

He recalled visits by British employers to Germany after the war. They invariably commented 'We don't know how it is but the German industrialists seem to like to have new machinery. They instal it even when they have no real reason.' The attitudes were different.

Decision taking in Britain was difficult. Either people didn't really want change or there was an obsession with the people who would suffer from its initial impact. This applied not only in management but also in government. In the case of the roads programme, for example, the parts of the country like the South-East where roads might contribute to growth were left to the very end. To decide where the third London Airport should go had taken thirty years and it would probably end up exactly where it was expected to put it in the 1950s. If one was obsessed with equity and disturbance one was not likely to make decisions favouring growth; and such decisions were made still more difficult by the great power of the labour force to resist change and the lack of willingness in management to override it.

Sir Austin Robinson had a question which he wanted to put to Dr Carli. In 1947 he had helped to draft the Vanoni Plan for Italian development in conjunction with Marsan and Saraceno. At that time there was a fear that Italy would go communist because of the stagnation of the economy; and the purpose of the Plan was to inject some dynamism by creating a picture of where Italy might get to in fifteen years and so changing business expectations. The Plan had been prepared at a point of inflexion in the path of growth of the economy. How far was the Italian government the cause of the growth that followed? What lessons could we draw from their experience?

In summing up, *Dr Carli* said his paper was to be regarded as a contribution to the analysis of differences in the adjustment process in countries with an early start. The process of reducing differences between European countries in economic levels was a lengthy one, and Europe would therefore have to live with very wide differences for a long time. If, for example, a division was made between the late-comers in the Mediterranean area and their northern neighbours, even a constant rate of growth 1 percentage point higher in the first group than in the second would still require forty-two years in the case of Italy and 128 years in the case of Turkey to level out the differences in prosperity. Persistent differences created tensions between countries in competition with one another and still greater tensions between social groups within them. Contact with other countries caused powerful and numerous groups to press for the level of income enjoyed abroad by their counterparts. Obvious examples were airline pilots, carrying out exactly the same duties in the same aircraft, and workers in the automobile industry, making the same model of car for the Common Market. Whether the claims of such groups were just or not, they could only be conceded at the expense of other groups in the same country and must inevitably produce more inflation than ever.

This situation was not new, but was now more evident because of common membership of the EEC and because society was much better informed on such matters. It helped to explain the increasing rate of inflation ever since the introduction of the European Monetary System. The weighted average rate of inflation had increased from 7.3 per cent in 1978 to 12 per cent in 1980 and, what was particularly significant, the standard deviation had risen over the same period from 3.2 per cent to 5.7 per cent. This pointed to a sharpening of the tensions he had described.

The clashes occurring *between* member countries of the Common Market, for example over agriculture and steel, had a similar origin, said Dr Carli. France and Italy wanted to index farmers' incomes at their protected level while the United Kingdom and Germany opposed this. Italy and the United Kingdom were in favour of government subsidies to their over-expanded steel industries while Germany was strongly opposed to all forms of government intervention, open or concealed. Within Italy, the highly efficient private sector had its eye on the quarter of the market for steel supplied by inefficient public enterprises and was hostile to government support for the latter.

A more hopeful development was the recognition by European governments that an extension of the public sector was a source of inflation because it reduced the area of the economy that was flexible. They were also coming to the conclusion that in the fight against inflation they would have to reduce the indexed part of government expenditure, including pensions, and to restrict the area covered by guaranteed government loans. Bank lending against such a guarantee paid no regard to the productivity of the investment and was in effect a credit extended to the government. Finally, there was a tendency towards de-regulation because there was general agreement that the jungle of regulations was so intricate that it formed an obstacle to development.

The new forms of struggle between social groups with which countries were now confronted had nothing in common with the Marxist model. But they were no less intense; and the violence of the struggle made itself felt inside the political parties as well as elsewhere. Both in Italy and in Great Britain the process of restructuring was affecting the socialist parties, which were discovering the merits of the market economy. He could only hope that they had more success than the efforts of government to restructure industry had had.

NOTES

1   C. F. Pratten, *Labour Productivity Differentials within International Companies*, Cambridge: Cambridge University Press, 1976.
2   E. F. Denison, *Why Growth Rates Differ*, Washington: Brookings Institution, 1967.

Concluding remarks

JAMES MEADE

My assignment is to survey our discussion of perspectives of economic policy over the past seventy years. But in a quite arbitrary manner I am going to restrict my terms of reference by looking back only sixty instead of seventy years, and also be omitting the war years 1939–45. Moreover, I am going to restrict my discussion to economic policy in the UK, although of course that cannot be divorced altogether from the international arrangements of which we were part.

That leaves me with three periods: three dramatically different periods. There is the dismal inter-war period; the period from 1945 to 1970 in which both the world and this country enjoyed a more successful economic history than ever before; and the period from 1970 to 1981 when it all went sour. I want to ask to what extent one can attribute the dramatically greater success of the second of these periods to government policy, and to what extent policy is responsible for the deterioration in the 1970s.

I think that everyone would agree that 1945 to 1970 was economically a far better time than the inter-war years. There was full employment, and the standard of living was high. Inflation, as Professor Matthews said earlier (p. 59), was bad compared with what we had known before; but it was after all very moderate compared with what we know now. I think, too, that we would all agree that there has been an enormous deterioration in economic performance since 1970. We have seen a much lower increase in productivity, and now very heavy unemployment combined with explosive inflation.

Let me begin with what happened immediately after the last war. There were, I think, four great changes in the structure which was set up then, compared with the policy arrangements in the inter-war period. First, there was Keynes and full employment. Both the

259

post-war Labour government and the subsequent Conservative government felt themselves committed to using demand management to maintain full employment. Of course, there had been the beginnings of an employment policy in the 1930s − all these things have their roots in the years before the war. But this commitment was quite different from anything which had gone before.

The second change was Beveridge and the welfare state. I include under that label education and health, social security, progressive taxation, the redistribution of income and wealth. There was a very marked change of emphasis: the Labour government in particular felt that the brave new post-war world should really try to fight against poverty, to redistribute income and wealth, and to provide welfare services and education and health for everybody.

The third change, which was undoubtedly very important, was the international settlement.

Fourth, there was nationalization: the idea that the 'commanding heights' of the economy should be taken into public ownership. Someone once described that as 'the great irrelevance'. That is how I intend to treat it, although I shall come back to nationalization briefly when I talk about Sir Arthur Knight's contribution.

The major gap in our discussions has been in the second area of policy which I have desribed. We have had no paper on the welfare state. I rather regret this because of the important distinction between the use of wages policies and the use of other welfare state policies as the means for dealing with low incomes − a matter which I shall discuss later. I shall start by confining my remarks to the first and the third of the post-war developments which I have just outlined, full employment and the international settlement.

Let me start with full employment. We achieved it with great success for a quarter of a century, and I am rather surprised when people sometimes feel disappointed with the degree of stability which we attained. A variation of between 1 per cent and 3 per cent in the rate of unemployment seems to me to be moderate. Indeed, we probably aimed at too low a level of unemployment. Between the wars, 10 per cent had been the minimum unemployment and 23 per cent had been the maximum. In the great Beveridge report on social security, all the figures were worked out on the basis of an average of 8 per cent unemployment. And the 1944 Employment Policy White Paper (Cmnd. 6527) also did the sums on the basis of average unemployment of 8 per cent. That was not ambitious enough. But to many people in the Treasury, it seemed like crying for the moon to start talking about an *average* of 8 per cent, when the minimum level of pre-war unemployment had been 10 per cent.

Sir Bryan's paper raised a question which has become much more important in the bad years since 1970. He emphasized the fact that demand management was being used to kill not one – not two – but four birds with one stone: to achieve full employment, the moderation of price inflation, equilibrium in the balance of payments and a stable background for growth. In fact, we did manage to get through this period, relying very largely on the one instrument to attain a fair degree of success for all four targets: but it took a good deal of luck.

But we now live in a period when the choice of instruments and targets has become absolutely basic. The question with which we have been struggling at this conference is the right use of demand management: do you use it to fight inflation, or do you use it for maintaining full employment? That's what is behind the current polarization of policy. If you cut out all the mumbo-jumbo of monetarism, what is going on at the moment is an enormous decrease in the demand for labour in order to throttle inflation. The people who argue that demand management should be used to achieve full employment are, to my mind, often rather blind to the argument in favour of the present policy: which is that if you did that, inflation would explode and you would have to start again dampening down the economy.

A good moderate might challenge the balance of policy. But the only real hope of achieving full employment without an explosive inflation is to do something radical about the fixing of money wage rates. This is the great dilemma, around which a great deal of our discussion revolved.

Now both Sir Bryan Hopkin and Sir Henry Phelps Brown raised in their papers the question whether the achievement of full employment in the first two post-war periods I am discussing was really due to the adoption of Keynesian policies. Might it not have been due to need for reconstruction, for instance? After the war, when I was in Whitehall, everyone was preparing for the great post-war slump, when we would turn on the Keynesian taps. It didn't happen.

One point which was made in the discussion – one with which I have immense sympathy – was that it may not have been simply the reduction of tax rates and increases in public expenditure which maintained full employment, so much as the expectation that the government would take effective measures to preserve the level of real demand for goods and services if ever the need should arise. That expectation may have helped to maintain business confidence and sustain investment. But whether you share that view or not — however far you believe that post-war success was due to Keynesian policies — I think it is absolutely certain that if it were not for the danger of a wage explosion, we would certainly have tried to deal with the present world recession by cutting taxes and raising public expenditure.

A great change took place towards the end of the 1960s and in the early 1970s. We have discussed three reasons which led to this change. I would put a good deal of emphasis on the overheating of the economy by Mr Edward Heath, although this is not the most important reason as I see it. Mr Heath's policies meant that we went into this period with enormous excess demand. But more important was what Sir Henry Phelps Brown called 'the hinge'. Somehow or other, in most of the countries of the Western world there seems to have been a rather sudden change in the attitude of people negotiating wage rates. Some kind of break in continuity took place — a change in the factors which caused people to press for higher wages. But the third and most important thing which happened was the oil crisis, and the concomitant rise in raw material prices. That undoubtedly and inevitably caused an increase in the cost of living which wage earners were not willing to accept. This caused a wage explosion which was an attempt to maintain real wages when there was a necessity for them to fall or at any rate not to rise as fast as before.

I want in passing to note that it is not the shortage of energy which has induced Mrs Thatcher to cause unemployment. She is not causing unemployment to save energy. She is causing it in order to prevent wage increases. Now it is perfectly true that we may never be able to return to earlier rates of employment and growth until we succeed in saving energy. And indeed the rise in energy prices may have triggered off the wage explosion. But it is the wage explosion which is at present being fought through higher unemployment.

That brings me to Sir Henry Phelps Brown's paper, which discussed what I think is the central issue: the way in which wages are fixed. I drew five points from his paper and from the discussion.

First, in this country voluntarism was absolutely accepted. Government did not try to interfere in union affairs until 1971, and it is only since then that we have been discussing whether the state should take powers to control trade unions. Secondly, there has been a great increase in the power of the trade unions since 1906. Only one member of the conference was bold enough to state that this power was now excessive; but I agree with him that it is now so great that it must in future be subject to some form of social constraint. Third, Sir Henry emphasized the fact that now wage claims seem to be less affected by unemployment, and by supply and demand in the labour market, than they were. Fourth, we noticed the long series of attempts at incomes policy. Fifth, there has been a shift from national to decentralized pay agreements, reached in firms, in companies and on the shop floor.

The major question which arises from all this is whether we can somehow get a change in this wage fixing machinery which will enable us to maintain full employment without a wage explosion. In a number of the discussions we have had, we have been presented with a choice between two strategies, one of which I might call the orthodox Keynesian strategy and the other the neo-Keynesian strategy. The first involves using demand management to maintain full employment. If that leads to explosive inflation, you then have an incomes policy, to control wages and prices. That's what most governments have tried to do up to now. The neo-Keynesian solution, which might conceivably resolve the dispute between monetarists and Keynesians, and which is the strategy which I prefer, involves using Keynesian demand management to maintain the total level of money demand for goods and services – for the products of labour, or for nominal gross national product – on a steady growth path. But we must then find a way of building into wage fixing the idea that wages affect employment. Can this be done? Is it possible to gain acceptance for the idea that wage rates must have a bigger role as instruments for regulating the job market, while the achievement of more equal distribution of incomes is left more than it is now to taxation and to social security – to all those welfare state measures which I mentioned earlier on?

The other very important issue in this area is the question whether we need more or less centralization in wage negotiations. As an economic theorist who really knows nothing about the labour market, I do feel that if we want unemployment to have a bigger influence on wage fixing, there is much to be said for encouraging the decentralization of wage bargaining.

Nobody knows the answers to these questions – although they are the most important questions which we face. It is absolutely essential that an answer be found if our type of civilization is going to continue, in my view.

But let me turn to the other two targets on Sir Bryan Hopkin's list: growth and the balance of payments. As far as growth is concerned, the maintenance of a steady rate of growth of real demand for goods and services which creates an atmosphere of confidence and a high level of demand for labour is undoubtedly a good background for growth. It is also the best atmosphere for getting rid of restrictive practices, and it is easier to get adjustment between industries when there are jobs for people to move to. The question of which policy instrument you use – whether you use interest rates or tax policy – is also very important for growth: on it depends whether you want to encourage investment or consumption. But while appropriate demand management can create a good background, whether or not growth takes place depends on many other factors, some of the most important of which were discussed in Sir Arthur Knight's paper. Should the government intervene to preserve lame ducks? Should it try to pick winners? Should it try to promote efficiency by encouraging small businesses and competition, or ought it to encourage large-scale monopolies which will take advantage of economies of scale? And should these large-scale activities be nationalized or should they be left to some form of socially controlled private enterprise? Or is it that question a 'great irrelevance'? I don't know the answers, and from our discussion I had the impression that nobody else really did, either.

In our discussion, though, we did not talk much about the other aspects of growth: education, training, social attitudes and so on. Dr Carli's paper is extremely relevant here. Are there social attitudes which differ from one country to another, and do we in Britain suffer from attitudes which make growth less likely? The awful conflict between Them and Us holds back many of the reforms which might make business more efficient.

Now that leaves the balance of payments. Let me go back, for a moment, to the post-war settlement. Let me ask the younger generation to try to put themselves in the position of somebody in government in 1945. Imagine yourself somebody called John

Maynard Keynes for example. We ended the war with no exports at all. All our imports were on Lend-Lease, and we relied on Lend-Lease entirely to feed the population and to revive the economy after the war. We ended the war with a whole battery of controls over imports and foreign exchange. Then President Trueman suddenly cut off Lend-Lease – probably quite rightly. There we were, with no way of paying for imports. We had used most of our foreign securities to pay for the war. We had a new Labour government, devoted to planning and controls.

But in spite of all this, we did not veto the post-war settlement – and indeed, we made a great positive contribution to it. It is difficult now to get back into the atmosphere of those post-war days, in which it would have been so easy to do just the opposite. Everyone remembered the 1930s, and thought that there would be a tremendous slump in America. Many people thought that there would be another Hawley-Smoot tariff, and that the US would once again retreat behind a barrier of import controls. In spite of that, the Western world set up the GATT and the IMF.

That was a rather remarkable achievement. It is also rather remarkable that, as Dr Lamfalussy tells us in his paper, even now – when we have a recession like that of the 1930s, and OPEC surpluses instead of reparation payments to accommodate – even now, capital movements have never been freer. Pause to think of what might have happened after 1945. Dr Tumlir tells us that the main structure of GATT has survived. Perhaps it is because, as with the nuclear deterrent, we are all so afraid of mutual destruction. Perhaps each of the main countries is frightened that if it gives in to protectionism, so will all the others, leaving everyone even worse off than before. But it is remarkable that the framework of the post-war settlement has survived. Let us keep our fingers crossed and hope that we can achieve domestic stability in time to re-build that framework before it finally collapses.

But can we hope to maintain an international system of multilateral free trade and payments? There are two ways of doing it. Let me give you extreme versions of each. You can have a single international currency, fixed exchange rates, free capital movements, free trade, and leave wages and prices to adjust themselves in the domestic market to give you full employment. That is one kind of international order. The alternative – which I think we should pursue – is that national governments should remain responsible for their own domestic demand management and wage fixing, aiming through them to achieve full employment. There should be free capital movements and free trade, but in this case adjustments of foreign exchange rates to accommodate differences in domestic stabilization policies are a necessary feature of the system. If you have such a policy, a country like ours will have to rely on fiscal policy rather than monetary policy for demand management, and use interest rate policy combined with exchange rate policy to promote growth and to stabilize the balance of payments.

In short, I think that the international order can be rebuilt. But like domestic economic stability it all depends on achieving a radical reform of our wage fixing arrangments. That is the problem which obsesses me these days. It does not just matter for Britain. When you look round the world, you find that the United States suffers from the same problem – though perhaps not quite as badly as us. Even Germany is afflicted. The *sine qua non* for our society is that we should somehow find a way of wage fixing without confrontation, which will enable us to maintain full employment without a wage explosion.

List of participants

Chris Allsopp	Fellow, New College, Oxford
Sir Fred Atkinson	Chief Economic Adviser, HM Treasury and Head of Government Economic Service 1977–9
John Black	Professor of Economics, Exeter University
Andrea Boltho	Fellow, Magdalen College, Oxford
A. J. Brown	Professor of Economics, Leeds University 1947–79
Sir Henry Phelps Brown	Professor of Economics of Labour, London School of Economics 1947–68
William Brown	Director, Industrial Relations Unit, Warwick University
Alan Budd	Director, Centre for Economic Forecasting, London Business School
Sir Alec Cairncross	Economic Adviser to HMG 1961–4; Head of Government Economic Service 1964–9
Frances Cairncross	Economics Correspondent, *The Guardian*
Guido Carli	Former Governor, Bank of Italy; President, UNICE
Sydney Checkland	Professor of Economic History, Glasgow University
Lord Croham	Permanent Secretary, HM Treasury 1968–74; Head of Home Civil Service 1974–7
Michael Dealtry	Bank for International Settlements
Christopher Dow	Executive Director, Bank of England 1973–81; now Adviser to the Governor
Sir Frank Figgures	Director-General NEDO 1971–3; Chairman, Pay Board 1973–4

267

Nick Gardner	Undersecretary, Department of Employment
Herbert Giersch	Director, Institut für Weltwirtschaft, Kiel, West Germany
Sir Bryan Hopkin	Professor of Economics, Cardiff University; Chief Economic Adviser, HM Treasury and Head of Government Economic Service 1974–7
Sir Arthur Knight	Chairman, Courtaulds Ltd 1975–9; Chairman, National Enterprise Board 1979–80
Andrew Likierman	Lecturer, London Business School
Erik Lundberg	Former Professor at Stockholm School of Economics; Former President of the International Economic Association
Hamish McRae	Financial Editor, *The Guardian*
Robin Matthews	Professor of Political Economy, Cambridge University
James Meade	Professor of Political Economy, Cambridge University 1957–68; Joint winner of Nobel Prize for Economics, 1977
Alec Nove	Professor of Economics, Glasgow University
Milivoje (Mića) Panić	Chief Economist, NEDO 1972–7; Director, External Policy Section, Bank of England Economic Intelligence Department
Joseph A. Pechman	Director of Economic Studies, The Brookings Institution, Washington, DC
Geoffrey Penrice	Deputy Secretary and Director of Statistics, Department of Employment 1978–81
Michael Posner	Chairman, Social Science Research Council
Lord Roberthall	Director, Economic Section, Cabinet Office 1947–53; Economic Adviser to HMG 1953–61
Sir Austin Robinson	Professor of Economics, Cambridge University 1950–65
Lord Roll	Chairman, S. G. Warburg and Co.
William Ryrie	Second Permanent Secretary, Domestic Economy, HM Treasury
Walter S. Salant	Senior Fellow Emeritus, Brookings Institution, Washington, DC

List of participants

Maurice Scott	Fellow, Nuffield College, Oxford
Peter Sinclair	Fellow, Brasenose College, Oxford
Brian Tew	Midland Bank Professor of Money and Banking, Nottingham University
Wendy Thompson	Secretary to the Economics Committee, Social Science Research Council
Jan Tumlir	GATT
Tom Wilson	Adam Smith Professor of Political Economy, Glasgow University
David Worswick	Director, National Institute of Economic and Social Research
John Wright	Fellow, Trinity College, Oxford

Index

Index

Subject index

Index

Index

Prices—*cont.*
  post-war increases, 59; retail, 34, 149, index, 34, 48; setting of, 4; theory of, 23; wrong forecasting by workers, 49
private sector, 9, 10; asset preferences, 50; expectation of government intervention, 59, 66; inflation, response to, 43; rented, loss of, 53; unemployment, weakness as cause of, 34;
productivity: decline in, 72; growth in, xii, 191; labour market organization, effect of, 101, 110; low, 57, 239, 251, 259; national, 85
protectionism, 8, 147, 148; infant industries and, 133; lack of, 6, 240; legislation, 116, 165; revival of, xii, 116, 175; textile industry and, 128
public, the, 1, 10; 'establishment', loss of respect for, 20; expectations, 89, of inflation, 47; opinion: polls, 95, preventing policy implementation, 31, 88, 133
Public Sector Borrowing Requirement (PSBR), 9, 47, 51
public sector: British, growth in, xii, 240–2, 245; housing, 53; spending, increase in, 34; works, to stablize employment, 6, 33; Woytinsky-Keynes proposal, 166

recession, 34, 42, 175
reconstruction, industrial, 115, 125–9, 133, 136, 143, 261; international, 170–4; national plans, 172
regional policy, 120, 121–3, 133, 136, 138, 142, 147–8; investment, influence on, 122–3; Special Areas, 81, 122, 131, capital-intensive industries in, 123; subsidies, 121
resources, xii, 185; allocation, 185, 218; shortage of energy, 187, 232
Royal Commissions, 8; 1867–9, 68; 1891–4, 68; Donovan, 89, 90, 92, 93, 95, recommendations, 90–1, 111; Monopolies, 129, 133; national incomes, 85; Samuel, 178; Trade Unions and Employers' Associations, Cmnd 3623, 96

searing experience, theory of, x, 55–6, 66
Second World War, 5, 34, 75, 98, 250
shop stewards, 69, 98; and pay negotiation, 89; rise in importance, 93
statistics, 9, 13, 15; price index, 9; production, 9; public expenditure, 58; strike, 256; wage index, 9
sterling, 78, 239; balance fluctuations, 58; controls, 197; crises, 75, 85, 239; external value, 83
strikes, 73, 79; General, 76, 77, 78, 79, 97; London Dock, 69; settlement procedures, 79; transport, 69; unofficial, 82, 90, 91

Sweden, 105–6, 108; as economic model, 64, 99; collective ownership, 64; differentials, 106; employer coordination, 111; protection in, 145; trade unions, 70, 73; wage-push, 106

tariffs, 2, 55; the Mckenna, 165
taxation, 54; consumption, to influence, 37; income, 6; income distribution, use in, 8; indirect, 6; progressive, 8; reduction in, 47; Selective Employment Tax (SET), 247
trade: terms, of, 9, 72, 79, 109, 190, 249; world, 234–7
trade cycles, xi, 71; Phillips curve, 71
trade policy, 2, 167, 168, 172
trade unions, xi, 34, 68, 82, 87; cooperation with labour governments, 86–7; expectation of government intervention, 66; membership, 73, 77; militancy in, 50, 95; need for change, 253; New Unionism, 68, 73, 77; non-acceptance of incomes policy, 65, 91; post-war strength, 53, 107, 262; register of, 92, 93; special legal position, 118
Trade Union Congress, 95, 99, 100, 252; General Council, 79, 87, 111; members, lack of authority over, 98
Treasury, 6, 7; agreement, 1915, 75; economists, number in, 18, 30, 31; forecasting machinery, 28

uncertainty, 61, 239; in economic forecasting, 14; in trade cycle, waves of, 71; inflationary conditions, increased under, 43; monetary targets, reduced by publishing, 45; planning and, 19; present, 145
unemployment, 61, 259, 262; 1930–9, x, 33, 120; balance of payments crises and, 53; definitions, varying, 65; exchange rate, effect of, 221; inevitable, regarded as, 33; insurance, 81; Keynesian view of, 64; maintainable rate, 67; natural rate of, 45, 48, 49, 53, 247; unemployment pay, 53; wages, role in lowering, 49
United States of America, 12, 164; balance of payments, 176, 178; bargaining, decentralization of, 106; capital controls, 198, 201, 207; capital movements, 203, 204, 205, 206; credit expansion in, 53; immigration restriction, 157; incomes policy, 60; industrial policy, 117; inflation, 229; interest equalization tax (IET), 198, 221; isolationism in, 162–3, 166; lending, decline in, as cause of world depression, 161, 173; monetary policy, 158–9; National Industrial Recovery Act, 168; New Deal, 167; plant contracts in, 89; prices, 176; Reconstruction Finance Corporation, 168; scale economies in, 128;

275